T0346811

MAGICAL SYMBOLS AND ALPHABETS

ABOUT THE AUTHOR

Sandra Kynes is a yoga instructor and Reiki practitioner, and a member of the Bards, Ovates, and Druids. She likes developing creative ways to explore the world and integrating them with her spiritual path, which serves as the basis for her books. She has lived in New York City, Europe, England, and now coastal New England where she lives in a Victorian-era house with her family, cats, and a couple of ghosts. She loves connecting with nature through gardening, hiking, bird watching, and ocean kayaking. Visit her website at www.kynes.net.

SANDRA KYNES

MAGICAL SYMBOLS

AND

ALPHABETS

A PRACTITIONER'S GUIDE TO SPELLS, RITES, AND HISTORY

Llewellyn Publications
Woodbury, Minnesota

First Edition
Fourth Printing, 2024

Book design by Donna Burch-Brown
Cover design by Kevin Brown
Editing by Patti Frazee
Interior art by Laura Tempest Zakroff

Llewellyn Publications is a registered trademark of Llewellyn Worldwide Ltd.

Library of Congress Cataloging-in-Publication Data
Names: Kynes, Sandra, author.
Title: Magical symbols and alphabets : a practitioner's guide to spells,
  rites, and history / Sandra Kynes.
Description: First edition. | Woodbury, Minnesota : Llewellyn Publications,
  2020. | Includes bibliographical references and index.
Identifiers: LCCN 2019051221 (print) | LCCN 2019051222 (ebook) | ISBN
  9780738761923 (paperback) | ISBN 9780738762005 (ebook)
Subjects: LCSH: Occultism. | Witchcraft. | Magic. | Signs and symbols. |
  Alphabets.
Classification: LCC BF1439 .K96 2020 (print) | LCC BF1439 (ebook) | DDC
  133.4/3—dc23
LC record available at https://lccn.loc.gov/2019051221
LC ebook record available at https://lccn.loc.gov/2019051222

Llewellyn Worldwide Ltd. does not participate in, endorse, or have any authority or responsibility concerning private business transactions between our authors and the public.

All mail addressed to the author is forwarded, but the publisher cannot, unless specifically instructed by the author, give out an address or phone number.

Any internet references contained in this work are current at publication time, but the publisher cannot guarantee that a specific location will continue to be maintained. Please refer to the publisher's website for links to authors' websites and other sources.

Llewellyn Publications
A Division of Llewellyn Worldwide Ltd.
2143 Wooddale Drive
Woodbury, MN 55125-2989
www.llewellyn.com

Printed in the United States of America

OTHER BOOKS BY SANDRA KYNES

Llewellyn's Complete Book of Essential Oils

365 Days of Crystal Magic

Crystal Magic

Plant Magic

Bird Magic

Herb Gardener's Essential Guide

Star Magic

Mixing Essential Oils for Magic

Llewellyn's Complete Book of Correspondences

Change at Hand

Sea Magic

Your Altar

Whispers from the Woods

A Year of Ritual

Gemstone Feng Shui

FORTHCOMING BOOKS BY SANDRA KYNES

Herbal Remedies for Beginners

Tree Magic

CONTENTS

PART SEVEN: THE WITCHES' ALPHABET AND OTHER MAGICAL SCRIPTS

INTRODUCTION

ALTHOUGH WE MAY NOT BE aware of them, symbols are an integral part of daily life in the form of road signs, laundering instructions, mathematical functions, and of course, emojis. While these symbols communicate information, they do not hold a great deal of significance. However, in art, myth, religion, and magic we find symbols that convey deep meaning and provide guidance.

Throughout time, people have used symbols to explain unusual events, the natural world, and the mystical Divine. Symbols were—and still are—used to express abstract ideas. Although the use of symbols found in Lascaux Cave in France and Altamira Cave in Spain date to approximately 30,000 BCE, more recent discoveries in Africa are pushing it back even further to around 70,000 BCE.[1] It seems as though we are hard-wired for using symbols.

Having dedicated her life to studying the Neolithic and Bronze Age cultures of Europe, scholar and archeologist Marija Gimbutas (1921–1994) considered many of these ancient symbols as "an alphabet of the metaphysical."[2] Conveying information with symbols was especially important before written language and in later times when most of the population was illiterate. Symbols were easy to understand and served as simple abbreviations for concepts. They also served to veil information from the uninitiated.

Swiss psychologist Carl Jung (1875–1961) wrote about the deep significance of symbols and the fact that we tend to be drawn to them because somewhere within our psyches

---

1. Alexander Marshack, *The Roots of Civilization: The Cognitive Beginnings of Man's First Art, Symbol and Notation* (Wakefield, RI: Moyer Bell Ltd., 1991), 57; Nicholas St. Fleur, "Oldest Known Drawing by a Human is Found in South Africa," *The New York Times,* September 13, 2018, 10.
2. Marija Gimbutas, *The Language of the Goddess* (San Francisco: HarperSanFrancisco, 1991), xv.

we are aware of their importance. Since most symbols are multilayered—operating on the emotional, intellectual, and spiritual levels—they awaken a response within us. Mythologist, writer, and lecturer Joseph Campbell (1904–1987) noted that symbols help us "to identify with the symbolized force."[3] According to Campbell, a symbol provides a means to access the reality of the symbolized concept and in some ways to join with or embody it.

From the Greek *symbolon*, the word *symbol* has had a variety of meanings, one of which relates to the principle of complementation.[4] In this sense, the symbol complements or is part of something greater and, as an abbreviation, it serves to convey the meaning or truth of it. However, in verb form, *symballein*, symbol can mean "hidden" or "veiled."[5] In magical systems, symbols do both; they make information accessible but can also camouflage it. For example, the ogham or runes can look like simple line designs, but to the initiated who can discern the characters, they hold a wealth of information.

While some of the symbols explored here are used more widely than others, they all offer unique approaches for bringing magic into our lives. This book serves as an introduction to various systems of symbols and alphabets and enables you to begin using them in your own practices. For those already using some of them, it may provide more information to better understand their context, history, and relevance. Also included is information and suggestions for magical, ritual, and mundane use that is meaningful to twenty-first-century Pagans and Wiccans.

Intended to inform and inspire, this book serves as a foundation upon which you can continue to build knowledge. Because most of the systems included are more extensive than space allows, you may want to further your study. Whether or not you pursue any of the systems more deeply, this book will serve as a convenient reference for years to come.

Each section covers a separate system, beginning with the astrological symbols. While they are most often equated with high or ceremonial magic and, of course, astrology, the purpose of this section is to acquaint you with a more Pagan/Wiccan-centric application. The second section explores the elements, which are often just a cursory component of ritual and magic. We will see how expansive the underlying concept of the elements is and how we can fully access their power. Although related to astrological symbols, the third section explores the "fixed" stars. This is a special group of fifteen stars that have been regarded as particularly potent for magic since ancient times.

---

3. Joseph Campbell with Bill Moyers, *The Power of Myth* (New York: Doubleday, 1988), 217.

4. Kenan B. Osborne, *Sacramental Theology: A General Introduction* (New York: Paulist Press, 1988), 60.

5. Udo Becker, *The Continuum Encyclopedia of Symbols*, trans. Lance W. Garmer (New York: Continuum International Publishing Group Inc., 2000), 5.

Sections four and five examine the ogham and runes, respectively. While the exact origins of these systems may be lost in the proverbial mists of time, these sections follow their circuitous histories, separate fact from fantasy, and present realistic and meaningful suggestions for their use. Section six explores sigils and their development from magic squares to the word method for creating them. It also presents several new approaches to creating these unique symbols. Finally, section seven looks at magical alphabets with a special focus on the one known as the witches' alphabet.

As you work with symbols, you will find they provide power as well as simplicity. This doesn't mean that we should dispense with our magical and ritual accoutrements; however, the objects we use can be more fully empowered with symbols. In addition, incorporating symbols into our everyday lives provides continuity and enables us to live more deeply in the magic around us. Although I have written about many of these systems before, delving into more intense research has been an interesting and exciting journey that has deepened my understanding and appreciation for symbols.

While we can simply use symbols to boost the energy of spells and ritual, learning the fullness of their history provides insight on how we can employ them in a way that is relevant today. It provides a base upon which we can continue to build knowledge as we develop our skills and unique expression in the craft.

PART ONE
ASTROLOGICAL SYMBOLS

The purpose of this section is to explore the historical roots of astrology and its symbols, rather than explain how to create and interpret astrological charts or readings. Instead, we will examine the relevance of these symbols in magic for twenty-first-century Pagans and Wiccans independent of astrology.

Closely tied to personality traits and the strengths associated with them, the zodiac signs are commonly used to channel energy for magic according to birth sign. Most often viewed through the lens of the four elements and long lists of correspondences, the power of the constellations and planets often seem to get lost. We will explore how astrological symbols can be used to energize spells and rituals and cultivate aspects of personal life. While the sun signs and planets we are born under may hold special meaning and power for us, the energy of these celestial bodies is available for anyone to use regardless of birth sign.

CHAPTER 1
DISTANT ROOTS

GREEK INFLUENCE ON ASTRONOMY was widespread; however, the Greeks were not the earliest stargazers. The Babylonians, Persians, Egyptians, Indians, and Chinese also studied the heavens. Because the moon is the closest satellite to Earth and most impressive to the unaided eye, it was the focus of early astronomy and astrology.

As early as the second millennium BCE, the Chinese were coordinating their twelve zodiac signs with twenty-eight lunar mansions—segments of the sky that marked the position of the moon. The Hindus of India had a similar system by which they tracked the moon's progress across the sky, dividing its path into lunar mansions. Dating to approximately the same time, Mesopotamian astronomy focused on the moon and eclipses for their lunar-based calendar. The Mesopotamians were not concerned with the movement of the planets until the development of omen literature around 1000 BCE, which initially applied to royalty and not the common folk.[6] The later Babylonian omen astrology was based on the premise that celestial influence concerned both important and mundane events.

Babylon, the most famous city in Mesopotamia, was the capital of the southeastern region, which was the location of the former country of Sumer. As the Babylonians expanded their astrology beyond the planets and moon to the stars, they adapted the constellations that had been recognized by the Sumerians. Weather phenomena were also included in observations and predictions. In addition, Babylonian astrology and omen literature differed from earlier astrology because of the premise that the heavens did not direct events; instead, it provided signs. Intended not only for the rich, it was used by

---

6. Jim Tester, *A History of Western Astrology* (Woodbridge, England: The Boydell Press, 1996), 13.

farmers for guidance in planting and harvesting. As the city rose to prominence, the name *Babylonian* came to identify an entire culture and area.

The Babylonians eventually recorded the movement of planets as evidenced by thousands of cuneiform tablets, which indicated that they carefully studied the Sumerian constellations and invented a zodiac for mathematical astronomy. The zodiac is an exclusive club of constellations that appear along a band of sky, called the *ecliptic*, which circles the earth. This band traces the sun's annual arc. To say that the sun is in a sign of the zodiac means that the sun's position is between the earth and that constellation. Because of this, the zodiac constellations are also called *sun signs*.

The twelve constellations on the ecliptic became the focus of Babylonian astronomy and astrology, replacing the earlier seventeen constellations that occurred along the path of the moon. Astronomers neatly divided the 360-degree circle of the ecliptic into twelve equal 30-degree segments. First used by the Babylonians in the fifth century BCE, the system also included mathematical calculations for the planetary and lunar positions.[7] By incorporating the zodiac constellations into their system, a new form of astrology was developed, and the older omen texts were rewritten and enhanced. Symbols for the planets and zodiac constellations were used in astronomy, astrology, and magical texts.

The Chaldeans were a Semitic people who lived in the southern area around Babylon. Their leader, Nabopolassar (reign c. 625–605 BCE), seized the opportunity to become king of Babylon in 625 BCE and set up a Chaldean dynasty of rulers who remained in power until 539 BCE when the Persians moved in and took over.[8] The term *Chaldean* became synonymous with *Babylonian* and was used by some ancient writers in reference to the scholars and priests of the region who were renowned for their knowledge of astronomy and astrology. Despite their prestige, ancient tablets found in the cities of Uruk and Babylon indicated that astronomy and astrology were mostly a sideline pursuit, not a full-time job. Because of the widespread belief in demons, astrologers often functioned as exorcists too.

The Persians aided the dissemination of Babylonian astronomy and astrology by taking it with them when they moved on to conquer other lands. Although the early Egyptians mapped the stars for calendric purposes, they did not take to the Babylonian style of astrology that the Persians brought with them. Change came later in Egypt during the Greek occupation.

---

7. Ulla Koch-Westenholz, *Mesopotamian Astrology: An Introduction to Babylonian and Assyrian Celestial Divination* (Copenhagen, Denmark: Museum Tusculanum Press, 1995), 163.

8. The Editors of Encyclopaedia Britannica, "Babylonia," Encyclopaedia Britannica, Inc., July 12, 2016, https://www.britannica.com/place/Babylonia.

Along with the movement of trade goods, information filtered around the Mediter-ranean and east to India and China. As mentioned, early Hindu astrology was based on the position of the moon; however, they adapted some of the Babylonian omen astrology into their system. As for China, despite attempts by a few early twentieth-century academics to corroborate a Babylonian influence, they stayed with their own celestial system.[9]

According to the Greeks, astrology was introduced to them by the Chaldean scholar and priest Berosus (c. 330–250 BCE) who founded a school on the Aegean island of Kos in 290 BCE.[10] The Greeks used his ideas and refined the work of the Babylonians and Egyptians as they incorporated it into their own. In addition, the Greeks equated the planets with their deities and applied the concepts of the elements and planetary rulership. Rulership was based on each planet's distance from the sun and how quickly it appeared to move through the zodiac. The sequence of planets and their rulership was also applied to the days of the week and hours of the day. Later, Greco-Roman mathematician and astronomer Claudius Ptolemaeus (c. 100–170 CE), better known as Ptolemy, suggested that stars and constellations possessed "natures" that were similar to one or two of the planets. Greek scholar, biologist, and physicist Theophrastus (c. 372–287 BCE), is credited with associating the celestial bodies with plants and crystals and integrating them into the practice of medicine.

By the first century BCE, Roman interest in astrology had piqued. Many texts on the subject from this period were attributed to the gods Hermes and Aesculapius, both of whom were associated with healing. Although these texts have not survived, they are known from references in the work of later astrologers. One text that survived was by Roman poet Marcus Manilius (first century CE). While his instructional poem entitled *Astronomica* focused on the zodiac, fixed stars, and horoscope houses, it contained little about the planets.

THE RETURN TO EUROPE

After the decline of the Roman Empire, Europe entered a chaotic period called the *Dark Ages* (c. 500–1000 CE) when the advancement of learning and knowledge came to a screeching halt. Scholars who fled the disruption took the observations and ideas of

---

9. David W. Pankenier, "On Chinese Astrology's Imperviousness to External Influences," *Astrology in Time and Place: Cross-Cultural Questions in the History of Astrology*, ed. Nicholas Campion and Dorian Geiseler-Greenbaum (Newcastle upon Tyne, England: Cambridge Scholars Publishing, 2015), 3–26.

10. James Herschel Holden, *A History of Horoscopic Astrology*, 2nd ed. (Tempe, AZ: American Federation of Astrologers, Inc., 2006), 7.

ancient stargazers with them to the Middle East. Eager to expand their knowledge, Arab philosophers and scientists welcomed the newcomers and Baghdad became an important center of learning where European texts were translated into Arabic. Philosopher, mathematician, and astronomer Stephanus of Alexandria (c. 550–622 CE) was a mover and shaker who collected books on astrology and was known for his treatise on alchemy. After spending some time in Baghdad, he moved to Constantinople, which was becoming another melting pot of wisdom. Like Stephanus, other scholars were on the move, disseminating knowledge wherever they traveled.

As astrology filtered back into the West, it was met with condemnation by the powerful Christian church. Nevertheless, astrology took hold in tenth-century Spain because of the influence of the Moors who ruled the country for about eight hundred years. Although astrology was controversial, many Islamic astronomers regarded it as a branch of their science. As it became more popular among laypeople, astrological symbols personifying the planets and zodiac constellations were incorporated into Islamic art. Objects decorated with these motifs were believed to have talismanic power.

Impatient for knowledge, European scholars traveled to Spain and the Middle East where much of the ancient work that had been translated from Greek into Arabic was being translated into Latin. As a result, astrological studies in Europe exploded during the twelfth and thirteenth centuries. Paduan physician and scholar Pietro d'Abano (1257–1316) was one of many influenced by the newly translated Arabic texts. He wrote books on medicine, astrology, and philosophy, and played an important role in the further development of astrological medicine. His denial of the existence and influence of spirits and demons and his belief that celestial bodies could shape human affairs landed him in trouble with the Church. Drawing hundreds of astrological symbols on the Padua city hall did not endear him to local authorities, either. Tried twice by the Inquisition, he was eventually found guilty but died in custody before sentencing.

According to a prevailing belief at the time, angels and demons inhabited the cosmos. Best known for being the first to write about the Arthurian legend in his *Historia Regum Britanniae* (*History of the Kings of Britain*), English cleric and chronicler Geoffrey of Monmouth (c. 1100–1155) explained that God created the universe, angels lived above the stars, and demons lived above the moon.[11] Astrologers of the day saw it a little differently, explaining that celestial intelligences and planetary spirits populated the universe. There

11. Nicholas Campion, *A History of Western Astrology Volume II: The Medieval and Modern Worlds* (New York: Continuum US, 2009), 69.

was also a belief that as a person's soul descended from heaven—the place of its origin—it gained attributes from the planets.

Despite its doctrine, the Church sometimes turned a blind eye and people figured out how to stay under the radar of its scrutiny. This included the clergy, especially in rural monasteries where natural magic was believed to enhance learning. Working with the natural world, natural—white—magic included the study of stars, stones, herbs, and animals. Magic was considered an offshoot of astrology and vice versa. Natural magic was regarded as the opposite of demonic—black—magic.

Often lumped with divination, astrology was denounced by Church leaders, but when couched in terms of being a philosophy, it was not considered so problematic. Divination was frowned upon because it was regarded as an attempt to know God's plan. Nevertheless, magic, astrology, and divination grew in popularity during the Middle Ages and books on these subjects were often disguised as philosophic or religious texts. Attesting to the widespread familiarity of astrology, *The Canterbury Tales* by Geoffrey Chaucer (c. 1342–1400) is peppered with references to astrology, as is other literature of the time.

The fifteenth and sixteenth centuries were a golden age for astrology in Europe. This was the period during which German physician and scholar Heinrich Cornelius Agrippa of Nettesheim (1486–1535) produced his famous work, *Three Books of Occult Philosophy*. Studying and moving around Europe in 1510, Agrippa sent a letter to Abbot Johannes Trithemius (1462–1516) looking for advice and explaining that he was an "explorer of the mysterious forces in nature."[12] The abbot encouraged him to continue his occult studies, and with like-minded friends, Agrippa formed a secret society. Later, as a professor of philosophy and theology at the University of Dôle in Burgundy, France, his lectures brought him under the suspicion of heresy. Agrippa defended himself with the shield of "theology" for his work. He became an influential thinker and writer of his time.

Focusing on natural magic, Agrippa attempted to reconcile it with Christian theories. Ultimately, he wanted to comprehend the workings of nature. This went hand in hand with a prevailing belief that an understanding of the material and spiritual could be found in the celestial bodies because the stars and planets were regarded as perfect.

Although it outwardly condemned astrology and magic, the Church also flirted with these subjects. It wasn't only lowly monks tucked away in remote monasteries, abbots and popes also took part in a clerical underground that explored the realm of magic. Occasionally,

---

12. Marc van der Poel, *Cornelius Agrippa: The Humanist Theologian and His Declamations* (New York: Brill, 1997), 16.

the people they might otherwise have condemned were employed by the Church and royalty, as was the case with Agrippa becoming a counselor to the Holy Roman Emperor Charles V (1500–1558).

Agrippa's mentor, Johannes Trithemius, was abbot in Sponheim and later the Schottenkloster monastery in Würzburg, Germany. In 1508 Trithemius published *De Septum Secundeis* (*The Seven Secondary Intelligences*), in which he explained that each planet had its own personality, character, and consciousness.[13] Although freewheeling abbots such as Trithemius had to move on from time to time to avoid scrutiny of their sideline practices, they were not subjected to the discipline or punishment laid down by their more strict and dogmatic brethren.

For a time, science and astrology coexisted and even some of the founders of modern astronomy such as Nicolaus Copernicus (1473–1543) and Johannes Kepler (1571–1630) also engaged in astrology. Universities established chairs of astrology and in some colleges the topic was included in the curriculum for medical students. Astrological medicine continued to grow in popularity and became almost *de rigueur* for physicians, clerics, and lay people. Books were written on the rules of astrological medicine and included information on zodiac signs, the powers of the planets, the position of the moon, and the fixed stars. Even the famed English herbalist Nicholas Culpeper (1616–1654) wrote several books on astrology and integrated it into his herbal practice.

Eventually, the Scientific Revolution spurred a divergence between astronomy and astrology. While this moved astrology outside the realm of science, its influence and popularity never waned. In the following chapters, we will see how to work with the energy and symbolism of the planets and zodiac constellations for magic and ritual.

---

13. Campion, *A History of Western Astrology*, 118.

CHAPTER 2
THE PLANETS

ANCIENT STARGAZERS NOTICED that some stars seemed to wander rather than follow a fixed path. The Greeks called these *planetes*, "wandering stars," from the verb *planasthai*, meaning "to wander."[14] Believing the planets to be divine beings that moved by their own will, the Greeks gave them great credence, along with the ability to influence not only human lives but to bestow power to the stars that did not wander—the constellations.

However, Ptolemy and Agrippa had different philosophies on the relationship between stars and planets. According to British astrologer, geologist, and author Vivian Robson (1890–1942), Ptolemy noted that rather than being ruled by a planet, a star could have a nature or influence akin to it.[15] Agrippa theorized that the stars were a source of power for the planets rather than the other way around.

Previously mentioned for being tried by the Inquisition, Pietro d'Abano is sometimes attributed with writing a book entitled *Heptameron (Magical Elements)*, which included incantations and rites for conjuring angels for each day of the week. According to the book, each planet was believed to have an associated angel, intelligence, and spirit that could be conjured through complicated rituals. Today, planets are more frequently used in accordance with their associated energies rather than angels and spirits.

Just as the moon phases can be used for timing spells and rituals, so too can the planets. This association of the planets with the days of the week dates to the Babylonians/Chaldeans. However, in ancient times only five planets were known: Jupiter, Mars, Mercury,

---

14. Sam Mickey, *Whole Earth Thinking and Planetary Coexistence: Ecological Wisdom at the Intersection of Religion, Ecology, and Philosophy* (New York: Routledge, 2016), 97.

15. Vivian Robson, *The Fixed Stars & Constellations in Astrology* (Abingdon, MD: The Astrology Center of America, 2005), 98.

Saturn, and Venus. Often called *luminaries*, the sun and moon were included in the planetary system because they were regarded as spheres that revolved around the earth.

The easiest way to use planetary energy for timing events is according to their associated days of the week. Like calling on the power of a rune or element, a planet's symbol can be drawn on objects for spells or carved on a candle for meditating on the planet's associated qualities. Planetary energy can be used to enhance dreamwork, divination, and psychic work, as well as mundane events.

Table 1.1 offers highlights for planetary themes. Refer to the individual entries on each planet for full details. While the three "new" planets (Neptune, Pluto, Uranus) do not have days of the week in traditional planetary work and astrology, there are suitable days for them. The argument against using these planets is that they are too far away to be of influence, however, the stars are a great deal farther, yet they are believed to have power. Follow your heart and work with the energy of these planets if you feel they are appropriate for you.

TABLE 1.1 PLANETARY THEMES		
Day	**Planet**	**Aspects**
Monday	Moon	Creativity, emotions, divination, dreamwork, inspiration, intuition, love, psychic work, spirituality, transformation
Tuesday	Mars	Action, courage, defense, determination, energy, initiative, motivation, passion, protection, skills, tenacity, willpower
	Pluto	The afterlife, changes, dreamwork, memories, renewal, spiritual advancement, transformation
Wednesday	Mercury	Adaptability, communication, expression, ideas, the intellect, messages, omens, success, travel, wealth, wisdom
Thursday	Jupiter	Abundance, ambition, achievement, authority, confidence, growth, justice, leadership, luck, opportunities, prosperity
	Neptune	Awareness, creativity, dreamwork, intuition, passion, prophecy, psychic abilities, spirits, talents
Friday	Venus	Affection, aesthetics, compassion, cooperation, harmony, love, passion, relationships, sensuality, sexuality, sympathy
Saturday	Saturn	Binding, banishing, boundaries, cycles, discipline, justice, knowledge, obstacles, responsibility, stability

TABLE 1.1 PLANETARY THEMES		
Day	**Planet**	**Aspects**
	Uranus	Change, creativity, independence, innovation, inventiveness, motivation
Sunday	Sun	Growth, healing, leadership, manifestation, motivation, power, prosperity, protection, renewal, strength, well-being, wisdom

PLANETARY HOURS

More complex than timing by day of the week is timing by planetary hour. Like our standard day, a planetary day has twenty-four hours, but that is where the similarity ends. Unlike a standard day that runs from midnight to midnight, a planetary day runs from sunrise to sunrise. It is split between twelve hours of daytime from sunrise to sunset and twelve hours of nighttime from sunset to sunrise. For this to work, the length of the hours within daytime and nighttime vary. And of course, sunrise and sunset times change throughout the year.

Before panicking, sunrise and sunset times can be found in many places online including a table for an entire year at the US Naval Observatory website.[16] There are also calculators online, as well as software and apps that provide complete tables, which make it so much easier to use planetary hours. Whether or not you want to do the calculations yourself, it is helpful to understand how it works. Before you start, you will need the sunrise and sunset times for a given day, plus the sunrise for the following day.

As an example, we will use Sunday sunrise and sunset times of 5:25 a.m. and 7:51 p.m. and the following sunrise of 5:22 a.m. The duration of the daytime hours (from 5:25 a.m. to 7:51 p.m.) is 14 hours 27 minutes. The duration of the nighttime hours (from 7:52 p.m. to 5:22 a.m.) is 9 hours 31 minutes.

The next step is to convert the duration times to minutes. In our example, daytime is 867 minutes and nighttime 571 minutes. Because a planetary day is divided in half with 12 hours each, divide the daytime and nighttime minutes by 12 to get the length of an hour for each half of the day. In our example, the daytime hour is 72 minutes long and the

---

16. Available at http://aa.usno.navy.mil/data/docs/RS_OneYear.php; accessed May 18, 2018.

nighttime hour is 47 minutes long. The final step is to calculate when each hour begins. Continuing with the example, the first hour begins at sunrise, 5:25 a.m., and runs for 72 minutes, which means the second hour begins at 6:37 a.m., and so forth. At sunset, the length of the hour changes to 47 minutes. Now you can see why an app or online calculator is a wonderful tool.

The planet associated with the first hour of a day is the same as the planet of the day. For example, the day and first hour on Sunday is associated with the sun. From here, the planetary hours follow an order established by the Babylonians / Chaldeans, which was arranged according to how they were perceived to move; slowest to fastest. The order is Saturn, Jupiter, Mars, Sun, Venus, Mercury, Moon. In our example, the first hour on Sunday is the sun, the second hour is Venus, and so forth. After the fourth hour—the hour of the moon—the order resets to start at the beginning with Saturn. Table 1.2 provides a list of the planetary hours.

TABLE 1.2 SCHEDULE OF PLANETARY HOURS						
Hour	**Sunday**	**Monday**	**Tuesday**	**Wednesday**	**Thursday**	**Friday**	**Saturday**
Daytime Hours							
1	Sun	Moon	Mars	Mercury	Jupiter	Venus	Saturn
2	Venus	Saturn	Sun	Moon	Mars	Mercury	Jupiter
3	Mercury	Jupiter	Venus	Saturn	Sun	Moon	Mars
4	Moon	Mars	Mercury	Jupiter	Venus	Saturn	Sun
5	Saturn	Sun	Moon	Mars	Mercury	Jupiter	Venus
6	Jupiter	Venus	Saturn	Sun	Moon	Mars	Mercury
7	Mars	Mercury	Jupiter	Venus	Saturn	Sun	Moon
8	Sun	Moon	Mars	Mercury	Jupiter	Venus	Saturn
9	Venus	Saturn	Sun	Moon	Mars	Mercury	Jupiter
10	Mercury	Jupiter	Venus	Saturn	Sun	Moon	Mars
11	Moon	Mars	Mercury	Jupiter	Venus	Saturn	Sun
12	Saturn	Sun	Moon	Mars	Mercury	Jupiter	Venus

Hour	Sunday	Monday	Tuesday	Wednesday	Thursday	Friday	Saturday
TABLE 1.2 SCHEDULE OF PLANETARY HOURS							
Nighttime Hours							
1	Jupiter	Venus	Saturn	Sun	Moon	Mars	Mercury
2	Mars	Mercury	Jupiter	Venus	Saturn	Sun	Moon
3	Sun	Moon	Mars	Mercury	Jupiter	Venus	Saturn
4	Venus	Saturn	Sun	Moon	Mars	Mercury	Jupiter
5	Mercury	Jupiter	Venus	Saturn	Sun	Moon	Mars
6	Moon	Mars	Mercury	Jupiter	Venus	Saturn	Sun
7	Saturn	Sun	Moon	Mars	Mercury	Jupiter	Venus
8	Jupiter	Venus	Saturn	Sun	Moon	Mars	Mercury
9	Mars	Mercury	Jupiter	Venus	Saturn	Sun	Moon
10	Sun	Moon	Mars	Mercury	Jupiter	Venus	Saturn
11	Venus	Saturn	Sun	Moon	Mars	Mercury	Jupiter
12	Mercury	Jupiter	Venus	Saturn	Sun	Moon	Mars

WORKING WITH THE PLANETS

Working with the energy and symbolism of the planets is like calling on the power of the elements or runes. Whether or not you use planetary days or hours, their symbols can be used anytime for boosting the energy of spells, making talismans, enhancing rituals, and for any mundane purpose that seems appropriate to you. Using the symbols in meditation and/or visualization also aids in cultivating the traits associated with a planet.

Although the source of the planetary symbols used today is sometimes attributed to Roman scholar and author Gaius Julius Hyginus (c. 64 BCE–17 CE) from a text entitled *Poeticon Astronomicon*, others attribute them to the work of a later author. This is because the symbols were not found in early copies of Hyginus's book but appear in the 1539 edition printed by German publisher Johannes Soter (c. 1519–1543). In the following entries, you will see that although many of the modern symbols come from medieval manu-scripts, they have roots in Egyptian, Greek, and Roman traditions. Along with the modern symbols, two variations are included in the illustrations, however, there are many more that you may want to research further. Information on associated plants and crystals is also included, along with suggestions for using the energy of each planet.

Jupiter

The largest planet in the solar system, Jupiter was named for the supreme Roman god. Also known as Jove, he was a powerful sky and thunder god. Fundamentally, this planet relates to authority, learning, growth, achievement, and luck. The main forces at work in everyday life are ambition, leadership, honor, confidence, and justice. The energy of this planet can instill a sense of justice and the need to uphold principles that guide the desire to rule. It aids in being reliable, self-confident, and appropriately assertive.

The energy of Jupiter can be employed to attract abundance and prosperity. Carve its symbol on a candle for spells to stimulate opportunities and achieve success. For business purposes, draw it on a piece of paper and keep it where you handle finances to help build wealth. Paint it on a piece of amethyst as a reminder to be generous and treat others with dignity. This symbol aids in cultivating discipline and kindness for using power and author-ity wisely. Draw it on a piece of paper, and then wrap it around a diopside crystal for heal-ing rituals. Wear the symbol on a piece of jewelry, made of tin if possible, when seeking justice.

Figure 1: The modern/1539 symbol of Jupiter (left)
with fourteenth-century (center)
and sixteenth-century (right) variations.

Although the modern symbol for Jupiter comes from the late medieval tradition, it may be based on the ancient Greek symbol for the planet: the letter Z (for Zeus) with a horizontal line through the middle. According to other theories, the symbol is a glyph rep-resenting an eagle—Jupiter's bird. It also resembles one of the alchemical symbols for tin, the metal associated with Jupiter. However, the fourteenth-century symbol is one of the alchemical symbols for the metal lead. The sixteenth-century symbol represents an orb and scepter—symbols of power.

Some of the plants associated with Jupiter include anise, betony, borage, cedar, cinquefoil, clove, meadowsweet, myrrh, oak, and sage. Crystals include amethyst, ametrine, diopside, emerald, lepidolite, sugilite, turquoise, and red zircon. Jupiter is associated with the metal tin and the elements air and fire. In astrology, it is the ruling planet of Sagittarius and Pisces.

Mars

Mostly known as the Roman god of war, Mars was also associated with agriculture and second in importance to Jupiter. Fundamentally, this planet relates to energy, action, initiative, motivation, and male sexuality. The main forces at work in everyday life are courage—physical and moral—tenacity, and caution. The energy of Mars helps to build initiative, inspire others to action, and see things through to completion.

The energy of this planet is helpful when a call to action is needed for defense or to halt aggression. Paint the symbol of Mars on a piece of bloodstone to carry with you to bolster courage and appropriate assertiveness. Mars energy is helpful for honing skills and personal growth. It is an aid for strengthening determination and willpower, especially to resolve conflicts. This includes personal battles and self-imposed obstacles. Carve the symbol on a red candle for spells relating to passion and desire, but be careful of what you wish for. Using the energy of this planet for retribution escalates anger and discord.

Figure 2: The modern/1539 symbol of Mars (left)
with seventeenth-century (center)
and eighteenth-century (right) variations.

Representing the shield and spear of the god of war, the modern and medieval symbol is derived from the Greco-Roman period (c. 330 BCE–395 CE). Later variations were based on the same theme. The modern symbol for Mars is also the male or masculine symbol.

Some of the plants associated with Mars include anise, asafetida, basil, blackthorn, coriander, ginger, hawthorn, juniper, and rue. Crystals include bloodstone, citrine, hematite, red jasper, pyrite, sard, and red zircon. Mars is associated with the metals iron and steel and the element fire. In astrology, it is the ruling planet of Aries and Scorpio.

Mercury

Known as the messenger of the gods, Mercury was the Roman god of communication, commerce, and wisdom. Fundamentally, this planet relates to the intellect—the reasoning mind—ideas, and the power of self-expression. The main forces at work in everyday life are mental abilities, self-expression, and tact. The energy of Mercury supports a quick wit and good communication skills. It boosts action and ideas and supports an aptitude for business or teaching.

Call on Mercury for help whenever you need to improve communications ranging from developing clarity of speech to opening energy channels with another person. Inscribe Mercury's symbol on a gray or dark blue candle for spells to boost business success or general wealth. Draw the symbol in the air in front of you before a divination session for support in deciphering messages and omens. Use it on your altar when seeking inspiration and wisdom. For smooth travel, wear a piece of jewelry with the symbol. Paint it on a piece of moss agate for healing. Mercury is also instrumental for recalling memories, stoking creativity, and cultivating adaptability.

Figure 3: The modern/1539 symbol of Mercury (left)
with John Dee's (center)
and another sixteenth-century (right) variation.

The modern and medieval symbol is derived from the Greco-Roman period and represents the head and winged cap of Mercury atop his caduceus (staff). Medieval alchemists also used this symbol to represent the metal mercury. In Dee's symbol, the crossed lines represented the cross of materiality, a concept used by medieval alchemists for the union of the elements.

Some of the plants associated with Mercury include ash, dill, elder, hazel, mandrake, marjoram, mistletoe, rosemary, and sage. Crystals include agate, amber, cat's eye, citrine, fluorite, peridot, and topaz. Mercury is associated with the metals aluminum and mercury, and the elements air and water. In astrology, it is the ruling planet of Gemini and Virgo.

The Moon

While the Roman goddess Luna represented the moon, Diana, goddess of the hunt, was also a powerful lunar deity. Fundamentally, the moon relates to intuition, spirituality, emotions, domestic activities, and women's rituals. The main forces at work in everyday life are memories, dreams, imagination, and creativity. The energy of the moon stirs the imagination and aids in finding the muse that resides deep within the soul. Lunar energy opens the channels for being in tune with the needs of others.

The moon is a powerful ally for any type of magic. Inscribe its symbol on a white candle to draw down energy when you want to heighten intuition, creativity, or sensitivity. Use it on a blue candle to enhance contact with spirits. Incorporate the symbol with items used for dreamwork, divination, and psychic work to boost your abilities. For protection spells, draw the moon's symbol on a small piece of paper, sprinkle it with rosemary leaves, and then burn it in your cauldron. To dispel negativity, paint it on a piece of smoky quartz and place it wherever needed or keep it with you to overcome obstacles. Place the symbol and a piece of moonstone on your altar when seeking love or transformation.

Moon energy is also powerful when coordinating magic with its phases. The new moon is a quiet period, a time for divination and personal workings. It is a time for incubation and holding power. The waxing moon is a time for growth, gathering knowledge, and inspiration. Magic begun now culminates at the full moon. The waxing phase is conducive for creativity because of the high energy and clarity of vision it brings. It is also advantageous for teaching. The energy of the full moon is intense. It is a time for sending forth intentions because of the high-powered energy that can propel them to manifest. The waning phase is a time for turning inward and reflecting. It is a time for reaping what was put forth during the waxing phase. The waning phase is a good time for banishing spells and releasing what is unwanted. It is also conducive for deep rest.

Figure 4: The modern/1539 symbol of the Moon (left)
with fourteenth-century (center)
and sixteenth-century (right) variations.

The modern and many medieval symbols for the moon are derived from ancient Greek tradition. The fourteenth-century symbol comes from the medieval alchemical tradition with long lines representing streams of light. This symbol is similar to the ancient Greek alchemical symbol for selenite. The sixteenth-century symbol represents waxing and waning.

Some of the plants associated with the moon include aloe, bergamot, birch, blackberry, jasmine, lemon balm, moonwort, rosemary, and willow. Crystals include angelite, clear calcite, diamond, moonstone, quartz, selenite, smoky quartz, and turquoise. The moon is associated with the metal silver and the element water. In astrology, it is the ruling planet of Cancer.

Neptune

Best known as the god of the sea, this Roman deity also presided over fresh water. Fundamentally, Neptune relates to creativity, intuition, illusion, and prophecy. The main forces at work in everyday life are vitality, passion, and creative expression. The energy of Neptune supports the development of talent and putting it out to the world through a full range of the arts: visual, music, dance, writing, and poetry.

This planet's energy is especially powerful for expanding awareness and developing psychic abilities, including clairvoyance. For help in tapping into the subconscious mind, paint Neptune's symbol on a piece of labradorite when engaging in divination or shamanic work. Carve it into a light green or indigo candle when working with other realms. Paint it on an amethyst crystal for aid in contacting spirits or when working with spirit guides. To boost dreamwork, draw or sew Neptune's symbol on a small organza bag, place a piece of turquoise in it, and then hang it on your bedpost or place it on a bedside table.

Figure 5: The modern/early twentieth-century symbol of Neptune (left)
with late nineteenth-century (center)
and alternative early twentieth-century (right) variations.

All of the symbols created for Neptune represent the sea god's trident. Plants associated with Neptune include ash, dune grass, reeds, seaweed, and water lily. Crystals include amethyst, angelite, aquamarine, celestite, labradorite, lapis lazuli, lepidolite, and turquoise. This planet is associated with the element water. When used in astrology, Neptune is the ruling planet of Pisces; Jupiter is the traditional planet.

Pluto

This planet is named for the Roman god and ruler of the underworld. Fundamentally, this planet relates to transformation, regeneration, and rebirth. The main forces at work in everyday life are changes, personal transformation, and spiritual advancement. Although Pluto was downgraded to dwarf planet status, its energy is anything but small. Pluto's energy can be intense, making it a challenge to keep in check; however, when used wisely it becomes a catalyst for change.

Because Pluto is associated with death, the underworld, and afterlife, its energy is effective at Samhain for commemorating ancestors and loved ones who have passed. As part of your sabbat ritual, draw Pluto's symbol on a piece of paper to place on your altar with a sprig of bittersweet and a piece of jet. To aid dreamwork, paint the symbol on a piece of garnet to place under your pillow. For help in accessing deeply held memories and the inner workings of the self, paint the symbol on a piece of tourmalated quartz to hold during meditation. Carving the symbol on a black candle symbolizes the restful darkness of incubation and aids when seeking change or renewal in any aspect of life.

Figure 6: The modern/early twentieth-century symbol of Pluto (left)
with mid twentieth-century (center) and late twentieth-century (right) variations.

The modern symbol was adapted from French-American author, composer, and astrologer Dane Rudhyar (1895–1985) who described it as representing the transcendence of mind moving from matter to spirit. Canadian-American astrologer Paul Clancy (1897–1956) popularized the symbol through his *American Astrology* magazine. The mid twentieth-century symbol is based on an alchemical symbol for salt, which was also used to represent light and dark. The late twentieth-century symbol plays on the theme of Pluto/Hades as god of the underworld.

Some of the plants associated with Pluto include basil, belladonna, bittersweet, cypress, nettle, and reed. Crystals include amethyst, garnet, jet, labradorite, obsidian, spinel, tourmaline, and tourmalated quartz. Pluto is associated with the element water. When used in astrology, it is the ruling planet of Scorpio; Mars is the traditional planet.

Saturn

This planet is named for the Roman god of agriculture, the harvest, and time. Fundamentally, Saturn relates to cycles, boundaries and limitations, and responsibility. The main forces at work in everyday life are earnestness in work, the importance of discipline, and the limits of time. The energy of this planet is particularly supportive for those who are sensitive, studious, and observant. It also provides stability.

For an energy boost, carve Saturn's symbol on a dark blue or gray candle to use during a binding spell. For banishing, draw it on a piece of paper, wrap it around a few pine needles, and then burn it in your cauldron. When seeking justice, wear Saturn's symbol as jewelry or keep a drawing of it with you for meetings with lawyers or during court appearances. For aid in overcoming obstacles, hold the symbol between your hands as you visualize whatever is holding you back, and then let the image slowly fade from your mind. Using the energy of Saturn for retribution amplifies problems and creates obstacles.

Figure 7: The modern/sixteenth-century symbol of Saturn (left)
with fifteenth-century (center)
and mid twentieth-century (right) variations.

The modern and medieval symbols were derived from symbols of the Greco-Roman tradition, which represented a scythe or sickle, relating to Saturn as a god of seed sowing and time. The mid twentieth-century symbol is a modern interpretation by Austrian mathematician and astronomer Otto Neugebauer (1899–1990).

Some of the plants associated with Saturn include beech, belladonna, comfrey, henbane, monkshood, pine, rowan, Solomon's seal, and thornapple. Crystals include apache tears, azurite, carnelian, brown jasper, obsidian, sardonyx, serpentine, and black tourmaline. Saturn is associated with the metal lead and the elements earth and water. In astrology, it is the ruling planet of Aquarius and Capricorn.

The Sun

In Roman mythology, the god Helios represents the sun. Fundamentally, the sun relates to the self, power, success, and hope. The main forces at work in everyday life are warmth, fulfillment, and joy. The energy of the sun stimulates a love of art and an appreciation of beauty. It aids in being versatile and loyal and helps in finding a meaningful path.

The sun is especially beneficial for sending healing energy and thoughts to anyone in need. Carve its symbol on a yellow candle for healing circles to attract nurturing energy and blessings. Paint it on a piece of amber to wear or carry with you as a protective amulet. For confidence in a leadership role, wear or carry a piece of tiger's eye marked with the sun's symbol. In a spell to attract prosperity and success, use the symbol with dried marigold or sunflower petals. Meditate on the symbol to awaken wisdom.

Figure 8: The modern/sixteenth-century symbol of the sun (left)
with fourteenth-century (center)
and fifteenth-century (right) variations.

The modern symbol for the sun was introduced during the Italian Renaissance and based on an esoteric Christian tradition where it represented the seed of potential within spirit. The fourteenth-century symbol was an alchemical representation of the sun. Some fifteenth-century astrologers used a diamond shape divided into sections.

Some of the plants associated with the sun include chrysanthemum, daisy, gorse, heliotrope, marigold, oak, saffron crocus, St. John's wort, sunflower, and witch hazel. Crystals include amber, golden beryl, orange calcite, chrysoberyl, citrine, diamond, sunstone, tiger's eye, and yellow topaz. The sun is associated with the metal gold and the element fire. In astrology, it is the ruling planet of Leo.

Uranus

Uranus was named for the primordial Greek sky god Ouranos. Fundamentally, this planet relates to independence, innovation, change, and the ability to blaze new trails. The main forces at work in everyday life are originality, creativity, and non-traditionalism. The energy of this planet helps to deal with change and to thrive during transitions—even ones that may be difficult. Uranus fosters the ability to find different approaches to problematic situations.

Providing the jolt needed to get out of a rut, the energy of Uranus is perfect for initiating major or subtle changes. Draw its symbol on a piece of aventurine to carry with you until things begin to move. Use the symbol in spells aimed at stoking ambition and reaching goals. Before a divination session, carve the symbol on a dark blue candle and focus attention on your third-eye chakra to sharpen intuitive skills. To improve family relationships, paint the symbol on several pieces of quartz, and then place them around your home. Meditate on the symbol to cultivate a sense of freedom and a hopeful future.

Figure 9: The modern/early twentieth-century symbol of Uranus (left)
with late nineteenth-century (center)
and early twentieth-century (right) variations.

Discovered in 1781 by British astronomer William Herschel (1738–1822), many of the symbols for Uranus incorporate a stylized letter *H*. Dutch astrologer Adolph Ernestus Thierens (1875–1941) depicted an esoteric symbol of Uranus as an awakener of the soul.

The plants associated with Uranus are ash and rowan. Crystals include amazonite, aventurine, Herkimer diamond, labradorite, and quartz. Uranus is associated with the element air. When used in astrology, it is the ruling planet of Aquarius; Saturn is the traditional planet.

Venus

This planet was named for the Roman goddess of love and beauty. Fundamentally, it relates to love, harmony, refinement, aesthetics, and sensuality. The main forces at work in everyday life are affection, passion (in all its forms), cooperation, sympathy, and appreciation of the arts. The energy of Venus encourages a warm and friendly disposition. It is also an aid for keeping in tune with the physical body.

Associated with the goddess of love, the energy of Venus is the perfect planet to call on for love. Use white paint to draw the symbol of Venus on a piece of rose quartz for attraction spells and romance charms. When placed in the bedroom, it can help fire up passion and sexual energy. To kindle compassion and affection, dip your finger in rose water, and then draw the symbol over your heart. When harmony and unity are lacking in the workplace, draw the symbol on a small piece of paper and place it under a celestite crystal on your desk. Also, keep the symbol in the workspace where you engage in creative activities.

Figure 10: The modern/1539 symbol of Venus (left)
with sixteenth-century (center)
and seventeenth-century (right) variations.

From the medieval tradition, the modern symbol is derived from the ancient Greek astrological system and represents the hand mirror of Aphrodite, reflecting wisdom and self-knowledge. It is also the symbol for female. The sixteenth-century symbol by Italian mathematician and astronomer Francesco Giutini (1523–1590) is similar to others of the same period that seem to suggest a rising motion. The seventeenth-century alchemical symbol for Venus could also be drawn upside down.

Some of the plants associated with Venus include apple, bergamot, blackberry, colts-foot, lilac, lady's mantle, rose, strawberry, and willow. Crystals include cat's eye, celestite, desert rose, diamond, emerald, jade, lapis lazuli, rose quartz, and turquoise. Venus is associated with the metal copper and the element earth. In astrology, it is the ruling planet of Libra and Taurus.

CHAPTER 3

THE ZODIAC CONSTELLATIONS

MODERN ASTRONOMY RECOGNIZES eighty-eight constellations, some of which are based on the forty-eight ancient Greek star figures described by Ptolemy. The other forty constellations are based on European star atlases from the fifteenth through seventeenth centuries. As mentioned, only a few of the constellations are members of the zodiac because they fall within the ecliptic.

TWELVE OR THIRTEEN FOR MAGIC?

Because we are focusing on the magical aspects of the zodiac, it is important to note that there are thirteen constellations that fall within the ecliptic. Located between Scorpio and Sagittarius is the constellation Ophiuchus (pronounced oh-fee-oo-kus). Most astrologers use the conventional twelve constellations and associated dates that were established over two thousand years ago. As a result, Aries is the first sign of the zodiac in astrology beginning at the spring equinox; however, Pisces is the constellation that is on the ecliptic "behind" the sun during the equinox.

The change of constellations at the equinox is due to a phenomenon called *precession of the equinoxes* or simply *precession*. Discovered by Greek mathematician and astronomer Hipparchus (c. 190–127 BCE), this ongoing shifting of stars is due to the earth's tilted axis and wobble. The wobble is caused by the gravitational pull of the sun and moon, which shifts the earth's orientation in space.

In astrology, the zodiac is comprised of time segments that are approximately thirty days long. However, the actual time that it takes the sun to pass through—or in front of—each constellation varies because the ecliptic often crosses a small part of them. For example, Virgo has the most time of forty-five days and Scorpio the least at seven days.

Despite these differences, magic and astrology are not incompatible. If you are into astrology and feel more comfortable with the traditional dates, use those for your magic.

TABLE 1.3 DATES OF CONSTELLATIONS ON THE ECLIPTIC			
Constellation	Actual Dates for the Zodiac	Days on the Ecliptic	Traditional Dates Used in Astrology
Pisces	Mar 12–Apr 18	38	Feb 19–Mar 20
Aries	Apr 19–May 13	25	Mar 21–Apr 19
Taurus	May 14–Jun 19	37	Apr 20–May 20
Gemini	Jun 20–Jul 20	31	May 21–Jun 21
Cancer	Jul 21–Aug 9	20	Jun 22–Jul 22
Leo	Aug 10–Sep 15	37	Jul 23–Aug 22
Virgo	Sep 16–Oct 30	45	Aug 23–Sep 22
Libra	Oct 31–Nov 22	23	Sep 23–Oct 23
Scorpio	Nov 23–Nov 29	7	Oct 24–Nov 21
Ophiuchus	Nov 30–Dec 17	18	
Sagittarius	Dec 18–Jan 18	32	Nov 22–Dec 21
Capricorn	Jan 19–Feb 15	28	Dec 22–Jan 19
Aquarius	Feb 16–Mar 11	24	Jan 20–Feb 18

WORKING WITH THE CONSTELLATIONS

Although the zodiac constellations have periods during which their influence is especially strong, their energy can be drawn upon as needed at any time. As with the planets, meditating on a zodiac symbol can help cultivate traits associated with that constellation. Regardless of which sign you were born under, wearing a piece of zodiac jewelry can act as a talisman to aid you. Drawing the energy of a constellation into a piece of jewelry, crystal, or something crafted for a spell can boost the energy of your intention and will-power.

The power of the constellations can also be used to boost astral travel or journeying. Our bodies consist of layers: the physical, etheric, and astral. The astral body, sometimes called the *star body*, is often described as shimmering like a multitude of tiny stars. There is disagreement as to whether the aura is part of the astral or etheric bodies or both. At any rate, the astral body is our vehicle of consciousness and astral travel is generally defined as any state in which the consciousness is immersed somewhere different from the physical body.

Whatever constellation you are working with, paint its symbol on a crystal or other object. When you are ready to travel, hold it between your hands. Raise energy in your physical body, and then visualize it rippling out through the etheric and astral bodies. Visualize the stars in your astral field twinkling as you receive energy from the constellation.

Constellation energy enhances contact with astral familiars that you may encounter during these travels. It also augments work with power animals and spirit guides. Dreamwork can also benefit from star energy. Unlike other practices for which we raise energy, in dreamwork we want to avoid too much active energy that will keep us from reaching a deep sleep. Draw the symbol of a constellation on a small piece of paper to slip under your pillow. In addition to the symbol, include a keyword or two about your intention for dreamwork. On the following evening, create sacred space, and then burn the paper, ideally outdoors under the stars or wherever it can be done safely.

For ease of use by non-astrologers, the following entries on the constellations are presented in alphabetical order. (Also, I may have been a librarian in a past life because I like presenting information this way.) Each entry includes historical details and illustrations of the modern symbols along with a couple of variations.

While suggestions are provided for magical and mundane use of the constellations, these are by no means the only ways to tap into their energy. Let your creativity and intuition guide you to find uses that you can tailor to your personal practices.

Aquarius

With a name meaning "water bearer," Aquarius is usually depicted as a man carrying or pouring water from a large jar.[17] In ancient times, Aquarius became associated with abundant water because the sun rose in this constellation during the rainy season.

Aquarius initiates a period of inspiration, making it a good time to shake things up. Take this opportunity to meet troubles head-on for resolution and change. It is also a time to break free and follow your creativity. Set new goals, but don't forget about cooperation and the power of spiritual community. Spells focusing on healing and friendship get a boost during this period. The main forces at work in everyday life are friendship,

---

17. Editorial Staff, *Webster's Third New International Dictionary*, vol. 1, 108.

loyalty, innovation, and accomplishment. The energy of Aquarius can instill peace and understanding, boost creative expression, and aid in finding freedom. It is helpful when trying to get out of the proverbial rut.

Whether you want to expand creative talents, psychic abilities, or magical skills, call on Aquarian energy to prepare mentally and energetically by painting its symbol on a piece of amethyst. Hold the crystal between your hands for a few moments before continuing with your activity. Because several of its major stars are associated with luck, Aquarius adds extra energy to spells for luck. Carve the symbol into a yellow candle along with a keyword relating to the reason you are seeking luck. Draw the symbol on a piece of paper to keep with you when cultivating friendships or to promote cooperation when working with a group. Use the symbol with a pearl when seeking wisdom.

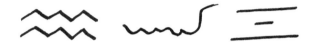

**Figure 11: The modern/late fifteenth-century symbol (left)
along with early fifteenth-century (center)
and early twentieth-century (right) variations.**

The modern and common medieval symbols for Aquarius were derived from ancient Egyptian forms. The Egyptians associated this constellation with the Nile River, the bringer of life-giving water. Many fifteenth- through seventeenth-century symbols suggest movement. The early twentieth-century symbol was derived from a second-century Roman depiction representing a channel or conduit.

Some of the crystals associated with Aquarius include amber, amethyst, aquamarine, aventurine, fluorite, hematite, jade, onyx, opal, pearl, clear quartz, and turquoise. Aquarius is associated with the element air. In astrology, its ruling planets are Saturn (traditional) and Uranus.

Aries

With its name meaning "ram" in Latin, this constellation represents the mythological ram with a golden fleece.[18] Like the terrestrial animal, it is associated with the gods Ares, Belenus, Hermes, Pan, Marduk, and Mars.

---

18. Ibid., 117.

Aries ushers in a period of high energy that is instrumental for getting things started. It is a time of vitality, independence, and for blazing new trails. Magic related to financial growth or leadership goals are especially effective at this time. This is also a period for working on assertiveness and developing personal strengths. The main forces at work in everyday life are energy, determination, willpower, and personal development. Aries energy can give ambition a boost to get projects started and provide the motivation to see them through to completion.

Aries the ram is associated with the Horned God and serves as a symbol of fertility and abundance. To give abundance or fertility spells a boost, draw the Aries symbol on a picture of a cluster of cherries. This constellation also offers a high degree of protective energy. To invite Aries to your property, paint its symbol on a piece of red jasper and place it near your front door or any place where you feel defensive energy is needed. To boost confidence, especially in business, wear or carry a piece of bloodstone with the symbol. For help in overcoming obstacles, draw it multiple times on a piece of paper in the form of a spiral to represent a ram's horn. Hold it between your hands as you visualize the obstacle dissolving, and then burn the paper in your cauldron.

Figure 12: The modern/sixteenth-century symbol of Aries (left)
with fifteenth-century (center)
and late nineteenth-century (right) variations.

With roots in the Greco-Roman period, the symbols for Aries depict the horns of a ram and represented the most powerful gods.

Some of the crystals associated with Aries include brown and fire agate, bloodstone, red jasper, lapis lazuli, clear quartz, ruby, and sardonyx. Aries is associated with the element fire. In astrology, its ruling planet is Mars.

Cancer

To the ancient Greeks and Romans this constellation represented the crab that Hera sent to distract Hercules from his tasks. Although its name is Latin for "crab," medieval astronomers represented the constellation as a crayfish.[19] Cancer was occasionally referred to as a dark sign because its stars are so faint.

Cancer brings in a period of nurturing energy that focuses on the family and home. It also fosters and supports psychic abilities while providing protection. This is a time of fertility that encompasses procreation and creativity. It provides an opportunity to use your sensitivity for developing and sharpening intuition. The main forces at work in everyday life are family, the home, emotions, loyalty, and introspection. Amplifying sensitivity and sympathy, Cancer's energy provides support for and connections with other people. It also helps overcome shyness.

Because the crab is an inhabitant of the shoreline and at home between the worlds, the energy of Cancer is an aid for astral travel and shamanic work. Wear or have its symbol with you when engaging in these activities. The crab's sideways movement represents the ability to side-step daily routines and tap into the subconscious. Carve the symbol into a light blue candle for meditation before dreamwork. To boost psychic abilities or stoke the imagination, dissolve a pinch of sea salt in water, dip your finger in, and then draw Cancer's symbol on your third-eye chakra. Paint the symbol on a piece of rose quartz to use in a romance spell or as a love charm. Paint it on a piece of moonstone and place on your altar during esbat rituals to amplify the energy.

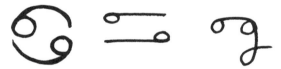

Figure 13: The modern/early twentieth-century symbol of Cancer (left)
with fifteenth-century (center)
and seventeenth-century (right) variations.

With roots in the Greco-Roman period, the modern symbol represents the rounded body and pincers of a crab. During medieval times, the symbols were more schematic in style and focused on the two arms and pincers. Some of the symbols from the seventeenth century also represented movement.

Some of the crystals associated with Cancer include agate, beryl, moonstone, opal, pearl, rose quartz, and selenite. This constellation is associated with the element water. In astrology, its ruling planet is the moon.

---

19. Ibid., 325.

Capricorn

Although Capricorn the Sea Goat is a faint constellation, observation of it dates to the Babylonians who referred to it as a goat fish. This concept began with the Sumerians who depicted Enki—their primordial god of wisdom, waters, and fertility—in this manner. The name *Capricorn* is Latin and means "goat-horned."[20] The Greeks associated the constellation with their forest deity Pan, who had the legs and horns of a goat.

Capricorn presides over a period that is conducive to working with the material side of life, advancing oneself, setting goals, and achieving success. Magic focused on career during this time can bring positive changes. The main forces at work in everyday life are ambition, discipline, organization, skills, and responsibility. The energy of Capricorn aids in dealing with practical matters and maintaining stability.

Capricorn is associated with the Horned God and abundance. Use its symbol on a ritual altar to represent the God, or in spells to boost prosperity. Paint it on a piece of calcite to use in spells to strengthen willpower and manifest success. To remove or ward off negativity, draw Capricorn's symbol on a small piece of paper, burn it with a few pine needles or a pinch of thyme, and smudge areas where needed. Carve the symbol on a white candle and use it to focus your mind or aid in grounding energy after ritual. For help in interpreting messages or omens, paint the symbol on a piece of garnet, and then hold it as you meditate on possible meanings. Paint it on a piece of obsidian jewelry to wear while practicing psychic abilities.

**Figure 14: The modern/sixteenth-century symbol of Capricorn (left)
with fifteenth-century (center)
and seventeenth-century (right) variations.**

The symbol calls on the duality of a goat fish and represents the combination of a billy goat beard and goat or fish tail. Through the centuries there have been many fanciful and flowing variants with faint echoes to ancient Egyptian symbols.

---

20. Ibid., 333.

Some of the crystals associated with Capricorn include azurite, calcite, garnet, malachite, obsidian, clear and smoky quartz, and black tourmaline. Capricorn is associated with the element earth. In astrology, its ruling planet is Saturn.

Gemini

Meaning "twins" in Latin, Gemini represents Romulus and Remus, the brothers who were credited with founding the city of Rome.[21] The Greeks regarded this constellation as Castor and Pollux, sons of the Spartan queen Leda.

Gemini ushers in a period focused on changes, adaptability, communication, and creativity. The energy of this constellation aids in staying alert and using the knowledge at hand to work out problems or to get to the truth of a situation. The main forces at work in everyday life are balance, flexibility, relationships, and all forms of communication. The energy of Gemini aids in resolving problems or difficult situations and builds negotiating skills for gaining the best possible outcome.

Like the number two, twins can represent anything of a binary nature and serve as a dynamic symbol of opposites. While two can represent division, it also represents the strength of unity. Because of this, the energy of Gemini can double the power of spells. Carve the Gemini symbol on two candles and as you light them say:

> *"Candles burn, cauldron bubble;*
> *Gemini, this spell to double."*

Proceed with your work and when you are finished, repeat the rhyme and blow out the candles. For help in adapting to transitions in your life, paint the symbol on a piece of topaz to wear or keep with you. To enhance communication skills, use it with carnelian. Meditate on the symbol when you need help discerning the truth in a situation.

Figure 15: The modern symbol of Gemini (left)
with fifteenth-century (center)
and late nineteenth-century (right) variations.

---

21. Ibid., 944.

Like most symbols, those for Gemini varied throughout time, however, they all reflect the concept of doubling and duality. The roots of these symbols date back to the Greco-Roman period.

Some of the crystals associated with Gemini include aquamarine, carnelian, cat's eye, chrysocolla, citrine, lodestone, clear quartz, serpentine, and topaz. Gemini is associated with the element air. In astrology, its ruling planet is Mercury.

Leo

One of the earliest recognized constellations; Leo was prominent during the summer solstice, giving it—and lions in general—a connection with the sun. Leo represented the mythological lion of Nemea that was slain by Hercules who wanted to gain its power by wearing its pelt. Leo's name is Latin and means "lion."[22]

The lion symbolizes strength, power, leadership, and authority. Leo brings in a period for fostering these qualities, but it must be done with integrity and care to avoid an overabundance of pride and ambition. A true lion is a guardian who provides guidance. The main forces at work in everyday life are confidence, growth, affection, loyalty, and protection. The energy of Leo provides a burst of vitality that can be most effective when directed toward positive change that benefits others.

Channel the vigor of Leo's energy for your garden by drawing its symbol on several stones and placing them amongst the plants. To boost spells, use lemon juice to draw the symbol on a small piece of paper. When it dries, it will be invisible. Hold the paper between your hands and visualize what you want to achieve. Just before releasing your energy, hold the paper close enough to a candle to warm it but not burn it. When the symbol becomes visible again, allow the paper to catch fire, and then drop it into your cauldron. To build courage and confidence in your skills as a leader, carry or wear yellow danburite marked with Leo's symbol. Use the symbol with sunstone to foster personal growth.

Figure 16: The modern/fourteenth-century symbol of Leo (left)
with thirteenth-century (center)
and seventeenth-century (right) variations.

22. Ibid., vol. 2, 1294.

Representing the lion's mane and/or tail, these symbols were derived from the Greco-Roman period.

Some of the crystals associated with Leo include amber, yellow beryl, carnelian, citrine, yellow danburite, peridot, sunstone, tiger's eye, and topaz. This constellation is associated with the element fire. In astrology, its ruling planet is the sun.

Libra

Originally considered part of Virgo by the ancient Greeks, the combination of these two constellations was associated with Themis, the goddess of justice. To the Romans, Libra represented the scales of justice. Its name is Latin and means "balance."[23]

Libra brings in a period for attaining balance and promoting fairness. This is a time to focus on fostering peace in relationships. Cooperation and unity are also hallmarks of Libra. This is a good time for spells involving love and romance. The main forces at work in everyday life are balance, harmony, fairness, and community. The energy of Libra aids in self-awareness and the realization that even the smallest action can have an impact on others. Libra also fosters civility and social graces.

Just as ancient people equated Libra with goddesses of justice, the energy of this constellation can be called upon for support in legal matters or to simply right a wrong. Draw Libra's symbol on a picture of a marigold to burn in your cauldron as you visualize a positive outcome to your situation. Alternatively, paint the symbol on a piece of jade to carry with you when meeting with lawyers or going to court. To foster harmony throughout your home, paint the symbol on several pieces of dual-colored agate, and then place them in areas of the house where your family spends time together. Inscribe the symbol on a pink or lavender candle to use in love spells or to gaze upon as you open your energy to attract romance.

Figure 17: The modern/fourteenth-century symbol of Libra (left)
with sixteenth-century (center)
and early twentieth-century (right) variations.

23. Ibid., 1304.

Representing weighing scales and balance, the modern/fourteenth-century and sixteenth-century symbols have roots in the Greco-Roman period. The early twentieth-century symbol was derived from the first-century CE Egyptian tradition.

Some of the crystals associated with Libra include agate, beryl, desert rose, diamond, jade, lapis lazuli, moonstone, opal, peridot, rose quartz, and smoky quartz. Libra is associated with the element air. In astrology, its ruling planet is Venus.

Ophiuchus

With a Greek name meaning "snake handler," Ophiuchus is intertwined with the dual constellation of Serpens the serpent.[24] In myth, this set of constellations represented Asclepius, the god of healing, who was usually depicted holding a staff around which one or two serpents coiled.

According to modern interpretation, the main forces at work with Ophiuchus are healing, strength, unity, and seeking truth. This constellation can be instrumental in activating Kundalini energy. Depicted as crisscrossing snakes running up the spine, this energy resembles the staff of Asclepius and the symbol of modern medicine.

Before being cast as evil incarnate, snakes were regarded as agents of healing. The snake was one of the most powerful creatures associated with the Great Goddess—the other was the bird. Because of this, I like to think of Ophiuchus as representing the Minoan snake goddess of Crete, who was powerful and nurturing. The energy of this constellation supports the cycles and changes that occur throughout life. Paint the Ophiuchus symbol on a piece of white quartz to keep with you during times of transition. When seeking truth and wisdom, paint it on a piece of tiger's eye to hold during meditation. For healing work, inscribe the symbol on a green candle to use during meditation, reiki sessions, or other types of energy work.

Figure 18: Ophiuchus has one symbol.

Although Ophiuchus was known in ancient times, the only symbol is modern because the constellation was not used in astrology as part of the zodiac. The symbol suggested by

---

24. Ibid., 1584.

British Astrologer Walter Berg (1947–) represents Ophiuchus holding a snake; the line on the left represents the serpent's tail; on the right is its head.

Some of the crystals associated with Ophiuchus include bloodstone, lapis lazuli, tiger's eye, and white quartz. When used in astrology, its ruling planet is sometimes noted as Chiron, a minor planetoid in the outer solar system.

Pisces

The Babylonians, Greeks, and Romans regarded Pisces as a pair of fish joined by a cord. This constellation is associated with the Roman myth of Venus and Cupid, who tied themselves together with a rope and shape-shifted into the form of fish to escape the monster Typhon. Pisces's name is Latin meaning "fish" and is the plural of *piscis*.[25]

Associated with water, Pisces brings a period that is conducive for dream and psychic work, as well as honing divination skills. It is a time of sensitivity, compassion, and creativity. Use this period to engage in charity work or to focus energy toward helping others. The main forces at work in everyday life are intuition, kindness, community, and clarity. Rather than duality, the energy of Pisces emphasizes the strength of unity and sharing. It fosters adaptability for working together toward collective goals.

Associated with secrets, the energy of Pisces aids in maintaining appropriate confidences and detecting deceits. Paint the Pisces symbol on a piece of black tourmaline to keep with you when in the presence of someone you believe is not being truthful. To foster creativity and boost the imagination, keep the symbol visible when engaging in creative work. Throughout the ancient world, fish were a symbol of fecundity and the feminine principle. To the Greeks, a fish was one of the symbols of Aphrodite. To call on the power of Aphrodite or other goddesses, inscribe the Pisces symbol on a light blue candle for spell work and esbat rituals.

Figure 19 : The modern/fifteenth-century symbol of Pisces (left)
with sixteenth-century (center)
and seventeenth-century (right) variations.

---

25. Ibid., 1723.

Although some of the symbols for Pisces are more elaborate than others, they represent the two tethered fish and were ultimately derived from the Greco-Roman period.

Some of the crystals associated with Pisces include alexandrite, aquamarine, bloodstone, blue lace agate, fluorite, jade, and black tourmaline. Pisces is associated with the element water. In astrology, its ruling planets are Jupiter (traditional) and Neptune.

Sagittarius

Rooted in Sumerian myth, this constellation was adopted by the Babylonians. According to cuneiform inscriptions, it was called the *Strong One*. Greek astronomer and mathematician Eratosthenes (c. 276–194) associated the constellation with Crotus, the son of Pan. The name *Sagittarius* is Latin and means "archer."[26]

This constellation ushers in a period for thinking about the bigger things in life and the ability to be unafraid to follow the beat of your own drum. The energy of Sagittarius aids in working on matters concerning the self, sexuality, and spirituality. This is a good time to follow intuition, engage in dreamwork, and go on travels that broaden your horizons. The main forces at work in everyday life are hopes and dreams, focus, discipline, and resilience. The energy of Sagittarius encourages aiming high and targeting goals that may seem out of reach. It also aids in picking up, rethinking, and starting over, when necessary.

To enhance dreamwork, draw the Sagittarius symbol on a small square of fabric to place under your pillow. In the morning, hold the fabric against your third-eye chakra to heighten your ability to interpret potential messages. When dealing with issues relating to sexuality, paint the symbol on a piece of red jasper to keep by your bedside until things are resolved. Wear a piece of jewelry with the symbol for support in pursuing higher education, honing skills, or seeking any form of self-improvement. Inscribe the symbol on a dark blue or purple candle to help raise consciousness through spiritual meditation. To give spells and rituals a boost, draw the symbol on four small pieces of paper, and then place them in the cardinal directions on your altar. Visualize energy arising from each symbol and forming a cone of power to be released at your direction.

---

26. Ibid., vol. 3, 1999.

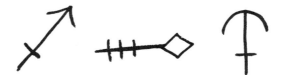

Figure 20: The modern/fifteenth-century symbol of Sagittarius (left)
with fourteenth-century (center)
and seventeenth-century (right) variations.

With roots in the Greco-Roman period and first century CE Egypt, the symbols for Sagittarius are variations of an arrow and/or bow.

Some of the crystals associated with Sagittarius include amethyst, azurite, iolite, red jasper, labradorite, obsidian, sodalite, and turquoise. This constellation is associated with the element fire. In astrology, its ruling planet is Jupiter.

Scorpio

Regarded as a scorpion by most ancient stargazers, this constellation was a symbol of protection to the Egyptians and Babylonians. According to Egyptian mythology, Isis escaped from the murderous Seth under the protection of seven scorpions. This constellation's name is Latin and means "scorpion."[27]

Scorpio brings a period of deep emotion that is often associated with sex, darkness, death, and power. It provides access and opportunity to deal with these aspects of ourselves that we usually keep hidden. The energy of Scorpio can serve as an incubator for creativity, spirituality, transformation, and psychic skills. The main forces at work in everyday life are control, determination, passions, and creativity. The intense energy of Scorpio, which is often misunderstood or misused, can be channeled into healing and success.

Because Scorpio is associated with death, the otherworld, and rebirth, it is a powerful symbol to use at Samhain. Paint it on a piece of carnelian and a piece of black tourmaline and inscribe it on a white candle for your altar to represent the power of transformative cycles. When you feel in need of protection, carry or wear a Scorpio pendant to repel negativity. To aid in developing psychic abilities, use an eyeliner pencil to draw the symbol over your third-eye chakra and meditate on it before each practice session. As you become confident in your skills, simply visualize the symbol on your forehead. Intensify passion

---

27. Ibid., 2307.

and sensuality in the bedroom by drawing the symbol in red ink on a piece of paper and placing it under the mattress.

Figure 21: The modern/fifteenth-century symbol of Scorpio (left)
with sixteenth-century (center)
and seventeenth-century (right) variations.

Depicting the shape of a scorpion and its stinger, the modern symbol for Scorpio comes from the medieval manuscript tradition, which was derived from the Greco-Roman period. Through the centuries, others presented more of a pictograph version of the scorpion.

Some of the crystals associated with Scorpio include bloodstone, carnelian, labradorite, rutilated quartz, topaz, and black tourmaline. Scorpio is associated with the element water. In astrology, its ruling planets are Mars (traditional) and Pluto.

Taurus

The name of this constellation is Latin and means "bull."[28] In Mesopotamia, this constellation was called the *Bull of Light* and equated with the god Marduk. In other mythology it was associated with the mightiest gods such as Amun, Jupiter, Mars, Mithras, Osiris, Poseidon, Shiva, and Zeus.

Taurus ushers in a period when love and money spells are particularly effective because whatever is started now tends to last. Creative work is enhanced by the vitality of this constellation's energy. The main forces at work in everyday life are strength, determination, and prosperity. With endurance and stability, this energy provides a foundation upon which comfort and long-term plans can be built.

Associated with the home, security, and comfort, the strength of this constellation's energy is a good choice for protection. Paint its symbol on four stones, and then place them in the cardinal directions on your property. For personal protection, wear the symbol with lapis lazuli jewelry.

---

28. Ibid., 2344.

For help in sharpening intuition, inscribe the symbol on a green candle and use it to focus your attention during meditation. Also use it on a green candle to enrich divination sessions. In situations that require patience, take a few minutes by yourself and use your finger to trace the symbol on one of your palms. To attract abundance and build wealth, paint the symbol on a piece of malachite to keep with your financial papers. To enhance the energy of ritual, draw it on a piece of paper or any object on your altar. Afterward, hold the object or paper to help ground excess energy.

Figure 22: The modern/fifteenth-century symbol of Taurus (left)
with two other fifteenth-century variations.

Most symbols for Taurus represent the bull's head and horns. From the medieval manuscript tradition, the modern symbol has roots in the Greco-Roman period.

Some of the crystals associated with Taurus include agate, chrysocolla, jade, lapis lazuli, malachite, pyrite, rose quartz, blue tourmaline, and turquoise. Taurus is associated with the element earth. In astrology, its ruling planet is Venus.

Virgo

Although its name is Latin and means "virgin," at one time the word *virgin* referred to a girl or young woman and not necessarily to her physical intactness.[29] To the Romans this constellation represented Ceres; to the Greeks, Demeter, and sometimes Persephone.

Virgo ushers in a period for using your head and putting your analytical mind to work, especially for business. The energy of Virgo aids in making long-range plans and helps to create the building blocks for success. The main forces at work in everyday life are resourcefulness, hard work, and getting things done. A boost from Virgo energy is especially helpful when juggling details, trying to get organized, or tracking busy family schedules.

The energy of Virgo can give a Lughnasadh ritual a boost and pay honor to the grain goddesses Demeter and Ceres. Inscribe the Virgo symbol on a yellow candle along with

---

29. Bonnie MacLachlan and Judith Fletcher, eds., *Virginity Revisited: Configurations of the Unpossessed Body* (Toronto, Canada: The University of Toronto Press Inc., 2007), 40.

the goddesses' names. Associated with cycles, the energy of Virgo can be instrumental in bringing closure to a situation and/or clearing space for something new. As part of a spell to draw abundance into your life, inscribe the symbol on a small piece of paper, sprinkle it with a pinch of dried dill leaves, and then burn it in your cauldron. To invite love into your life, attach a Virgo pendant to a piece of pink jasper jewelry or paint the symbol on the crystal and keep it with you. Paint the symbol on a piece of aquamarine for meditation when seeking emotional purification.

Figure 23: The modern/fifteenth-century symbol of Virgo (left)
with two other fifteenth-century variations.

The modern and other symbols that resemble the letter *M* from the medieval manuscript tradition may be stylized initials for Maria Virgo, "Virgin Mary," or designed from the letters in the Greek word *parthenos*, which means "virgin."[30] The fifteenth-century variation that resembles the letter *Y* was derived from the Greco-Roman period. It represents the grain carried in the arms of Ceres/Demeter.

Some of the crystals associated with Virgo include amethyst, aquamarine, diamond, jade, pink jasper, opal, sugilite, turquoise, and red zircon. This constellation is associated with the element earth. In astrology, its ruling planet is Mercury.

---

30. Cecilia Payne-Gaposchkin and Katherine Haramundanis, *Introduction to Astronomy* (New York: Prentice Hall, 1970), 13.

PART TWO

THE ELEMENTS

The four elements are so commonplace in Pagan and Wiccan ritual that their importance and power is often overlooked or underestimated. While we may simply bundle them with the cardinal directions, the elements are far more than props upon which to hang correspondences. We could say that the elements are a great deal more than elementary.

The elements have been regarded as abstract concepts, forces of energy, and states of matter. This section examines the ancient philosophies and theories behind the elements, including the suggestion from Aristotle (384–322 BCE) of a fifth element. We will also see how the elements have been a fundamental component of astrology, alchemy, medicine, and other practices. In addition to the elements in modern ritual and magic, we will explore their use for personal development and take a brief look at elemental beings.

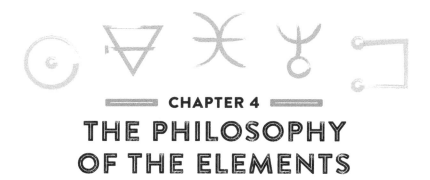

CHAPTER 4

THE PHILOSOPHY
OF THE ELEMENTS

WHILE THE ELEMENTS ARE often regarded as abstractions, they come from concepts relating to nature and represent types of energy. They stand at the center of creation and carry the primary archetypal energies that exist in all things. According to British psychologist, professor, and author David Fontana (1934–2010), many ancient people regarded the elements as "energy forces that sustained the world."[31] The elements also represented the three states of matter (earth, solid; water, liquid; air, gas) and the agent of transformation of matter (fire).

From ancient times to the Renaissance, the elements were believed to relate to the human condition, health, and personality traits. Because ancient philosophers and scientists regarded humans as the universe in miniature, it was believed that the physical body held within it the essence of all cosmic elements.

The four elements were viewed as the building blocks and organizing principles of the world. As such, they have been described as the manifestation of consciousness in nature and as the vibration of nature and spirit. With roots in both the physical and conscious spheres, they were believed to function within a person's inner and outer worlds as guides and teachers for awareness and consciousness.

The elements have been a fundamental component of astrology, alchemy, medicine, and magic. In addition, the suits of the tarot are based on the elements and convey their related powers. The famous Rider-Waite tarot and many later decks assigned the elements

---

31. David Fontana, *The Secret Language of Symbols: A Visual Key to Symbols and Their Meanings* (San Francisco: Chronicle Books, 2003), 180.

as fire for wands, water for cups, air for swords, and earth for pentacles. In myth, a symbolic mixture of the four elements has appeared in the form of the dragon. A dragon was said to be at home in the three permanent elements of earth, water, air (land, sea, sky) and, of course, it was well known for its ability to breathe fire.

Even in the twenty-first century, when we look through the lens of the four elements, we have a structure with which to see and understand the world around us and within us. The elements still provide the cornerstones to our world. The more we use them, the more we come to understand each related attribute on an intuitive level to the extent that they become very personal and part of us. Through this, we can attain a deeper self-knowledge that helps us understand our fundamental natures and consciousness. The elements can provide us with more meaning in ritual, put more power into our magical practices, and enhance our everyday lives.

THE ROOT OF EXISTENCE

One of the earliest theories on the elements is attributed to the Greek philosopher and physician Empedocles (495–430 BCE) in what he called *rizomata*, "roots."[32] He regarded the elements as four primal substances that possessed the power to both combine and separate all things in existence. Not only did they bring everything into existence, they were also responsible for the continual change and evolution of matter. Empedocles noted that everything in the universe existed because of some combination of the four elements. He also noted that nothing consisted purely and completely of just one.

Even though Empedocles was sometimes regarded as being on the fringe because he declared himself to have magical powers with the ability to change weather and raise the dead, his work was highly regarded, and influenced medical studies and science through the centuries. In fact, his great contribution to chemistry was his theory that a finite set of elements could form an unlimited number of compounds.

Regarded as the Father of Medicine, Greek physician Hippocrates (460–377 BCE) advanced the theory of the four humors, which were associated with the elements. The humors were the basis of a system to detail the workings of the human body. They also provided the means to diagnose and treat physical and emotional problems. In the body, the humors were expressed as blood, phlegm, bile (or yellow bile), and black bile. Their elements were air, water, fire, and earth, respectively. Disease was believed to be the result of the elements and their respective humors falling out of balance. In addition to their

---

32. Nigel Wilson, ed., *Encyclopedia of Ancient Greece* (New York: Routledge, 2010), 358.

relationship with the elements, Hippocrates described each humor as a combination of two of the four basic qualities, which were described as hot, cold, dry, and moist. His theory on the humors and elements remained an essential part of European medicine for more than two thousand years.[33]

According to British author, historian, and artist Fred Gettings (1937–2013), Hippocrates's concept was likely derived from an Eastern source because balancing the elements was not unique to Western medicine.[34] Both Indian Ayurvedic and Traditional Chinese Medicine maintained the belief that keeping the elements balanced within the body was important for physical and psychological health.

Although the Chinese elements differ from those of the West, theories about them were documented as early as 2000 BCE.[35] In addition to keeping them in balance, combinations of elemental energies were also important in the East. In Chinese myth, four mystical and powerful creatures were portrayed as a fusion of two elements. The phoenix was a combination of fire and air, green dragon was air and earth, tortoise was earth and water, and white tiger was water and fire. These creatures remain part of feng shui, which is a practice for working with and balancing elemental energy in one's environment.

Back in Europe, Aristotle combined and built on the theories of Empedocles and Hippocrates. He suggested that the four elements, like the humors, were a union of two of the four qualities of hot, cold, dry, and moist. This resulted in air being regarded as a combination of hot and moist, water with cold and moist, fire with hot and dry, and earth with cold and dry. In addition, Aristotle explored the notion that the four elements came from an unknown element that he regarded as more refined. This resulted in the fifth element having a higher importance than the others. Aristotle classified the first four elements with the lower region of nature and the earth. The upper region, the sky, was the domain of the fifth element. He called this element *aether*. Centuries later, German physician and scholar Agrippa referred to aether as "the Spirit of the World."[36]

According to Aristotle, the moon was the physical dividing point between the four base elements (below) and the finer element of aether (above). The elements of air, water,

---

33. Fiona MacDonald, *The Plague and Medicine in the Middle Ages* (Milwaukee, WI: World Almanac Library, 2006), 18.

34 Fred Gettings, *The Book of the Hand: An Illustrated History of Palmistry* (New York: Hamlyn Publishing, 1971), 39.

35. Becker, *The Continuum Encyclopedia of Symbols*, 98.

36. Heinrich Cornelius Agrippa of Nettesheim, *Three Books of Occult Philosophy: The Foundation Book of Western Occultism*, trans. James Freake, ed. Donald Tyson (St. Paul, MN: Llewellyn Publications, 2004), 721.

fire, and earth were terrestrial, which was their accepted and proper place in the universe. Aether—also spelled *ether*—was the element that existed where the divine dwelled, thus giving it a spiritual quality. This association with spirit is still referenced today in modern Paganism where the pentagram represents the four elements plus spirit. In addition, the center of the altar is commonly used to represent spirit and deities while the four elements with their cardinal directions hold the corners.

THE ELEMENTALS AND ALCHEMY

Early alchemists embraced Aristotle's theory of the four elements originating from a single source. The four elements were regarded as "differentiated matter" and their source as "prime matter" or "undifferentiated matter."[37] Alchemists believed that prime matter could be made to take on the characteristics of terrestrial matter. The agent or catalyst for this transmutation was called the *Philosopher's Stone*. According to Professor Lesley Cormack (1957–) of the University of Alberta, Canada, whether the Philosopher's Stone was "an actual object, the product of alchemical process, or a spiritual state depended on the theory followed by the individual alchemist."[38]

Used in alchemy, astrology, and philosophy, the medieval symbol representing the elements was drawn as a square with a triangle at each corner. Air and fire were represented by the top triangles, earth and water as the lower ones. The seventeenth-century ideogram for the art of alchemy consisted of a small circle representing water, within a square representing earth, within a triangle representing fire, within a large circle representing air. The quartered square was also sometimes used as an alchemical symbol to represent the elements.

Figure 24:. The early medieval symbol (left),
the seventeenth-century ideogram (center),
and the quartered square (right) represented the elements.

---

37. Andrew Ede and Lesley B. Cormack, *A History of Science in Society: From Philosophy to Utility*, 3rd ed. (Toronto, Canada: University of Toronto Press, 2017), 52.
38. Ibid.

According to German physician, pharmacist, and alchemist Johann Christoph Sommerhoff (1644–1723), the graphic origin of elemental triangles was the seal of Solomon, a six-pointed star more widely known as the Star of David.[39] (Refer to Part Seven for more about King Solomon.) Sommerhoff's *Lexion Pharmaceutico chymicum* (*Dictionary of Pharmaceutical Chemicals*) was an encyclopedia of symbols in which he identified the principle elements of alchemy.

The ancient Greeks used triangles and barred triangles to represent the individual elements. The triangles associated with fire and air point upward; earth and water point downward. The air and earth triangles are distinguished by an additional horizontal bar, which varies stylistically. Depicting the elements in this manner was adopted by many medieval alchemists and continues to this day in Pagan and Wiccan practice.

Figure 25: The most commonly used symbols left to right (top row): fire, air, water and earth. Variations are shown for the air symbol (second row) and earth symbol (third row).

According to Swiss psychiatrist Carl Jung, the elements were depicted as triangles because they could be joined into a circle and, once united, they "represent the whole physical world."[40] Jung also used the quartered circle to represent the self. Combined in the quartered circle, the elements create balance, unity, and wholeness. In Pagan and Wiccan ritual,

---

39. Fred Gettings, *Dictionary of Occult, Hermetic and Alchemical Sigils* (Boston: Routledge and Kegan Paul, Ltd., 1981), 106.

40. C. G. Jung, *Mysterium Coniunctions: An Inquiry into the Separation and Synthesis of Psychic Opposites in Alchemy* (Princeton, NJ: Princeton University Press, 1976), 460.

sacred space is created with a circle quartered by the elements and their associated cardinal directions. The quartered circle is also used as a symbol to represent the element earth.

Figure 26: Within a quartered circle,
the four elements represent unity and wholeness.

Regarded as the "cardinal points of material existence," equating and assigning the elements to the cardinal directions within a circle provides us with a place to acknowledge and work with the elements.[41] In the quartered circle, the center becomes a sacred place powered by the mighty forces of the elements. It is the *axis mundi*—world center—a place of union where heaven and earth are joined in our presence. This place is often regarded as the meeting point of the seven directions: east, west, north, south, above, below, and within. As a result, the circle that we cast for ritual and magic becomes a cauldron of energy that we can tap into and direct.

Figure 27: The elements can be depicted as circles,
left to right: earth, water, air, and fire.

A simplified quartered circle in the form of crossed lines has also been used to represent the unity of the elements along with their polarity of complementary and contrary pairings. Earth and water, and fire and air are complementary pairs. Earth and air, and fire and water are contrary opposites. Together, these complementary and contrary energies create an exquisite tension and cohesiveness that holds the universe in balance. Medieval alchemists also used the crossed lines as a symbol to represent the union of all five elements. The *quintessence*—fifth element—was the point where the four elements met, or rather, it was regarded as the point from which they radiated.

---

41. Juan Eduardo Cirlot, *A Dictionary of Symbols*, 2nd ed., trans. Jack Sage (Mineola, NY: Dover Publications, Inc., 1971), 95.

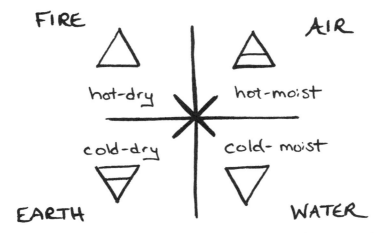

Figure 28: The complementary and contrary energies of the elements are depicted along with their two associated qualities.

CHAPTER 5

THE ELEMENTS
AND SELF-KNOWLEDGE

THROUGH THE CENTURIES, the elements have been associated with the fundamental aspects of personality. Greek philosopher Claudius Galenus (130–200 CE), better known as Galen, studied at the famous school of medicine in Alexandria, Egypt, and later traveled to Rome where he became a prominent physician and influential medical authority. Among his extensive work is a text entitled *The Doctrine of the Four Temperaments of Personality*, which was based on the theories of Empedocles and Hippocrates.

Galen's premise was that the elements and humors influenced a person's character and intelligence. He named the four humors sanguine, choleric, melancholic, and phlegmatic and defined the personalities as bold (air), angry (fire), sad (earth), and calm (water), respectively.[42] The theory of the Four Temperaments was a standard component in medical practice well into the Middle Ages. Remnants of Galen's treatise linger in our everyday language when we say that someone is in a good or bad humor.

Associating the elements with personality types has echoed down the centuries. Founder of analytical psychology, Carl Jung, identified four basic personality types and associated them with the elements: intuitive (fire), sensing (earth), thinking (air), and feeling (water). These archetypes are sets of traits or certain characteristics that correspond to an element's attributes. While people are a mix of personality types and their corresponding elements, Jung noted that one is usually more dominant than the others. Understanding which elements are at work within us can deepen our self-knowledge.

---

42. J. E. Roeckelein, comp., *Elsevier's Dictionary of Psychological Theories* (San Diego, CA: Elsevier Inc., 2006), 235.

The premise of the archetypes is that the things we do or are attracted to—by choice or subconsciously—are a result of the strong pull an element may have on us. When we strive for self-knowledge, we gain a better understanding of the forces that drive and sustain us, which in turn, supports and aids our spiritual paths and magic endeavors.

Because the continual interaction of the elements creates change, we are constantly evolving as we learn and grow throughout our lives. Through Jung's character types, we can discover the elements that resonate most deeply with us, which helps us live in sync with our true nature and with the natural world. In addition to helping us tap into the power of the element for which we have the most affinity, this knowledge also helps us recognize and foster qualities of the other elements.

Allow yourself adequate time alone to read the following entries on each element. Also, have a pen and paper or cell phone handy for taking notes. Alternatively, use a pencil and make notes or underline relevant words in the following section. My apologies to anyone who may be offended by the suggestion of writing in a book; however, I consider books to be tools.

Don't dwell or think too much as you read the entries. Simply mark or take note of the words or phrases that resonate strongly in describing who you are.

THE EARTH ARCHETYPE

Earth is the element of form and manifestation. People who have strong earth characteristics are, well, earthy. They are practical, reliable, and fond of tradition. They are instrumental in the process of handing things down from one generation to the next, including heirlooms, traits, or knowledge. Their children are well educated, not always through college but in the practical arts that support community. Earth people tend to become architects, craftspeople, designers, engineers, caregivers, and those who work with the land. They like to do things their way, but being honest souls they will not cheat or finagle to make this happen.

Earth people like routine and generally take a methodical approach to solving problems. While they may seem more cautious than most, it is because of their concern for the basic things in life and a drive to create a secure and stable foundation for themselves and others. Firmly rooted in realistic necessities, they are nurturers committed to home and family. Earth people are patient and their legacies endure the test of time. Commonsense is important. They are tenacious, well-balanced, and emotionally stable. Earth people are tactile and sensual and accept the wisdom of the body. They honor the natural world and its cycles. Those who don't understand earth people may see them as stubborn, dull, or resistant to change.

Magically, an earth person is the one who can pull things together. They can hold the energy of ritual until it is ready to be released. Being very grounded, they are the rock upon which others can stand.

THE WATER ARCHETYPE

People who have strong water characteristics are generally sensitive, empathetic, and caring. Holding friendship in high esteem, they know how to keep a confidence and betraying a secret is painful to them. Water people are protective and take great care where their children are concerned. Their emotions run strong, but when they are grounded, they can be very creative because of their unusual perspective on the world. While emotion runs deep, it also flows close to the surface, making them compassionate; however, this also leaves them open to the slings and arrows the world flings in their direction. Because of this, water people are easily wounded and tend to withdraw for self-protection; sometimes to the point where they may seem reclusive.

Water people are good observers with a combination of intellect, intuition, and imagination. They tend to become therapists, counselors, clergy, midwives, psychics, or artists (writers, actors, etc.). With a deep appreciation for beauty, they experience it on an almost sensual level. Water people can be self-conscious, especially when their perfectionism gets out of hand. Those who don't understand water people may see them as moody, secretive, over-sensitive, or fragile.

Magically, a water person is the channel who sends and receives messages. They can access the unseen realms to bring forth wisdom and information. They also tap into the power of the natural world.

THE AIR ARCHETYPE

The word *inspiration* has two meanings, and both are associated with the element air. To inhale relates to air and to have an idea is, of course, related to the mind. The person of air is someone for whom the mind is very important. Air people are rational, clever, witty, and entertaining. Putting logic before intuition, they may tend to think rather than feel their way through a situation. Their head generally rules the heart. Being cerebral and loving to talk, they are very sociable and enjoy having a good time. Often flamboyant, air people revel in recognition and have a good sense of humor.

More than being the center of attention, the air person loves an intellectual challenge. Their curiosity provides an endless stream of interests and often adventure. An air person needs stimulation and space, otherwise his or her restless nature kicks in. They avoid feeling trapped at all costs. Because they are good communicators, self-motivated, and do well under pressure, air people tend to become teachers, scholars, inventors, and media personalities. Those who don't understand air people may see them as self-centered, emotionally detached, and fickle. Ironically, because they may seem to blow with the wind they have been called "airheads."

Magically, the air person excels at planning rituals and spells. They hold knowledge that aids in interpreting messages and information.

THE FIRE ARCHETYPE

Fire people make things happen. They are always on the move. They have high ambitions and the intense energy to get where they are headed. After goals have been reached, fire people will set their sights on new mountains to climb, partly because they love being on the go and partly because they are easily bored. They are highly creative with things that have practical purposes. Fire people tend to be mavericks—assertive, daring, and strongly independent. They learn things quickly and are very focused. With a strong will and dominant nature, they are highly expressive and want things their way.

Fire people are known for their passion and romanticism. Often impulsive, they easily fall in love at first sight. In addition, their dramatic and larger-than-life characteristics make them attractive for friendship and intimacy. Because of their excitement, optimism, self-motivation, and vision, they tend to become leaders, salespeople, performers, and warriors. Those who don't understand fire people may see them as hot-tempered, obsessive, and impulsive.

Magically, a fire person is a catalyst. He or she is the spark that ignites energy to send forth intention and will with great power.

———

After reading the entries and taking notes, you may find that one element describes you a little more accurately than the others. This may confirm what you already know, or the information may be a surprise. Either way, acknowledge and embrace your predominant element because it may reveal your underlying temperament and strengths. Understanding this provides power for personal, spiritual, and magical growth.

By working with our energy, we can more effectively utilize a predominant element or strengthen another. One way to do this is by using the hand chakras, the energy centers located in the center of the palms. This is a very powerful area of the hand that we can use to work directly with the elemental energy in our bodies.

Before getting started, decide which element you want to work with. Cut two small triangles, circles, or squares of paper that fit in the center of your hand, and then draw one of the element's symbols on each piece of paper. Alternatively, use an eyeliner pencil and draw the symbol directly on the center of your palms.

If you are using pieces of paper, set them aside for a moment while you activate the energy of the palm chakras. One method is to rub the palms together to create heat, which will open the chakras. Once the chakras are activated and your hands feel warm, place the pieces of paper in your hands and sit with your palms facing upward on your lap.

Another method, which is better if you have drawn the symbols on your palms, is to sit with your hands on your lap, palms facing up. Close your eyes and visualize spirals on both palms. As they become clear in your mind's eye, see them rotate until you can feel a steady stream of energy spiraling through your palms.

Whichever method you use, close your eyes and imagine the energy of your chakras surrounding and embracing the symbol in your hands. Focus your attention and visualize the element as you think of its associated qualities that you want to amplify or foster. Pay attention to any sensations that may occur.

Allow the visualization to continue for as long as necessary, and then let the images and sensations fade. Sit in stillness for a minute or so. To deactivate the hand chakras, visualize them as flowers. Because the chakras are traditionally depicted as lotus blossoms, slowly close your fingers into your palms as you visualize the petals of flowers closing. While the chakras will stop spinning, the body will hold the energy. Take a few minutes to write down your thoughts and observations so you can review them later. Like wisps of a dream, illuminating thoughts can quickly disappear.

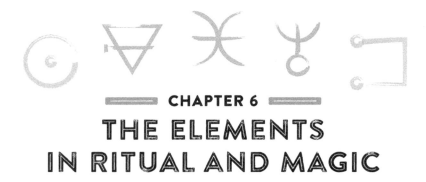

CHAPTER 6

THE ELEMENTS IN RITUAL AND MAGIC

FOR PAGANS AND WICCANS, the elements are fundamental symbols that help us attune with the natural world. As we work within a quartered circle for ritual and magic, we become that radiating point at the center with the elemental quarters opening and fine-tuning our minds and energy. The following meditation can be an aid for tapping into the energy of the elements whether you are just beginning to work with them or have done so for years. It is also helpful whenever you feel the need to realign your energy with the elements.

This meditation can be instrumental when preparing for ritual and magic because it helps us harmonize with all four elements by creating a path for our minds and energy to follow. Begin by clearing everything from your altar. Look through the graphics in this chapter, choose a symbol for each element, and then draw them on separate pieces of paper. Place one of the symbols in each quarter of your altar. You can align them with the cardinal directions according to your personal practice or place the symbols randomly.

Focusing on each element individually, you can decide on the order of elements ahead of time or spontaneously choose them as you proceed with the meditation. Alternatively, you can simply follow the order given here. Allow yourself as much time as necessary with each element.

ELEMENTS MEDITATION

Sit comfortably in front of your altar and close your eyes for a few minutes as you clear your mind. When you feel ready, open your eyes and focus your attention on the symbol in the earth sector of your altar. Earth represents the body, the physical. Earth is the element of form and manifestation. This element is our foundation. Its energy is the simplicity of everyday life. It is the profound beauty of existence. Earth represents stability and nurturing. In ritual and magic, earth represents the practice. Feel the energy of earth.

Move your gaze to the symbol in the water sector of your altar. Water represents emotions and intuition. It is both comforting and mysterious. It gives shape to our inner worlds and meaning to our existence. Water encompasses and completes us. Cleansing and pure, water quenches the thirst and helps everything grow. It represents healing and change. In ritual and magic, water represents the channel through which we send and receive. Feel the energy of water.

Let your eyes move to the symbol in the air sector of your altar. Air represents the mind and perception. It is inspiration and illumination. Air is the storehouse of knowledge and keeper of memories. It encompasses all forms of communication through which we can share the wonder and awe of our journey in this life. Air joins us when we enter this world and is our constant companion until the end. In ritual and magic, air represents the wisdom that shapes and the knowledge that motivates. Feel the energy of air.

Finally, move your gaze to the symbol in the fire sector of your altar. Fire represents sensation and energy. It is the spark of life and the power of faith. It provides illumination for self-examination. Fire is a double-edged sword that can destroy and yet it is a brilliant force that purifies and provides new beginnings. In ritual and magic, fire represents culmination and transformation. Feel the energy of fire.

———

After you have worked with all four elements, take time to remain with any thoughts or feelings that may have surfaced. If you keep a journal, record these thoughts. When you feel that your meditation is complete, ground and center your energy while you enjoy the wisdom and balance of all four elements working within you.

Metaphorically, the elements provide an intermixing of energy for ritual and magic. It begins with air, which supports an idea and the planning of a ritual or spell. Fire or water can lead the way to purify and make sacred the place and time to enact it. Earth brings the idea or intention into reality to do the ritual or spell. While water opens an energy channel, fire provides the spark that ignites the energy to send forth intention and will. Water is also the conduit through which information can come to us and air provides an explanation for whatever is received. Finally, earth draws away and grounds excess energy, providing a smooth re-entry into mundane reality.

THE SYMBOLS IN MAGIC

As mentioned in the introduction, symbols provide simplicity as well as power. Whatever you draw, paint, or inscribe with an elemental symbol, take time to infuse it with that element's energy. As you hold the object, gaze at the symbol for a moment or two, and then close your eyes. Use all your senses as you visualize that element and draw its energy into your body. When it feels as though the energy is reaching a peak, visualize it moving down your arms as you release it into the object. Afterward, take a moment or two to ground and center your energy, and then proceed with your work.

Two of the most common objects used to represent the elements for ritual and spell work are candles and crystals. In addition, coordinating a candle's color or a type of crystal with an element enhances the energy of your work. If you prefer not to mark up a crystal, draw or paint the symbol on a piece of paper, and then wrap it around the stone.

The Element Air

Air is the element of the mind, intelligence, and knowledge. It stimulates energy for learning and enlightenment. Air also strengthens memory. This element is an aid when you need to concentrate and focus willpower. Use air to bring order to your thoughts and clarity for better communication. Supporting eloquent communication makes air instrumental in relationships and in business. Use air to initiate action or inspire motivation for your career or business.

This element is also helpful in spells to attract money or when seeking fairness or justice. Air can ignite the imagination, bringing inspiration and creativity to your endeavors. It supports the refinement of intuition. Associated with psychic abilities, air is especially helpful in developing clairvoyance and in furthering divination skills. It supports shamanic work, astral travel, and contacting spirits. Use it for support when releasing things from your life. Afterward, air can help bring a sense freedom for new beginnings. This element fosters harmony and healing. The power of air is also an aid in weather magic.

Figure 29: Common triangle and circle symbols representing air,
along with one devised by American astrologer Nicholas deVore (1882–1960).

For air, use candles of the following colors: light blue, gray, lavender, pink, red, silver, white, or bright or light yellow. Some of the crystals that are effective for working with air include: blue lace and tree agate, ametrine, angelite, aragonite, aventurine, celestite, chrysoberyl, desert rose, moldavite, opal, clear quartz, sodalite, sphene, staurolite, blue topaz, and blue tourmaline.

The Element Earth

Earth is the element of form and manifestation. As a foundation, it provides stability and strength and keeps us grounded in the physical world. It supports the family and home, bringing warmth and peace. Use it in spells to attract abundance and increase prosperity. Also use this element to raise protective energy at home or when traveling. Earth is instrumental to ward off and break hexes and subdue any form of negative energy. This element's nurturing energy aids personal growth, as well as growth in our gardens. It also helps us when contacting nature spirits.

Associated with comfort, earth helps to quell anxiety and keep our lives balanced. It is also instrumental for healing and well-being. Use earth in spells for success in business or employment and for justice in legal matters. Call on earth's gentle energy when you need to foster patience or to accept a situation you cannot change. Associated with the sense of touch, this element can emphasize sensuality and aid in dealing with sexual issues. Use earth for fertility spells and for support during pregnancy and childbirth. An element of cycles, earth also aids in dealing with the death of a loved one.

Figure 30: Common triangle and circle symbols representing earth, along with the square used by seventeenth-century alchemists.

For this element, use candles of the following colors: black, brown, green, or white. Some of the crystals that are effective for working with earth include: moss agate, andalusite, cat's eye, chrysocolla, fluorite, hematite, jade, jasper, jet, labradorite, lodestone, malachite, rutilated and smoky quartz, salt, staurolite, black or brown tourmaline, and turquoise.

The Element Fire

Fire is the element of purification and transformation. It clears the way for releasing what we no longer need in our lives and aids in moving forward with a fresh start. This element sparks the imagination with creative energy and stokes intuition. Call on the energy of this element to strengthen divination skills and to develop psychic abilities. Fire is instrumental for consecrating ritual space and activating energy. It provides motivation to handle everyday tasks and the determination to reach for the stars. Employ this element in protection spells and for defense when seeking justice.

Call on fire to provide clarity in situations that require concise communication and truth. Associated with destruction, fire is also instrumental for healing. Fire stimulates ambition but warns us to temper it with honor, so we use our talents and influence with wisdom and grace. Employ this element to build confidence and courage when in a leadership role. The heat of this element generates passion—for one's purpose or goal in life as well as sexual.

Figure 31: Common triangle and circle symbols representing fire, along with the dotted triangle variation used by seventeenth-century alchemists.

For this element, use candles of the following colors: gold, orange, pink, red, white, or yellow. Some of the crystals that are effective for working with fire include: fire and red agate, amber, golden beryl, bloodstone, orange and red calcite, carnelian, citrine, red jasper, obsidian, fire opal, peridot, pyrite, quartz, ruby, spinel, sunstone, topaz, red tourmaline, and red zircon.

The Element Water

Water is the element of the emotions and intuition. Associated with sensitivity, it enhances psychic abilities and is especially supportive for clairvoyance. Because of this, water brings new dimensions to divination practices. Tapping into the subconscious mind, it aids dreamwork and helps in remembering dreams. It also fosters restful sleep. Water is especially powerful for shamanic work and lunar magic. It can also be used to reverse spells.

Call on the energy of water to initiate changes in your life. This element is an aid when you need to adapt to transitions not of your making. The purification properties of water foster serious introspection and spiritual renewal. Because of its association with compassion and empathy, water serves to strengthen friendships and reconcile troubled ones. Offering healing and growth, water provides nurturing during sorrow and restores the body, mind, and spirit to healthy balance. It is also instrumental for holding secrets.

Figure 32: Common triangle and circle symbols representing water, along with the dotted triangle variation used by seventeenth-century alchemists.

For this element, use candles of the following colors: aqua, black, blue, gray, blue and sea green, indigo, lilac, purple, silver, turquoise, violet, or white. Some of the crystals that are effective for working with water include blue lace agate, angelite, aquamarine, azurite, chrysocolla, fluorite, garnet, jade, ocean jasper, jet, lapis lazuli, larimar, moonstone, opal, pearl, quartz, sapphire, selenite, blue topaz, blue and watermelon tourmaline, and turquoise.

ELEMENTAL BEINGS

An exploration of the elements would not be complete without mentioning elemental beings. Unlike Empedocles who noted that nothing consisted purely of one element, by the Middle Ages there was widespread belief that such creatures existed. Despite a popular notion that elementals were devils, alchemists viewed them as semi-material spirits of the elements. Swiss physician and alchemist Theophrastus Bombastus von Hohenheim (1493–1541), who called himself Paracelsus, standardized the names and advanced the concept of elementals. (Read more about Paracelsus in Part Seven.)

Having collected folklore handed down from antiquity, Paracelsus provided a description of these mysterious beings in his treatise *A Book on Nymphs, Sylphs, Pygmies and Salamanders and Other Spirits*. Although it has a different connotation today, the term *pygmy* comes from the Greek *pygmaois* meaning "a type of goblin."[43] Nowadays, elementals are more commonly known as undines (water), sylphs (air), gnomes (earth), and salamanders (fire).

Paracelsus wanted to figure out their function in nature. While he regarded elemental beings as anthropomorphic, he believed they had a parallel evolution to humans. According to Paracelsus, they inhabited a separate realm from us but could pass into ours. A great deal has been written about them since the Middle Ages. According to some theories, elementals are sentient beings, not spirits. Some theories also regard elementals as being composed of just one element. Regardless of what they are, their presence can be felt and occasionally seen.

In my own experience, I can understand why they have been regarded as tricksters or mischievous sprites. One of the most memorable events with them took place when I was in Ireland. After a stormy night, my friends and I were enjoying a warm, sunny day and tried to perform a ritual on an ancient hill fort. Honoring the forces of the weather, Germaine began by saying, "Hail, wind and rain," meaning a salutation of "hail and welcome" to simply acknowledge the rain and wind of the previous night. Before anything further could be said, we were pelted with hail and rain and nearly blown off the hill. As fast as it started, the sky was clear and blue again without a trace of the storm. Coincidence? We didn't think so.

Despite that experience, I do not believe that the elementals were being vindictive or mischievous. Being mostly of one element—comprised of, living in it, or whatever—I think they lack balance and perspective and simply delivered what they probably thought we were requesting. Because of this, I think it is very challenging to enlist their aid in magic or ritual. When I sense their presence, I simply acknowledge them and wish them well. The decision to work with elemental beings is a personal one.

---

43. Marko Pogačnik, *Nature Spirits & Elemental Beings: Working with the Intelligence in Nature* (Forres, Scotland: Findhorn Press, 2009), 59.

PART THREE
THE FIFTEEN FIXED STARS

Stars are mainly thought of in relation to the zodiac and often skipped over for magical practices, which is unfortunate because they are a powerful source of energy and wisdom. Alchemists and magicians in the Middle Ages were particularly interested in fifteen special stars that were also known as the *Behenian*. Although these stars are occasionally included in modern Pagan literature, it wasn't until I was working on my book *Star Magic* that I became aware of their power. In this section, we will see how these fifteen stars can enhance ritual, magic, and other practices.

CHAPTER 7
SPECIAL STARS

FOR MILLENNIA, STARS HAVE been a source of wonder, mystery, and magic. While today we know that the visual effect we call *twinkling* is a way to tell the difference between a star and a planet, people during ancient and medieval times did not. They did, however, notice a difference in behavior among the lights in the sky.

The Egyptians called stars *the imperishable stars* and the planets, *the stars that never rested*.[44] Similarly, Greek astrologers called planets *the wanderers*. In medieval Europe the stars and planets were called *fixed stars* and *wandering stars*, respectively.[45] The fixed stars rose and set as did the sun and moon, but they stayed in the same pattern in relation to other stars.

In the sixteenth century, physician and scholar Heinrich Cornelius Agrippa noted that astrologers and alchemists in the Middle East regarded a group of fifteen stars as particularly powerful for magic. In his writing on the subject, Agrippa mentioned that his information was based in part on the work of Thebit, whose full name was Al-Sabi Thabit ibn Qurra al-Harrani (836–901). Thebit was born in what is now Turkey and made his mark as an astronomy and mathematics scholar in Baghdad. He translated numerous Greek manuscripts into Arabic and during the Middle Ages some of his work was translated into Latin.

In addition to Thebit, Agrippa mentioned that he used information from *The Book of Hermes*, a text ascribed to a shadowy wise man that was regarded as having a mystical connection with his namesake deity. According to American scholar and author Stephan

---

44. Pat Remler, *Egyptian Mythology A to Z*, 3rd ed. (New York: Chelsea House, 2010), 22.
45. Maurice A. Finocchiaro, *The Routledge Guidebook to Galileo's Dialogue* (New York: Routledge, 2014), 24.

Hoeller (1931–), the early Greek god Hermes was analogous with Thoth, the Egyptian god of wisdom, and together they were melded into an archetypal wise man that was called *Hermes Trismegistus*, "thrice-greatest Hermes."[46] This mélange of Greek and Egyptian religion and magic served as a source for both Hermeticism and Gnosticism. Without mentioning his Pagan roots, early Christians praised Hermes as a great sage who predated Moses but similarly received knowledge directly from God. Well into the Middle Ages, Hermes was lauded as a great astrologer, master alchemist, and an adept magician. It is no surprise that Agrippa name-dropped this learned wiseman as one of the sources for his own work.

While the potency of the special fifteen stars may have had something to do with their positions in the sky at certain times of the year, the exact reason for this belief is not known. It is likely that the high esteem for these stars originated in the Middle East, not only because Agrippa used the work of Thebit, but he also referred to the stars as *Behenian* and *Behenii* (plural). The English translator of Agrippa's work, James Freake (c. 1600s), noted that Agrippa used the term *behenian* "as a synonym meaning Arabian."[47] According to some sources, the word was derived from Arabic, meaning "root," and was used when referring to certain stars because they were the root or source of power. The Medieval Latin *behen* was derived from the Arabic *bahman*, which is the name that was used in parts of the Middle East for the root of the Indian ginseng plant (*Withania somnifera*).[48] During medieval times, this root was used magically to protect against evil and medicinally as a remedy for various ailments. The word *bahman* also meant "intelligent" and "supreme intelligence."[49]

The Behenii were commonly used throughout the Middle Ages and Renaissance in magic and astrology. Gradually, they fell out of favor because some had negative and destructive associations. However, according to Australian astrologer, teacher, and author Bernadette Brady (1950–), these stars have been rediscovered and are being employed as a source of knowledge to add more detail and depth to astrological readings. She also noted that the negative aspects ascribed to some of the stars merely point to aspects of which a person may need to be mindful.

---

46. Stephan A. Hoeller, "On the Trail of the Winged God: Hermes and Hermeticism Throughout the Ages," *Gnosis: A Journal of Western Inner Traditions*, vol. 40 (Commack, NY: Gnosis, 1996), 20–28.

47. Agrippa, *Three Books of Occult Philosophy*, 396.

48. Daniel F. Austin, *Florida Ethnobotany* (Boca Raton, FL: CRC Press, 2004), 529.

49. F. Steingass, *Persian-English Dictionary: Including Arabic Words and Phrases to be Met with in Persian Literature* (New York: Routledge, 1998), 212.

To help draw down the power of these stars, Agrippa and the Hermetic texts suggested the use of plants and gemstones that were commonly used in ritual and magic. Likewise, the sigils—symbols—for these stars were used as talismans to attract and hold celestial energy. Agrippa provided details on how to make a ring with a star's crystal, and then activate it with a handful of herbs. He also noted that instead of making a ring, a star's sigil could be inscribed on a crystal or simply drawn on a piece of parchment paper.

Although the sigils that appear in Agrippa's work were in common use during the Middle Ages, variations have been found in other texts. One of these is the thirteenth-century manuscript *De quindecim stellis* (The Fifteen Stars), attributed to Hermes Trismegistus and part of the Ashmole collection in the Bodleian Library at Oxford University, England. It was one of many manuscripts bequeathed to Oxford by Elias Ashmole (1617–1692), founder of the Ashmolean Museum. He was an antiquarian with a keen interest in astronomy, astrology, and magic who wrote alchemical texts under the pseudonym James Hasolle—an anagram using the letter *J* in place of the letter *I* as was common at the time. The star sigils are also found in a fourteenth-century manuscript in the Harley collection of the British Museum. The collection was named for English statesman Robert Harley (1661–1724), Earl of Oxford, who amassed material for his personal library. The Harley collection also contains work attributed to Thebit. Variations of the sigils have been found in other manuscripts as well.

USING THE STARS IN MAGIC

When a star's sigil is inscribed on an object, it helps to hold the energy until it is needed. Like other symbols, star sigils can be carved into candles for ritual or painted on gemstones and other items for use as talismans. The sigils can be incorporated into charms or any object used for spells. They can be written on paper and burned as part of a spell to release and direct the star's energy. The sigils can be used like any image we hold in our minds to focus intent and willpower. They can also provide support for ritual and divination and, of course, astrology and astral travel.

When you begin working with a star, draw its sigil on a piece of paper, place it on your altar, and meditate on it. Gaze at it for a few minutes, and then close your eyes as you hold the image in your mind. Take note of feelings or thoughts that arise, but do not dwell on them or try to analyze them. Repeat this a few times before drawing down the energy of the star. Details on how to draw down energy are covered later in this chapter.

As a common component in ritual and magic, candles provide the opportunity to incorporate color magic with the energy of the stars. Although the color of some of the brightest stars can be seen with the unaided eye, most appear white or bluish white. The most common star colors are blue, blue white, white, yellow white, yellow, orange, and red.

Because a star is not always just "a" star, more than one color can be used for an additional energy boost. A star may be binary—two stars that revolve around each other—or a group of stars, each with a different color. For example, the star Algol is a triple star; one is blue white, one orange, and the third white. In the case of blue white or yellow white stars, use candles that are pale blue or light yellow. Color information is included in each star's entry in the next chapter.

Whether or not you coordinate colors, you can still draw a star's sigil on a candle to use in your magic work or ritual. A sigil can be drawn with a felt tip pen on a crystal or other object too. If you want to charge a crystal without marking it up, draw the sigil on a piece of paper, and then wrap it around the stone. If you are working with plants, draw a sigil on a piece of paper to place under a living plant or dried leaves and/or flowers. Dried plant material that has been charged with star energy can be used to stuff a small pillow for dreamwork or placed in a sachet for any other purpose. For extra measure, draw or sew the sigil on the pillow or sachet. If a fresh or dried plant is not available, an essential oil works just as well because it carries the essence of the plant. In a pinch, if you cannot find a plant associated with the star you are working with, a photograph can be used.

Using a candle or other object with a sigil during divination or other practice provides a way to draw a star's energy into your session. If you are working at night, and depending on the time of year, you may want to go outside and see the star in the sky, which can enhance your experience.

DRAWING DOWN THE POWER OF STARS

Just like drawing down the moon in an esbat ritual, the energy of the stars is easy to access. The best way is by using the chakras. In addition to the seven major chakras within the body, there are several others that are especially helpful when working with the energy of the cosmos. Three of these are called the *stellar* or *celestial chakras* and are located above the head. A fourth, called the *earth star chakra*, is approximately three feet below the ground, connecting us with the energy of the earth. As Pagans, we may not have put a name to it, but we are usually aware of this chakra when working with the energy of the natural world or when grounding energy after ritual.

The first of the stellar chakras is called the *causal chakra*. Aligning with the spine about three or four inches above the head, it functions as a portal to regulate the flow of energy from the cosmic level to the personal, helping to prevent energy overload. The next is called the *soul star chakra*. Located about six inches above the head, it functions as a connection beyond the body to the stars. According to some beliefs, this is the entry and exit point for the soul. The third chakra is called the *stellar gateway*. It is approximately twelve inches above the head and provides a multi-dimensional connection with the cosmos and divine energy.

When we draw down star energy, we become a conduit for it. We internalize it, shape it with our intentions through visualization, and then send it out along with our willpower. We can also send it into an object to create a talisman or we can charge candles, tools, and other equipment for ritual, spells, and other practices. Marking the object with a star's sigil aids in holding the energy.

When you are ready to begin, choose one of the stars and draw its sigil on a piece of paper, candle, or other object, and then place it on your altar. Stand with your hands comfortably at your sides. Gaze at the sigil for a few minutes, and then close your eyes as you hold its image in your mind.

Bring your awareness down to the soles of your feet. Sense the power of the earth star chakra keeping you connected with Mother Earth. Imagine that you have roots extending from your feet down through the floor, through the earth star chakra, and deep into the earth. Feel the stability of the planet and your connection with her. Imagine drawing this energy up through your body. By doing this, you can tap into a continuous flow of energy that will enhance but not deplete your own. This also keeps you grounded and centered.

Bring your awareness up through your body to the crown of your head. Feel your energy extending up through the three stellar chakras. Sense the lightness of air above you and the vastness of the sky. Feel it lift you. Know that in addition to being part of the earth, you are part of the stars. Become aware of the difference between these two energies: one keeping you rooted and stable, the other lifting you to a higher purpose.

Bring the star's sigil into your mind's eye, and then raise your arms out to the sides to shoulder height. Just as you drew earth energy up through your feet, visualize drawing down the energy of the star. Feel it move through the stellar chakras and into your crown chakra. Pull the energy down through you and then hold it within your body. While you are doing this, visualize the purpose for the candle, crystal, or other object you want to charge. When you feel that you cannot contain the energy any longer, pick up the object and hold it between your hands. Release the energy by visualizing it moving down your arms into the object.

After a moment or two, imagine the movement of energy fading like stars in the morning sky. Let the remaining energy ripple down to your feet as you bring your awareness to your connection with the earth. When you feel that all excess energy has been grounded, slowly open your eyes. If you are not planning to use the charged object immediately, wrap it in a cloth and leave it on your altar until it is needed.

CHAPTER 8

WORKING WITH THE FIFTEEN FIXED STARS

EACH OF THE FOLLOWING entries includes information about a star's name, color, and details on how to find it in the sky. Although most of the fixed stars are visible in the Northern and Southern Hemispheres, the directions to locate them are from a northern perspective. In addition to the traditional crystals, suggestions for alternative stones have been included. Because some of the traditional plants associated with the stars are poisonous, substitutes have been provided.

Most of the illustrations in this chapter contain three sigils: one that was in common use during the sixteenth century from Agrippa's *Three Books of Occult Philosophy*, one from the thirteenth-century manuscript, *The Fifteen Stars*, attributed to Hermes Trismegistus, and one that I created using a method outlined in Part Six of this book.

While each entry provides suggestions for ways to use the sigils, let your intuition guide you to meaningful and personal ways to work with a star's energy. You may want to experiment with making your own sigils too.

ALA CORVI

Located in the constellation Corvus the Crow, the name *Ala Corvi*, which means "wing of the crow," has caused confusion because it could refer to two different stars: Algorab or Gienah. In various translations of Agrippa's work both have been cited as Ala Corvi.

Gienah is a blue white star and the brightest in the constellation. Its name comes from an Arabic phrase meaning "the right wing of the raven."[50] *Corvus* is the genus name for

---

50. Mark R. Chartrand, *Night Sky: A Guide to Field Identification* (New York: St. Martin's Press, 1990), 138.

both ravens and crows. Algorab is a double star on the crow's other wing. Its primary star is yellowish white and the other is a rare purplish color. This star's name comes from the same Arabic phrase as Gienah and means "raven."[51]

Corvus is a constellation of the Southern Hemisphere that is visible in the north in late spring and early summer. Its most recognizable pattern is a trapezoid of four stars. Corvus is low in the sky near the horizon below Virgo. To find it, look to the northeast to locate the Big Dipper. Follow the curve of the dipper's handle to a bright star, which is the fixed star Arcturus. Follow the same curve to the next bright star, which is Spica in Virgo. Continue to follow that imaginary line south to Corvus.

In medieval magic, Ala Corvi was used to drive away evil spirits. Today this star is called on for protection and defense. A crystal inscribed with its sigil makes a powerful amulet. This star is also effective to dispel all forms of negativity. Draw Ala Corvi's energy into the dried leaves of burdock or comfrey, and then burn a little to clear ritual space or to prepare an area for magic work. Sketch the symbol on a small piece of paper, and then place it anywhere in the home or at work to remove negative energy.

With the stars Algorab and Gienah depicted on the bird's wings, the energy of Ala Corvi can help you soar. To call on this type of support, inscribe the sigil on a candle and use it while engaging in creative work or spiritual practices.

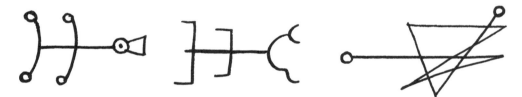

Figure 33: The sigils for Ala Corvi are from the sixteenth century (left),
thirteenth century (center), and the author's (right).

While onyx is the traditional gemstone associated with Ala Corvi, ruby or turquoise can be used too. Plants associated with this star include bur or burdock, which is also known as greater burdock; henbane; comfrey, also called common comfrey; and *quadraginus*, which is believed to refer to the yellow daffodil also known as lent lily. Boston fern can be used as a substitute for the poisonous henbane.

51. Richard Hinckley Allen, *Star-Names and Their Meanings* (New York: G. E. Stechert, 1899), 182.

ALDEBARAN

In the constellation Taurus the Bull, this star is visible from late autumn to early spring but is best seen in winter. To locate it, look north for the three stars of Orion's belt. Imagine a line that follows the angle of these stars to the northwest to the next bright star, which is Aldebaran. In depictions of the constellation, it represents the eye of the bull.

The name of this orange-red star comes from Arabic and means the "follower" or "attendant," because it appears to follow the Pleiades across the sky.[52] Aldebaran was one of the four royal stars of Persia and called the *Guardian of the East.*

Associated with steadfastness and courage, wear a crystal or carry a piece of paper inscribed with Aldebaran's sigil when you need to hold your resolve and take a firm stand. Linked with honor and honesty, this star is an aid in struggles where taking right action is necessary for the good of all.

When called upon to voice an opinion or idea, Aldebaran provides support in the form of clear, eloquent communication. Because of this star's association with intelligence, place an object marked with its sigil in a study area to help boost learning. Alternatively, the sigil could be lightly carved into a bookcase or drawn on paper and kept with schoolbooks. Use it in spells to foster success or wear it as an amulet during an important interview or meeting. Because Aldebaran represents the eye of the bull, use its sigil to foster clarity in divination and vision in psychic work.

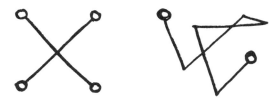

Figure 34: The sigils for Aldebaran are from the thirteenth
century (left) and the author's (right).

Traditionally, this star has been associated with ruby and carbuncle. *Carbuncle* is an old term that was used from ancient times through the Victorian era for any type of translucent red stone. It is generally accepted that the term most often referred to almandine garnet and ruby. In place of ruby or garnet, bloodstone and carnelian work well. The plants

---

52. Fred Schaaf, *A Year of the Stars: A Month by Month Journey of Skywatching* (Amherst, NY: Prometheus Books, 2003), 197.

associated with Aldebaran are milk thistle and matry-silva, which is believed to have been a folk name for woodruff or sweet woodruff.[53]

ALGOL

This star is part of the constellation Perseus the Hero, which is visible from late autumn to early spring. To locate Algol, look north to Orion's Belt, and then draw an imaginary line north to the first bright star, which is Capella. Forming a pattern that looks like a crooked, upside-down letter *Y*, Perseus is to the west of Capella. Of the two brightest stars in the constellation, Algol is the southern one.

The traditional name of this star was derived from Arabic and means "the head of the demon."[54] According to Greek mythology, the hero Perseus slew the snake-haired Gorgon Medusa. In depictions of this constellation, Algol represents Medusa's eye because the star seems to blink. This is because Algol is an eclipsing binary star. When the dimmer companion star passes in front of the brighter one, it produces a blinking effect. In fact, Algol is a triple star. The primary star is blue white, the second is orange, and the third is white.

In sixteenth-century Europe, Algol was known by the Latin names *Caput Larvae*, "the specter's head," and *Caput Medusae*, "the head of Medusa."[55] In ancient times Algol was linked with demons and considered one of the evilest stars in the sky. The reason for this may be because the Hebrews associated it with the independent and strong-willed Lilith, who was regarded as an abomination.

This once-feared star is now associated with strength and intense passion. Use its sigil in spells or rituals to amplify personal strength; however, remember to keep power in check and avoid turning yourself into an overbearing "demon." To increase passion, draw or sew the sigil on a small scarf or piece of cloth, and then dab it with a little rose essential oil. Use it to wrap diamond or red tourmaline jewelry to give to your lover. Of course, we can also be passionate about a creative project or other type of endeavor. Wear or carry Algol's sigil when engaged in these activities.

Because this star is associated with the forces of the natural world, it can be called upon to work with nature spirits or to foster a healthy garden. Carve its sigil on a fence or paint it on a few stones to place around your garden. Draw it on small stones to place in houseplant flowerpots. Also instrumental for breaking hexes, burn a little mugwort along

---

53. Agrippa, *Three Books of Occult Philosophy*, 100.

54. Bernadette Brady, *Brady's Book of Fixed Stars* (York Beach, ME: Red Wheel/Weiser LLC, 1998), 188.

55. Allen, *Star-Names and Their Meanings*, 332.

with a small piece of paper inscribed with the sigil. Since this star is associated with Lilith, use the sigil to honor her.

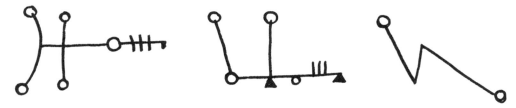

Figure 35: The sigils for Algol are from the sixteenth century (left),
thirteenth century (center), and the author's (right).

While diamond is the traditional gemstone for Algol, bloodstone or red tourmaline can be used. The plants black hellebore and mugwort are associated with Algol. Although black hellebore is often used as a garden plant, it is poisonous. For a substitute, use a white or pink five-petaled rose such as the redleaf rose.

ALPHECCA

Ranked as the fourteenth brightest in the entire sky, Alphecca is a double star with a white primary and a yellow secondary. Its name comes from an Arabic root word that means "break" or "broken," referring to the shape of its constellation, Corona Borealis, which is a broken circle.[56] The Latin name for this star is *Gemma*, which means "jewel."[57] During the Middle Ages it was called *Gnosia Stella* meaning "star of knowledge."[58] According to translator James Freake, Agrippa used the names *Elpheia* and *Elphrya* for it.[59] The source of these names is unknown.

To locate Corona Borealis, face north to find the Big Dipper. Draw an imaginary line east and slightly south from the end of the dipper's handle, through the top of a kite shape of stars. Look for a distinctive semi-circle; Alphecca is the brightest star in the group. It is visible from late spring through the summer.

Associated with artistic skills, Alphecca can be instrumental in discovering and developing talent. Draw its sigil on your tools or make a creative project of carving, sculpting,

56. David J. Darling, *The Universal Book of Astronomy: From the Andromeda Galaxy to the Zone of Avoidance* (Hoboken, NJ: John Wiley & Sons, Inc., 2004), 19.

57. Schaaf, *A Year of the Stars*, 117.

58. Allen, *Star-Names and Their Meanings*, 178.

59. Agrippa, *Three Books of Occult Philosophy*, 396.

or painting a picture of it. Alternatively, hide the sigil within your work. Draw down the star's energy into an ivy houseplant to foster and boost creative ideas.

Alphecca's influence can be called upon in spells to elevate social status, but only if such a change has been earned. Although it is associated with honor, don't draw down its energy if you are looking for loud kudos, because it will not work. Instead, wear or carry the sigil to mark quiet achievement for work that has a significant impact on others. Mark it on a piece of topaz or beryl jewelry to wear as your special gem. Carve it into a white candle for your altar to help find the wisdom you seek. Also, paint it on a red ribbon to tie a sprig of trefoil for a love spell.

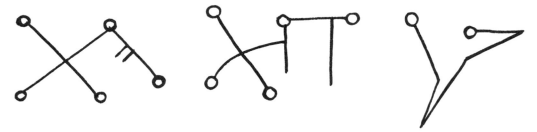

Figure 36: The sigils for Alphecca are from the sixteenth century (left), thirteenth century (center), and the author's (right).

While Agrippa suggested topaz as the gemstone to draw down the energy of Alphecca, beryl also works well. The plants associated with it include rosemary, ivy, and trefoil, also known as birds-foot trefoil. Red clover has also been suggested as the trefoil referred to by Agrippa.

ANTARES

Located in the constellation Scorpius the Scorpion, Antares is a bright red star that is best seen low on the southern horizon in early summer. It is the sixteenth brightest star in the entire sky.

The Babylonians called this star the *Breast of the Scorpion* and in Latin it was called *Cor Scorpii*, which means "scorpion's heart."[60] The name *Antares* comes from ancient Greek

---

60. William Tyler Olcott, *Star Lore: Myths, Legends, and Facts* (Mineola, NY: Dover Publications, Inc., 2004), 329.

and has been translated as "anti-Ares" and "the rival of Mars."[61] The latter name is believed to refer to Antares being similar in color to the planet Mars. In ancient Egypt, Antares was sacred to Isis and represented the scorpion goddess Selket. It was one of the four royal stars of Persia and was called the *Guardian of the West*.

While in the past Antares was associated with evil and destructiveness, it is now regarded as instrumental in raising awareness for potential self-destructive behavior. Although it should not replace professional help, wearing a crystal inscribed with Antares's sigil or holding it to meditate on problems can foster supportive energy. This star aids in subduing all forms of negativity. Place its sigil in areas of your home or workplace where you sense negative energy. To keep unwanted energy from entering your home, paint the symbol on the underside of a welcome mat and place it at your front door.

The energy of Antares can be used like a shield for dealing with difficult issues and for defense or protection. Place a piece of paper with the sigil in the bottom of your cauldron or other heat-resistant vessel and burn it along with a pinch or two of saffron. Gently waft the smoke around you as you visualize it creating a shield.

Figure 37: The sigils for Antares are from the sixteenth century (left), thirteenth century (center), and the author's (right).

Antares is associated with the gemstones sardonyx and amethyst. Jasper or sard can also be used to work with the energy of this star. Agrippa suggested the plants birthwort or long-rooted birthwort and saffron, also known as the autumn crocus.

ARCTURUS

This orange-red star is one of the two brightest in the spring sky and the fourth brightest of all. It is part of the constellation Boötis the Plowman. To find the constellation, follow the handle of the Big Dipper to the southeast and, according to the saying, "arc down to

---

61. Fred Schaaf, *The Brightest Stars: Discovering the Universe through the Sky's Most Brilliant Stars* (Hoboken, NJ: John Wiley & Sons, Inc., 2008), 217.

Arcturus," which is located at the bottom of a kite shape of stars. The constellation is visible in the spring and early summer.

While Agrippa knew this star as *Alchameth* or *Alchamech*, it was also called *Arctophilax*, "the bear watcher," referring to its proximity to the constellation Ursa Major, the Great Bear.[62] The Arabs called this star the *Keeper of Heaven* and the Chaldeans called it the *Guardian Messenger*.[63]

Arcturus is a guardian and protector—a night watchman of sorts. To use its protective power, draw down its energy to charge a piece of jasper. Go to each door in your house and use the stone to inscribe its sigil in the air. As you do this, visualize it creating an energy shield over the door. Alternatively, paint the sigil on four stones, and then place them at the corners of your property.

Also associated with guidance, meditate with the sigil to help sort out an issue. Sew or use fabric paint to add it to a dream pillow for aid in remembering and interpreting dreams. Whether you are a student or teacher, place a piece of paper with the sigil in your books for support in sharing knowledge or exploring new topics. Arcturus is also an effective aid and guide for people in leadership positions.

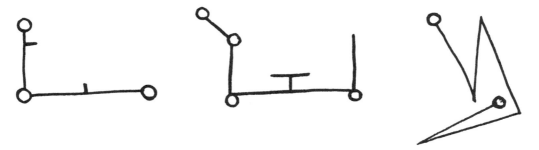

Figure 38: The sigils for Arcturus are from the sixteenth century (left), thirteenth century (center), and the author's (right).

While jasper is the traditional gemstone associated with this star, citrine, lodestone, and tourmaline also work well. Agrippa suggested the herb plantain, which is also known as broadleaf plantain. It is not related to the plantain that produces banana-like fruit.

---

62. Robson, *The Fixed Stars & Constellations in Astrology*, 139.
63. Olcott, *Star Lore*, 77–78.

CAPELLA

Sixth brightest of all the stars in the sky, Capella is part of the constellation Auriga the Charioteer. It is a binary star—the primary yellow, the secondary red—and its name is Latin meaning "female goat."[64] In depictions of the constellation, this star represents the heart of a goat that the charioteer holds on his shoulder. Agrippa called Capella the *Goat Star*. To ancient Romans this celestial animal represented the she-goat that suckled the infant Jupiter. To Babylonians, Capella was the star of Marduk, their powerful creator god. The Arabs called it the *Guardian of the Pleiades*.[65]

Although the Auriga constellation is visible from late autumn to early spring, January is the best time for viewing it. Looking north, locate Orion's Belt, and then draw an imaginary line north to the next bright star, which is Capella. The stars in Auriga form an uneven pentagon shape.

Capella has two very different aspects. On the one hand, it is associated with ambition and public position. For spells to support these, inscribe its sigil at the four corners of a piece of paper, and then write exactly what you seek in the middle of the page. Burn the paper as you visualize attaining your goal. To attract and increase wealth, draw the sigil on a piece of paper, and then wrap it around the largest-denomination bill you have in your wallet. Leave this on your altar for three days. While Capella aids in these gains, it also warns to not let them get out of hand.

Conversely, Capella is a star of compassion. For support when nurturing others, draw its sigil on a piece of paper, place it on your altar, and then sprinkle dried peppermint leaves over it. Allow it to stay in place for as long as you require Capella's help. Carry the sigil with you when engaging in community work or other related endeavors.

Figure 39: The sigils for Capella are from the sixteenth century (left),
thirteenth century (center), and the author's (right).

---

64. Allen, *Star-Names and Their Meanings*, 86.
65. Olcott, *Star Lore*, 66.

While sapphire is the traditional stone for working with Capella, amber, hematite, and jade work well, too, especially when used together. Plants associated with this star include horehound, also known as white horehound; mint, which could refer to peppermint or spearmint; mugwort; and mandrake, which is poisonous. Tobacco is generally suggested as a substitute for mandrake. In addition to finding it in cigarettes, it is often grown as a garden plant. Its cousins, jasmine tobacco and flowering tobacco, can be used as substitutes too. The herb thyme has also become associated with Capella.

DENEB ALGEDI

Deneb Algedi is the brightest star in the constellation Capricornus the Sea Goat. Best seen in early autumn, the stars of Capricornus form a wide arrowhead shape, which can be located low in the southern sky during the early evening hours.

Called *Cauda Capricorni*, "tail of Capricorn," by Agrippa, its traditional name comes from Arabic and means "the tail of the goat," which describes its location in depictions of the constellation.[66] It is a four-star system comprised of two white and two yellow-white stars. The name is often written with the alternate spelling of *Deneb Algiedi*.

In the past, this star was linked with opposites: sorrow and happiness, life and death. Today's interpretation associates it with the fullness of life and the importance of balance. Inscribe its sigil on a piece of paper and place it along with a pearl and a piece of jet on your Mabon or Ostara altar to symbolize balance.

Whenever you feel that your emotions or enthusiasm are getting out of hand, sit quietly for a couple of minutes as you gaze at the sigil. To banish sadness, draw it on a small piece of paper to burn with a pinch of marjoram. Deneb Algedi is also associated with integrity and justice. Mark its sigil on a piece of chalcedony and keep it with you as you work to right a wrong. Let it serve as a reminder that retribution is not the path to follow. Also, carry the chalcedony sigil any time your self-esteem needs supportive energy.

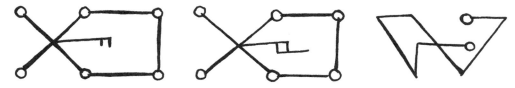

Figure 40: The sigils for Deneb Algedi are from the sixteenth century (left), thirteenth century (center), and the author's (right).

---

66. Chartrand, *Night Sky*, 126.

Chalcedony is the traditional gemstone; however, jet, opal, or pearl also work well. Associated plants include catnip, marjoram, mandrake, and mugwort. As mentioned, mandrake is poisonous—refer to the entry on Capella for substitutes.

THE PLEIADES

Collectively, the Pleiades are regarded as one of the special fifteen fixed stars. It is an open cluster of stars in Taurus, which is visible from late autumn to early spring. Six of the stars form a semi-circle surrounded by a soft glowing haze. To find the Pleiades, look north and locate Orion's Belt. Draw an imaginary line extending from these stars to the northwest just beyond Aldebaran. The next bright star is Alcyone in the Pleiades. The stars are bluish white.

Throughout time and in most cultures worldwide, the Pleiades have been observed, commented upon, and honored. Innumerable poets have written about the charm and mystery of these stars and have described them as drops of dew, diamonds, pearls, or doves. According to various sources, the name may have come from the Greek *peleiades* meaning "flock of doves," or *plein* meaning "to sail," referring to the heliacal rising of these stars that heralded the season for safe navigation.[67] In Greek mythology, the Pleiades were called the *Atlantides*—the daughters of Atlas—and were considered the virgin companions of Artemis. The Egyptians called them *Atauria*, which means "the stars of *Athyr*" (Hathor).

The Pleiades have been considered bringers of wisdom and peace. To foster calm, peaceful energy in your home, draw its sigil on multiple crystals and place them throughout your house. This also works well in the workplace. For love spells, inscribe the sigil on several light blue candles, and then cluster them together on your altar or wherever you perform magic work. If you want to pay homage to Artemis or Hathor, include a white candle with the sigil—or two candles, one for each goddess—in your esbat rituals.

The Pleiades are also an aid on the quest for knowledge, which often comes from within. Prepare for meditation by drawing the sigil on your palms with an eyeliner pencil or on two small pieces of paper to hold in your hands. Burn a little frankincense while you meditate. These stars are also instrumental for communicating with spirits. To enhance your contact, carve the sigil into a fennel bulb and place it on your altar when working with them.

---

67. Ian Ridpath, *Star Tales* (Cambridge, England: Lutterworth Press, 1988), 121.

Figure 41: The sigils for the Pleiades are from the sixteenth century (left),
thirteenth century (center), and the author's (right).

Clear quartz is the traditional stone associated with the Pleiades, but smoky quartz and blue topaz also work well. The plants associated with these stars are fennel and frankincense.

POLARIS

Commonly known as the *North Star* and the *Pole Star*, Polaris is visible all year. It is part of the constellation Ursa Minor, the Little Bear, which is easy to find because of the well-known shape within it called *the Little Dipper*. The four stars marking the bowl of the Little Dipper represent the body of the Bear and the three stars of the handle, its tail. Polaris is at the end of the tail.

Polaris is a yellow-white double star that has been used for navigation for millennia. It has been known by many names including *Lodestar*, the *Steering Star*, *Stella Maris* ("sea star"), and the *Gate of Heaven*.[68] Agrippa called this star *Cauda Ursae* ("tail of the bear").

Just as in medieval magic, Polaris is effective for protection, especially against spells that may be directed at you. Gather a few fresh chicory or mugwort leaves and carefully draw the symbol on each leaf with a felt tip pen. Let the leaves dry for a day or two, crumble them into pieces, and then burn them as you visualize a protective shield forming around you.

Always linked with guidance, this star is an aid for gaining a sense of where you want to go in life and how to get there. Draw the sigil on a picture of a bear to hold while meditating on your life's purpose. Keep a piece of lodestone inscribed with it in your car or luggage for guidance and protection when traveling.

---

68. Roy A. Gallant, *The Constellations: How They Came to Be* (Cincinnati, OH: Four Winds Press, 1979), 24.

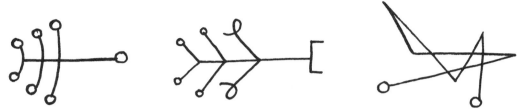

Figure 42: The sigils for Polaris are from the sixteenth century (left),
thirteenth century (center), and the author's (right).

Agrippa associated Polaris with lodestone, which he called *magnet* because of its magnetic properties. The plants to use with this star are succory, also known as chicory, mugwort, and periwinkle, which could refer to greater periwinkle or lesser periwinkle.

PROCYON

The seventh brightest in the sky, Procyon is a white binary star in the constellation Canis Minor, the Little Dog. Visible from December to March, the stars in Canis Minor form a line with a zigzag at one end. To find this constellation, look to the southeast for the brightest star in the sky, which is Sirius in the constellation Canis Major. Draw an imaginary line a little to the northeast from Sirius to the next bright star, which is Procyon. According to Greek myth, the constellations of Canis Minor and Major represented the hunting dogs of Orion.

The name *Procyon* was derived from Greek and means "before the dog" or "preceding the dog," referring to its position to the north of Canis Major.[69] It was also occasionally called *Antecanis*, which means the same thing in Latin.[70]

While in the past Procyon was linked with danger, today it is an aid for avoiding danger. Wear any of the crystals associated with Procyon inscribed with its sigil as an amulet. That said, it is important to use common sense to keep from harm. Procyon is also associated with power, wealth, and fame. The caution with this star is to be careful with fortune and success because it can easily slip away.

Procyon is most effective when taking the long view with slower but steady progress toward goals. If this approach works for you, make a white altar cloth, and sew or draw the sigil in the center. Use this cloth on your altar when performing any magic related to

---

69. Schaaf, *The Brightest Stars*, 165.
70. Ibid.

your goals. Associated with good health, use the sigil on objects to boost energy for a healing circle. Also, draw it on a crystal or piece of paper to keep with you when working with animals—the energy of the little dog will aid you.

Figure 43: The sigils for Procyon are from the sixteenth century (left), thirteenth century (center), and the author's (right).

While agate is the traditional gemstone, aventurine or jasper make good alternatives. Agrippa associated this star with marigold, which is regarded as the English marigold, and pennyroyal. Calamint can be used as a substitute for pennyroyal, which can be toxic. Water buttercup has also become associated with Procyon.

REGULUS

Regulus is part of Leo the Lion, which is one of the oldest-recognized constellations. Six stars form the shape of a backward question mark that represents the lion's head and mane. To find Regulus, draw an imaginary line from Polaris at the end of the handle of the Little Dipper to the two stars in the bowl of the Big Dipper, opposite the dipper's handle. Continue that line to the southwest to the star at the bottom of the question mark. Regulus is the brightest star in the constellation. Best seen in March, Leo is visible from spring to early summer.

Agrippa called this star *Cor Leonis*, which means "the heart of the lion."[71] In Latin, Regulus means "little king" or "little prince."[72] One of the royal stars of Persia, it was called the *Guardian of the North*. In the past, navigators used this star to determine longitude. Regulus is a triple star: the primary is bluish white, the second is orange, and the third is red.

As might be expected of a star in the lion constellation, Regulus is associated with power and strength. Like Procyon, it also comes with a warning: Once these attributes

---

71. Robson, *The Fixed Stars & Constellations in Astrology,* 195.
72. Olcott, *Star Lore,* 236.

are obtained they should never be used for revenge; otherwise, all that was gained will be lost. To boost the power of spells, draw the sigil multiple times in the shape of a backward question mark on a large piece of paper. Place candles and other objects used in your spell on top of it. When you are finished, tear the paper into small pieces and safely burn them.

For help in subduing anger or ameliorating sadness, carefully break open a capsule of Arabic / mastic gum (available in health food stores and pharmacies) and use the liquid to draw the symbol on a crystal. Hold the crystal and visualize the anger or sadness draining away. Just a note: don't confuse Arabic gum with gum Arabic, which is different and comes from a tree in the genus *Acacia*.

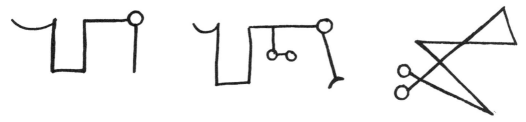

Figure 44: The sigils for Regulus are from the sixteenth century (left), thirteenth century (center), and the author's (right).

Depending on the translation of Agrippa's work, the stone(s) for Regulus is granite and / or garnet. In addition to garnet's name coming from the Latin *malum granatum*, meaning "seeded apple" or "pomegranate," it also shares etymology with granite in the Latin *granum* meaning "grain" or "seed."[73] Bloodstone or zircon also work well with the energy of this star. The associated plants are mugwort; mastic, which is also known as Arabic gum, a resin from the mastic tree; and sallendine, which most likely refers to greater celandine.

SIRIUS

Visible from December to March, Sirius is part of the constellation Canis Major, the Big Dog. Being the brightest of all stars, Sirius makes this constellation easy to locate by looking to the southeast. The two triangles of stars below Sirius represent the dog's head and its hindquarters.

---

73. Walter W. Skeat, *The Concise Dictionary of English Etymology* (Ware, England: Wordsworth Editions, Ltd., 1993), 186.

Sirius is a white binary star; the smaller of the two has been nicknamed the *Pup*. The name *Sirius* comes from Greek and means "scorching" or "searing."[74] In ancient times, this star rose just before the sun during the hottest period of the year, which is the source of the phrase "the dog days of summer." In Egypt, the rising of Sirius marked the annual flooding of the Nile, an occasion linked with the return from the dead of the god Osiris. The Egyptians called this star *Sopdet* and regarded it as the celestial manifestation of the goddess Isis.[75] In medieval medicine, Sirius was believed to ward off the plague, as well as provide a cure for dropsy.

This brightest of all stars is associated with marital peace, faithfulness, and passion. For spells to bolster these aspects of a relationship, squeeze the juice from several juniper berries or purchase the essential oil and use it to inscribe the symbol on a white candle or a red one to ignite passion. Prepare a green candle in the same way for a spell to attract money and wealth.

For help in bolstering communication skills, wear a piece of beryl or topaz jewelry marked with the star's sigil. Also regarded a guardian, draw the sigil on a small dog collar to wear as a bracelet or anklet and think of the energy as your guard dog. Carve the sigil on an altar candle to honor Isis.

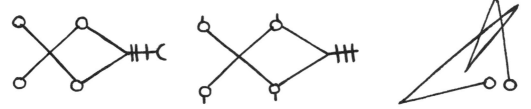

Figure 45: The sigils for Sirius are from the sixteenth century (left), thirteenth century (center), and the author's (right).

While the traditional gemstone for this star is beryl, topaz also works well. Plants associated with Sirius are mugwort; savin, more commonly known as juniper; and dragonwort or common bistort.

---

74. Ridpath, *Star Tales*, 40.

75. Jay B. Holberg, *Sirius: Brightest Diamond in the Night Sky* (New York: Springer, 2007), 4.

SPICA

Spica is one of two very bright stars in the spring sky. It is part of the constellation Virgo, which forms the shape of a stick figure low on the horizon. To find Virgo, follow the handle of the Big Dipper and, according to the saying, "arc down to Arcturus, and then speed on to Spica."

Spica is a bluish-white binary star. From Latin meaning "the head of grain," Spica represents a sheaf of grain in Virgo's left hand.[76] Like Polaris, this star was used for navigation in ancient times. Ptolemy's geographical reference for Spica was the Fortunate Islands—present-day Canary Islands—which may account for the star being referred to as "the Fortunate One."[77]

Representing a head of grain, Spica is a star of abundance. Use its sigil on a light blue candle for spells to attract security and abundance into your life. Draw it on flowerpots or fence posts to increase the bounty of your garden. On the Ostara altar, the sigil can represent the freshness of spring and maidenhood.

Associated with knowledge and insight, this star is especially effective for developing and refining psychic skills. Mark its sigil on a piece of tiger's eye jewelry to wear when engaging in these activities. To aid in dreamwork, keep the crystal on your bedside table. Burn a small piece of paper with the sigil along with a pinch of sage for a spell to bring success in legal matters. If you are going to court, burn the paper and use it for a light smudging beforehand. Also, use the sigil in spells for protection or to attract luck.

Figure 46: The sigils for Spica are from the sixteenth century (left),
and the author's (right).

While emerald is the traditional gemstone associated with Spica, tiger's eye also works well. Plants include sage, trefoil, periwinkle, mandrake, and mugwort. As mentioned, mandrake is poisonous; refer to the entry on Capella for substitutes.

---

76. Erik Gregersen, ed., *The Milky Way and Beyond: Stars, Nebulae, and Other Galaxies* (New York: Britannica Educational Publishing, 2010), 211.

77. James Evans, *The History and Practice of Ancient Astronomy* (New York: Oxford University Press, 1998), 102.

VEGA

This blue-white star is part of the constellation Lyra the Lyre, which is also regarded as a harp. Lyra consists of a small parallelogram of four faint stars. In depictions of Lyra, Vega is northwest just outside of this shape, representing the instrument's handle. To locate Vega, look overhead for the brightest star in the summer sky. Sometimes called *Wega*, it is the fifth-brightest star of all.

The name *Vega* was derived from the Arabic word "falling" or "swooping."[78] While the Arabs regarded Lyra as a falling or swooping eagle, in India it was considered a falling vulture. To ancient Egyptians, Vega was the *Vulture Star* associated with the goddess Ma'at, who was often depicted holding a vulture feather.

During medieval times, Vega was associated with magic and used for protection against witchcraft. Draw its sigil on a pointed clear quartz crystal to break hexes and send negative energy to ground. To subdue fears or concerns, draw it on eight pieces of paper, and then place them on the floor in a circle large enough to sit in. Visualize energy rising from the sigils, creating a safe dome around you as your fears dissolve.

If you feel the need to enhance your social awareness, wear or carry a piece of calcite marked with the sigil. Vega is also associated with artistic talent. Keep the sigil in your workspace to enhance creativity. Linked with hopefulness, wear a pendant with the sigil to help find the music in your heart.

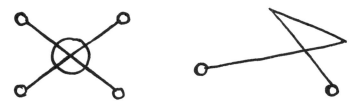

Figure 47: The sigils for Vega are from the thirteenth century (left) and the author's (right).

Agrippa associated this star with the gemstone chrysolite, which could refer to chryso-beryl, peridot, or topaz. Calcite or clear quartz can also be used to work with the energy of Vega. Plants include chicory, winter savory, and fumitory.

---

78. Olcott, *Star Lore*, 260.

PART FOUR
THE OGHAM

For centuries, almost everything about the Celtic ogham—its name, origin, and characters—has been disputed. Also spelled *ogam* and *ogum*, even the simple fact of how to pronounce the word has variations ranging from "OH-umm" to "OH-wam" to "OH-yam"—take your pick.[79]

Just like spelling and pronouncing the word *ogham*, there are several theories concerning the origin of the name itself. According to Celtic myth, the ogham was created by and named for Ogma. Known as Ogma the Eloquent, he was the god of learning, poetry, and speech. According to researchers, another contender for the origin of the name is the Greek word *ogmos*, which means "furrow" or "groove."[80] This refers to the straight lines of the first twenty symbols that resemble little furrows when carved into rock or wood.

In this section, we will explore the origin theories and development of the ogham and examine the types of inscriptions found on stones. We will see that although the ogham was written in stone, it was not a static alphabet and, over time, some of the characters were replaced or modified. After centuries of obscurity, the Celtic Revival brought the ogham to light where it captivated the attention of the world and became an integral part of some Pagan and Wicca practices.

---

79. Editorial Staff, *Webster's Third New International Dictionary*, 1569.

80. Ruth P. M. Lehmann, "Ogham: The Ancient Script of the Celts," *The Origins of Writing*, ed. Wayne M. Senner (Lincoln, NE: University of Nebraska Press, 1989), 160.

CHAPTER 9
ORIGIN THEORIES, INSCRIPTIONS, AND LANGUAGES

WHILE A CONNECTION WITH Greek may seem odd, the language was familiar to the Celts of Gaul (present-day France and other parts of Western Europe) who carried on a thriving trade with merchants in the Mediterranean region. Not only were they familiar with the Greek language, they also used it to record business transactions. This cultural contact has spurred other theories that attribute the development of the ogham from the Greek or Latin alphabets. One reason for this is that the ogham is a linguistic script with signs that render the sounds of a language. Although it is generally agreed that the *forfeda*—the fifth group of ogham symbols—was added at a later time to accommodate Latin and Greek sounds, it does not account for the original four groups of ogham coming from those alphabets.

Other origin theories associate the development of the ogham with the Norse runes, possibly because they may have come into use around the same time. Some of these speculations are fueled by the fact that the runes and ogham do not follow a conventional alphabetical order. Another reason for linking the two is based on the resemblance between the Scandinavian feather runes, a style used in some later runic writing, and the branch oghams found in *The Book of Ballymote*. However, according to Hans Hock (1938–), Professor Emeritus of Linguistics at the University of Illinois, the problem with this argument is that these example letters are creative variations and do not take into account the linguistics of the Celtic and Germanic languages.

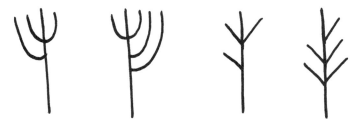

Figure 48: Creative variations produced similarities between the feather runes of Scandinavia (left) and the branch oghams (right).

The chief source of information on the ogham is *The Book of Ballymote*, which was compiled around 1391 for the McDonagh family of Ballymote Castle, Ireland.[81] This "book" is a collection of documents containing history, lore, legal, medical, and religious writings. Other books that contain information on the ogham include *The Yellow Book of Lecan* (fourteenth century), *The Book of Lismore* (late fourteenth or early fifteenth century), and *The Book of Leinster* (twelfth century).[82] Like *The Book of Ballymote*, these books are manuscript collections of prose, poetry, and other documents. The *Auraicept na n-Éces* (*Scholar's Primer* or *Handbook of the Learned*), also contains ogham tracts that are similar to the ones found in *The Book of Ballymote* and *The Yellow Book of Lecan*.

Although it is exciting to have older sources, the problem is that some details vary widely from one book to another. In addition, scholars believe that some of the documents were copied from much earlier sources. Any time a manuscript was copied, the information was open to mistranslation, reinterpretation, and embellishment. To err and tinker is human.

OGHAM INSCRIPTIONS

Despite a plethora of tangled theories and information, what we know for certain is that there are almost four hundred ogham stone inscriptions. Most ogham stones are located in Ireland, particularly the southwest, with a smattering in Scotland, Wales, the Isle of Man, and southwestern England. While there is still some disagreement about the age of the ogham writing on these stones, many scholars place their timeframe from the fourth to

---

81. Steven L. Danver, ed., *Popular Controversies in World History: Investigating History's Intriguing Questions. Prehistory and Early Civilizations*, vol. 1 (Santa Barbara, CA: ABC-CLIO, LLC, 2011), 56.

82. Michael Slavin, *The Ancient Books of Ireland* (Montreal, Canada: McGill-Queen's University Press, 2005), 45.

sixth centuries CE during the early spread of Christianity.[83] Carving ogham on stones continued longer on the Isle of Man with some dating to the eleventh and twelfth centuries.[84] In Britain and Scotland, some ogham stones also contain Latin inscriptions.

Most ogham stones are near ring forts, earthen mounds, cairns (mounds of stones built as landmarks or memorials), single-standing stones, stone circles, and Christian churches. Many of the inscriptions contain names and kinship lineages. Some of the stones are thought to have been either boundary markers that laid claim to the land or grave markers because some inscriptions resemble funerary prayers for the dead. Although burials have not been found beneath ogham stones, some of them appear to have been moved or repurposed, which may account for the absence of human remains.

Other types of inscriptions include tribal affiliations, eponymous deities of tribes, and personal descriptions such as "born of the raven."[85] Charles Graves (1812–1899), ogham scholar and professor of mathematics at Trinity College in Dublin, Ireland, noted that a few inscriptions referred to people who could be identified through genealogies in the *Book of Leinster*. Ogham inscriptions have also been found on small artifacts of ivory, bone, bronze, and silver. Although a few seventeenth- and eighteenth-century manuscripts appear to contain ogham symbols as margin notes, as an alphabet it is very cumbersome and was never used for long texts.

According to R. A. Stewart Macalister (1870–1950), professor of Celtic Archaeology at University College in Dublin, the magical use of ogham may have been an important function.[86] Although some of his theories are not supported by more recent scholarship, many agree that the ogham had some type of magical use. That said, while its use as a manual gesture alphabet of the Druids is still debated, it is generally accepted that the ogham served as a Bardic aide memoire. As such, it is not difficult to see that associations for memorization can also function as magical correspondences, which is how the ogham is widely used today. Also, some of the elaborate ogham variations from *The Book of Ballymote* seem to strongly suggest an esoteric or magical purpose.

THE LANGUAGES OF THE OGHAM

Ogham stone inscriptions provide the earliest written record of Archaic Irish, also called Primitive Irish, which is the oldest-known Gaelic language. According to Catherine Swift,

---

83. Lehmann, "Ogham: The Ancient Script of the Celts," 165.

84. Danver, *Popular Controversies in World History*, 47.

85. Ibid., 48.

86. R. A. Stewart Macalister, *The Secret Languages of Ireland* (New York: Cambridge University Press, 2014), 39.

professor of Irish Studies at Mary Immaculate College in Limerick, Ireland, the first twenty characters of the ogham accommodated the eighty or so sounds of Archaic Irish.[87] Although written in stone, the ogham was not a static alphabet. Over time, some of the characters were replaced or modified, especially when writing non-Archaic Irish words.

For example, the early twenty characters of ogham do not include the letter *P*. According to author and Celtic scholar James MacKillop (1950–), an upturned arrow was used in British ogham inscriptions for the P sound.[88] Even though this symbol pre-dates the forfeda, others have regarded it as a variation of the character Ifin.

The lack of the letter *P* is due to the early ogham having been written by speakers of the Goidelic language. There were two major branches of Celtic languages called *Goidelic* or Gaelic (Archaic Irish) and *Brythonic* or Gallo-Brittonic (Gaulish, Ancient British). One wave of Celtic migration that passed through Britain into Ireland spoke the Goidelic or Q-Celtic language. Q-Celtic used the K (or hard C) sound, whereas the later wave of Celts who settled in Britain spoke Brythonic or P-Celtic and used the P sound. While this is a simple explanation, there are far more complex differences between the two branches of Celtic languages.

In addition to these differences, Professor John Koch of the University of Wales noted that the evolving ogham script reflected a linguistic upheaval and transition in Celtic languages. Along with mistranslations and tinkering, is it any wonder that the information we have today is so tangled?

The ogham fell into obscurity until the nineteenth-century Celtic Revival (also referred to as the Celtic Twilight) in literature and art. Aimed at reviving ancient Irish folklore and traditions, the movement also fueled interest in this unusual alphabet. The enthusiasm for all things Celtic spilled into the twentieth century, and in the 1940s Professor Macalister published a two-volume work on ogham inscriptions. As mentioned, more recent studies do not support all of Macalister's work; however, he has been lauded for his meticulous drawings of ogham inscriptions. Some of the inscriptions that he recorded have since been lost to the weathering of the stones.

Also published in the 1940s, *The White Goddess* by Robert Graves (1895–1985) has served as the basis for a great deal of popular information on the ogham. However, despite being the grandson of ogham scholar Charles Graves, Robert took liberties with the history of the script and added embellishments, such as the thirteen-month ogham tree calendar.

---

87. Catherine Swift, "The Story of Ogham." *History Today* 65, no. 10 (October 2015), 4.
88. James MacKillop, *A Dictionary of Celtic Mythology* (New York: Oxford University Press, 1998), 351.

The appeal and fascination of the mystical ogham continues today. This alphabet has captured the imagination and curiosity of many of us who have incorporated it into our magical practices. While some interpretations and the tree calendar are modern constructs, they hold meaning because of the concepts they have come to symbolize. And therein lies the power of symbols: the significance of their meanings. However, it is important that we do not use modern interpretations to cloud the truth.

WRITING AND USING THE OGHAM

As mentioned, the ogham originally consisted of twenty symbols with five more added later. There is a marked difference between the first twenty and the others. The former are simple straight lines suitable for carving into wood or stone, while the latter are more complex and would not easily lend to being carved. The original twenty are referred to as *feda* and the additional five, *forfeda*, which means "supplementary letters."[89] The ogham symbols are divided into groups of five. The original four groups are called *aicmi* (plural for *aicme* meaning "family" or "class").[90] Each aicme is named for the first character in the group, for example, aicme Beith, aicme Huath, and so forth.

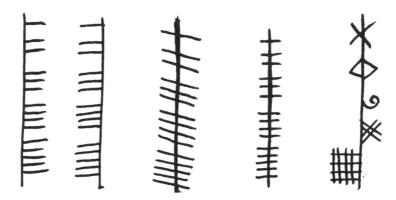

Figure 49: From left to right are aicme Beith, aicme Huath, aicme Muin, aicme Ailm, and the forfeda.

As with many facets of the ogham, the order of the first three letters is sometimes a point of contention. While the first aicme begins with the letters *BLF* (Beith, Luis, Fearn),

---

89. Peter T. Daniels and William Bright, eds., *The World's Writing Systems* (New York: Oxford University Press, 1996), 340.

90. Danver, *Popular Controversies in World History*, 56.

the order BLN (Beith, Luis, Nion) is regarded by some as the original. In fact, the ogham alphabet has been referred to as the Beth-Luis-Nin. However, Charles Graves believed that it was named for the first two letters with the word *nin* tacked on to function as "etcetera."[91]

Ogham symbols are written along a stem line. This line is also called a *druim*, which means "ridge" and refers to the edge of a stone along which inscriptions were often written.[92] The vowels were often represented as dots or simple indentations along the stem line rather than a line that crossed it.

A unique feature of the ogham is that it can be written horizontally or vertically. When written horizontally, it is read from left to right. When vertical, it is read from bottom to top. In later times, when written in manuscripts the starting point of the stem line was often distinguished with a *V* or curlicue shape. When inscribed on a stone, the inscription usually begins at the bottom left and follows the edge up, over, and down to the bottom right. When all four edges of a stone contain ogham symbols, it can be difficult to figure out where to begin reading. The effects of time and weathering further complicate the task.

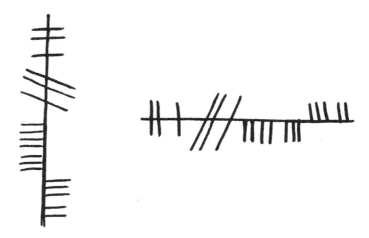

Figure 50: Various random letters are used to show how the different types of Ogham characters can be written vertically or horizontally.

91. Charles Graves, "On the Ogham Character," *Archaeologia Cambrensis, The Journal of the Cambrian Archaeological Association,* vol. 2 (London, England: J. Russell Smith, 1856), 80.

92. Danver, *Popular Controversies in World History,* 56.

CHAPTER 10
THE OGHAM IN MAGIC

WHILE DIVINATION IS A popular way to use the ogham, there are several other ways to incorporate these symbols into magic and ritual. For example, the ogham can be used as a magic cipher to boost spells. Rather than making a long inscription, use one or two keywords such as "love" or "guide me" to carve into a candle. Alternatively, keywords can be inscribed on a piece of paper. If magic or ritual is focused on a deity or person, write his or her name in ogham. The ogham is also a powerful aid when sending energy for healing. Of course, inscribing ogham symbols on a twig or piece of wood can add even more power to your ritual or magic work.

Like many symbols, ogham characters can be used as talismans to draw specific energy into an object. Coordinate the attributes of ogham characters and crystals, and then paint the symbol on your chosen stone(s). These can be used for spells or rituals or placed around the home and garden to enhance the energy and hold your intentions. Of course, crystal jewelry marked with oghams can be worn as an amulet. For example, the ogham character Onn painted on a piece of red agate or sardonyx can serve as a protective amulet, or the character Quert on a rose quartz crystal can be a love charm.

TABLE 4.1 OGHAM CHARACTERS ACCORDING TO LETTERS/SOUNDS

Name	Symbol	Letters/Sounds
Ailm		A
Amhancholl / Mór		Ae
Beith		B
Coll		C
Ebad		Ch
Duir		D
Edad		E
Ebad		Ea
Fearn		F
Gort		G

TABLE 4.1 OGHAM CHARACTERS ACCORDING TO LETTERS/SOUNDS

Name	Symbol	Letters/Sounds
Huath		H
Ioho		I
Ifin		Io
Luis		L
Muin		M
Nion		N
Ngetal		Ng
Onn		O
Oir		Oi
Peith		P

TABLE 4.1 OGHAM CHARACTERS ACCORDING TO LETTERS/SOUNDS		
Name	Symbol	Letters/Sounds
Phagos		Ph
Quert		q/kw
Ruis		R
Saille		S
Straif		st and z
Tinne		T
Ur		U
Uilleann		Ui

The ogham symbols can be used to help foster or strengthen traits or aspects of life that relate to an ogham character. A simple way to do this is to draw an ogham character on a small piece of paper, hold it between your hands as you meditate on what you want to achieve, and then carry the paper with you. For example, if your life is in transition you could carry the ogham Beith, or if maturity is an issue use Ruis. If you feel bogged down and you need to rise above whatever is causing a problem in your life, choose the symbol Ailm.

Most often used in ogham divination, staves (small sticks) or cards can be placed on an altar to emphasize the attributes of an ogham character for magic, meditation, and spells. Creating your own set of cards or staves allows you to make them uniquely personal. Cards can be designed on your computer, printed on heavy stock, and then cut to any size you like. If you are artistically inclined, you can draw it freehand. In addition to the ogham symbol and name, you might consider including a picture of the associated trees and plants, birds, and colors. Because of the variations in the way forfeda symbols are drawn, making your own cards or staves allows you to choose the ones that have more meaning to you.

OGHAM STAVES AND DIVINATION

While sets of ogham staves can be purchased, it is simple enough to make your own. As with other magical tools, making your own imbues them with your energy, which personalizes and makes them more powerful.

How to Make Staves

Collect twenty-five twigs or branches that have about the same thickness, but not too skinny because you are going to draw or inscribe the Ogham characters on the diameter of the wood rather than along the length. If you choose to include the symbols Phagos and/or Peith, you will need one or two more twigs. Refer to their respective entries in the next chapter for details on these symbols. The length of the twigs doesn't matter because you can cut them down to a uniform size.

Begin by removing any small side twigs and leaves. The bark can be stripped off or left on. If you strip the bark off, you can leave the wood in its natural state or use a little lemon oil to bring out a rich patina.

After cutting the twigs down to size, cut one end of each stave at a 45-degree angle. This slanted surface will be used to carve or paint an ogham character, however, you can draw the characters along the length of the twigs, if you prefer. The characters can also be burned into the wood if you have a fine-tipped wood-burning tool. When not in use, keep the staves in a pouch or wrap them in a soft cloth and tie it with a piece of yarn or ribbon.

Instead of twigs, squared pegs of wood can be used. Check your local hardware store for square dowels that you can cut into short lengths. When using dowels, the ogham characters can be written along the edge as they were on ancient stones. Another alternative is to make ogham tiles by cutting horizontal slices from a tree branch or large dowel that has about an inch diameter. In a pinch, or if you are working with children, Popsicle sticks can be used as staves.

As with other ritual or magic tools, consecrate your staves or cards before using them. Pass them through the smoke of incense or burning herbs such as sage, mugwort, or lavender. You may also want to crumble a dried tree leaf into the herbs. As you consecrate the staves or cards, call on the Celtic deities Ogma, Danu, and/or the Dagda to bless your tools.

OGHAM DIVINATION

As a system for guidance, ogham divination helps to bring awareness to a situation or problem. It may also point toward a certain direction or help you further an idea or plan.

While the single draw method of divination is simple, it is also effective. Sit in front of your altar or wherever you are comfortable and light a candle. Take time to relax and clear your mind. If you have a question or issue for which you seek guidance, think about it for a few minutes, and then ask for guidance. On the other hand, you can simply ask, "What do I need to know today?"

Randomly select one of the staves or cards, and then examine the attributes and qualities associated with that ogham character. Pay attention to your initial reaction but don't over analyze it. Leave the stave or card on your altar or carry it with you for a day or two. Alternatively, write the ogham symbol on a piece of paper and keep that with you.

For a more complex form of divination, use three staves. This method echoes the power of the three realms of the sky, earth, and sea. According to Irish folklore, oaths were sworn by the strength of the sky above, the earth below, and the sea that surrounds. Select three staves or cards one at a time and lay them out in front of you. The first one represents the sky and relates to an idea or aim. This ogham clarifies a goal, or it may point to a purpose or situation of which you may not have been aware. The second ogham represents the earth. It elucidates your present situation or state of mind in regard to the goal, purpose, or situation. The third stave represents the sea that surrounds and embodies the energy of action and change. This ogham reveals a potential path or paths to success in achieving your goal, or it may indicate what you need to do to make changes.

Information gained with the three-stave method may take a little while to figure out. Because of this, you may want to make note of your thoughts during the divination session and afterward spend time meditating on them. Don't rush the process. It may take a couple of days or even a couple of weeks for your reading to become clear.

CHAPTER 11

WORKING WITH THE ORIGINAL TWENTY OGHAM

As noted, the medieval sources for details on the ogham do not agree, which has resulted in centuries of trickle-down confusion. Because of this, there is a range of differences in ogham character names, their associated trees and plants, letters, and occasionally, how their symbols are rendered. While an attempt to untangle the details is beyond the scope of this book, I have tried to present as much information as possible with perspective and clarity.

Because the most popular use of the ogham is in relation to trees and plants, the following entries are based on the tree ogham. From my interest and study of birds, I have included details relating to the bird ogham to add more fullness and flexibility to the information. The colors associated with each ogham are also included. Color can be used in rituals and spells through candles or other objects. Candles are also particularly well-suited because the ogham symbols can be easily inscribed on them.

As you read and work with this information, it is important to remember that no one knows the true ogham used by the Celts. However, rather than regarding discrepancies in details from the various sources as points of contention, I believe they provide choice and flexibility. Just as the variations of ogham in *The Book of Ballymote* reflect great individuality and creativity, so too is our use of this system. Follow what your inner sense tells you.

Because the first four family groups are distinctly different and universally regarded as the original ogham, we will review them separately from the forfeda. For convenience, the symbols are presented in alphabetical order.

AILM / AILIM

This ogham is associated with fir and pine trees and the lapwing bird. It is also associated with the color light blue and the winter solstice. Ailm is a symbol of achievement and having a comprehensive perspective when setting goals. It is an aid for learning from the past, especially mistakes, and making necessary assessments before initiating important changes. To gain clarity and insight, carve this ogham into a light blue candle and use it when meditating on important projects or a situation. Associated with the energy and vitality of life, draw Ailm on a pine or fir cone to place on your altar when sending healing energy. Alternatively, arrange long fir needles on your altar in the pattern of this symbol.

The lapwing is a bird of protection and guidance that also supports and enhances divination. Draw the Ailm symbol on a picture of a lapwing to use in a protection spell or carry it with you as a talisman. Alternatively, place the picture with your divination tools to imbue them with the power of this bird.

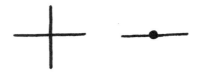

Figure 51: Ailm is shown in its two forms: linear (left) and dot (right).

When selected for divination or guidance, this ogham advises you to define goals or refine the ones you have already set. Ailm also indicates the importance of seeking clarity before acting on a situation or problem.

BEITH / BEITHE / BETH

This ogham is associated with the birch tree, the pheasant, the color white, and the winter solstice. Like the birch tree, this ogham is a symbol of beginnings. Carve Beith on a white candle to use for spells or meditations when you feel the need to make a fresh start in some aspect of your life. Draw it on a piece of parchment to carry with you during a time of renewal, when you are initiating changes in your life, or dealing with a challenging situation. Call on this ogham's association with purification by drawing it on the handle of a broom, and then use it to symbolically sweep away and clear negative energy before ritual. To remove anything unwanted from your life, draw Beith on a piece of paper, and then burn it as you visualize negativity being released.

As a solar bird, the pheasant represents warmth, fertility, and prosperity. Mark a pheasant figurine with the Beith symbol to place on your Yule altar to draw abundance and prosperity into the New Year ahead. Draw Beith on a picture of this bird for use in fertility spells or to boost creative inspiration.

Figure 52: Beith is shown written horizontally (left) and vertically (right).

When selected for divination or guidance, this ogham symbol indicates the beginning of something new in your life or the need to get moving and start something. Beith encourages you to make changes that help you live to your full potential.

Beginning on December 24, just after the winter solstice, the time of Beith runs until January 20. This ogham carries us through the turning of the year and prepares the way for renewal. To call on the energy of this ogham, paint it on a piece of carnelian. While the reddish color of this stone epitomizes the return of the sun, along with this ogham it will symbolically light your path.

COLL / CALL

This ogham is associated with the hazel tree and the color brown. Although Coll was not included in the bird ogham, the owl has become associated with it. Strongly linked with wisdom, Coll supports both learning and teaching. It fosters the pursuit of knowledge and offers insight for attaining more than superficial information. Carve this ogham on a brown candle to amplify the energy of ritual or to keep creative juices flowing. Draw this symbol on three hazelnuts to place on your altar during meditation to connect with inner wisdom. Draw it on a piece of paper to keep with you during a meeting or public event to enhance your communication skills. Use amethyst, red agate, or tiger's eye in spells to aid in drawing on the power of this ogham.

When drawn on a picture or figurine of an owl, Coll helps to open the psyche and find the bridge between the seen and unseen worlds. Also use this ogham with the owl as an aid for dreamwork and deciphering omens.

Figure 53: Coll is shown written horizontally (left) and vertically (right).

When selected for divination or guidance, this ogham tells you to cultivate deeper wisdom. It may also indicate that you have talents, perhaps related to teaching, of which you may not be aware. Spend time in meditation with this ogham to help you find those talents.

From August 5 to September 1, Coll marks a period that is associated with creativity, inspiration, and divination. The energy invested in creative projects and developing skills is doubled during this period. This is also a time when esoteric knowledge and great wisdom are more readily accessible.

DUIR / DAIR

This ogham is associated with the oak tree, the wren, and the colors black and dark brown. Like the oak, Duir is a symbol of strength and endurance. Carve it on a black or dark brown candle for spells to aid you when seeking justice in a situation or a legal matter. Paint this ogham on an acorn to carry with you when you need to bolster your courage. It will also aid you in feeling secure and confident. Draw Duir on three oak leaves or a picture of oak leaves to burn as you visualize achieving success in any endeavor. Paint the symbol on a piece of white quartz, chrysoberyl, or dioptase for help in finding truth. Supporting leadership, Duir is a good symbol to keep at the workplace.

Like the oak tree, the wren was closely associated with the Druids and said to be used for divination. In fact, the Welsh word *dryw* means both "wren" and "druid."[93] Write the word *wren* on a piece of paper, and then draw the symbol for Duir above, below, and on either side of it. Hold this paper between your hands when interpreting an omen or a message received through divination. Also do this before a divination session for aid in activating and opening the channels of communication.

Figure 54: Duir is shown written horizontally (left) and vertically (right).

When selected for divination or guidance, this ogham encourages you to keep moving forward. Great opportunities will come your way no matter how small they may seem at first if you hang in there and believe in yourself.

From June 10 to July 7, this ogham fosters a period of wisdom with an emphasis on inner strength. With strength comes confidence, which makes this a good time to work on any self-confidence issues. Like the mighty oak, we can be strong and wise and provide security to those around us. Use white quartz, chrysoberyl, or dioptase to draw on the power of this ogham.

---

93. Adele Nozedar, *The Secret Language of Birds: A Treasury of Myths, Folklore and Inspirational True Stories* (London: Harper Element, 2006), 150.

EDAD / EADHA / EADHADH

This ogham is associated with the aspen and white poplar, the swan, and the color red. It is also associated with the autumn equinox and Mabon. Edad symbolizes tenacity, endurance, and inner strength. Carve it on a red candle for spells to aid in overcoming problems or to dispel doubts. Draw the symbol on a piece of paper to keep with you for help in facing and subduing fear. Carve it on a white candle for meditation to help cultivate spiritual visions. This ogham also supports and enhances communication skills. To strengthen your intuitive abilities, hold a stave or other object inscribed with Edad for a couple of minutes before a divination session.

When used in conjunction with the swan, Edad can help you follow your true calling. Paint the ogham on a picture or figurine of this bird, and then visualize a great swan flying with you on its back. Pay attention to details, as these may provide clues for you. Long associated with shamanic work, this bird, along with Edad, can guide you through other realms and support your vision quests.

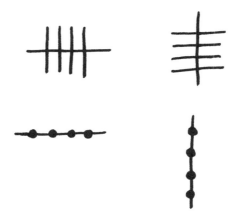

Figure 55: Edad is shown in its linear and dot forms written horizontally (left) and vertically (right).

When selected for divination or guidance, this ogham offers encouragement to stay on your chosen path or invest time in discovering the right one for you. It also tells you to not give up on something you truly believe in.

FEARN / FERN

This ogham is associated with the alder tree, the seagull, and the color crimson. Fearn is especially helpful for keeping energy grounded no matter how crazy life may be. Carve or paint it on a small piece of wood or a crystal to use as a protective charm. Keep it in a small decorative bag to carry with you or keep in your car. This charm can also be used to foster prophetic dreams by placing it on your bedside table. For clarity in divination, hold the charm between your palms before each session. Red garnet or lapis lazuli with obsidian are especially effective to work with the energy of this ogham. Fearn also aids in developing spiritual practices that hold strong personal meaning. Inscribe this symbol on a candle for support when contacting spirit guides.

When used in conjunction with the seagull, Fearn aids in communicating with deities and spirits. Draw the ogham on a picture or figurine of a seagull and hold it between your hands to provide clarity for messages and omens, especially those that seem particularly obscure at first. Also use this bird and symbol for spells to draw abundance into your life.

Figure 56: Fearn is shown written horizontally (left) and vertically (right).

When selected for divination or guidance, this ogham offers insight into issues that may have troubled you for a long time. Fearn also helps discover inner strength to remain steadfast in decisions that feel particularly right for you.

From March 18 to April 14, Fearn helps keep energy grounded for mundane issues while fine-tuning intuition and magical skills. This is also a time to enjoy your uniqueness and focus on the spiritual aspects of life. It is an opportune time for seeking spiritual guidance.

GORT

Gort is associated with ivy, the mute swan, and the color blue or sky blue. This ogham teaches us about strength and endurance, death, and immortality. It is a symbol of esoteric or hidden knowledge. Draw this ogham on a piece of paper to keep with you or in your work space when practicing new skills. As a boon to learning, keep it with you when attending classes or lectures or any time you are working to develop talents. Inscribe it on a blue candle to burn for introspection or for help when making important decisions. Because Gort is associated with ivy, which frequently grows in a spiral pattern, use pieces of the mineral serpentine marked with this ogham to create a spiral shape on your altar, which will symbolize your spiritual journey through the wheel of the year.

Although the romantic stories of the mute swan not making a sound until just before death are not true, it is, nevertheless, a magically powerful bird. Keep an image of a mute swan marked with the Gort symbol on your altar to help awaken to your beauty and power. It will also help to cultivate intuition. This bird and ogham combination is effective to boost love spells or to break enchantments.

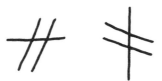

Figure 57: Gort is shown written horizontally (left) and vertically (right).

When selected for divination or guidance, Gort tells us that growth can be a slow and sometimes indirect process. Because of this, it is important to keep focused on your purpose and accept a slower pace as long as there is progress toward your goal.

From September 30 to October 27, Gort provides a time to enter the darkness within and find the symbolic jewels that are hidden there. Use clear quartz to work with the energy of Gort and find your hidden jewels of knowledge. During this time, combine Gort and the mute swan to foster change and manifest what you desire.

HUATH / HÚATH / UATH

Huath is associated with the hawthorn tree, the night raven or night crow, and the color purple. A symbol of healing and hope, this ogham is instrumental for dealing with the bumps and bruises of daily life. To connect with the power of Huath, place a piece of lapis lazuli, blue lace agate, or fluorite under a hawthorn tree or hold the stone as you visualize the tree in bloom. Leave one of these crystals or the ogham on a piece of paper as a gift to the tree when taking anything from it. Draw this ogham on a picture of hawthorn flowers for spells to attract love and passion, or place it under your bed to stoke the fires of sexual pleasure. Also associated with defense, this ogham can be used as a protective amulet to wear or hang in your home. Huath is also effective to overcome obstacles and dispel any form of negativity.

The terms *night raven* and *night crow* refer to the black-crowned night heron, a bird known for its crow-like calls and nocturnal habits. Believed to possess the power of the otherworld, this bird is an ally for astral and shamanic work, especially when combined with Huath. Draw the ogham symbol on a picture of this bird for help in developing psychic skills or to foster transformation.

Figure 58: Huath is shown written horizontally (left) and vertically (right).

When selected for divination or guidance, Huath indicates the need for patience because many obstacles turn out to be temporary impediments. Instead of feeling held back, this ogham tells us that good things come to those who wait. Use your time wisely by cultivating your skills.

From May 13 to June 9, this ogham holds the energy of enchantment that began at Beltane and continues to Midsummer's Eve. Paint Huath on a few garden stones or crystals to leave as offerings to fairies and other nature spirits. If possible, place them under a hawthorn tree where they will amplify your intention and aid in contacting these beings.

IOHO / IDHO / IODHO / IODAHDH

Ioho is associated with the yew tree, eaglets (young eagles), and the color white. It is also associated with the winter solstice. Like the yew, Ioho is linked with death and endings, which are a normal part of the bigger cycle of life and renewal. Place three pieces of white quartz marked with this ogham and three yew berries on your altar for help in turning inward during the dark of the year. This will also help foster self-nurturing energy. Burn the berries at Yule but leave the crystals on your altar until the New Year. Inscribe Ioho on a white candle to use in dark moon rituals, which helps incubate positive energy for the new cycle ahead. Also use this ogham to aid in past-life work.

When used with the eaglet, Ioho can help you adapt to changes and seize opportunities with confidence. Write the ogham symbol and a few keywords about your goals or changes taking place in your life on a picture of a young eagle. Hold the paper against your heart as you visualize your desired outcome. This ogham and bird combination can also provide the spark of inspiration to get creative juices flowing or ignite fiery passions with your lover.

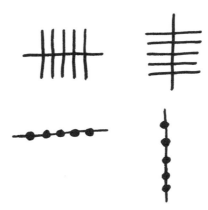

Figure 59: Ioho is shown in its linear and dot forms written horizontally (left) and vertically (right).

When selected for divination or guidance, Ioho advises you to strive for personal transformation that supports and furthers your potentials, even if it requires a major change in direction. Don't be fooled by illusions; follow the path that feels grounded and appropriate and it will enable you to be your true self.

LUIS

Luis is associated with the rowan tree, ducks, and the color gray. Linked with the awakening of early spring, the power of this ogham is its ability to activate energy. Draw Luis on a piece of paper, fold it several times, and then tie it with a ribbon or piece of string. Burn this little bundle to activate the energy of a spell or place it on your altar to boost the energy of a ritual. Luis is especially effective when working toward independence. Carry a stave or card with you as a protective amulet. Inscribe this ogham on a gray candle to use for insightful meditation. Draw Luis on a picture of a rowan tree, and then burn it in a ritual to express your dedication and devotion to your chosen deity. Also do this to acknowledge the blessings in your life.

Draw this ogham symbol on a picture of a duck for prosperity spells to call on this bird's age-old symbolism of abundance and comfort. Paint the ogham on a duck pendant or other piece of duck jewelry to wear as a protective amulet. As a water bird, the duck is associated with emotions and, along with Luis, it can help bring clarity and stability.

Figure 60: Luis is shown written horizontally (left) and vertically (right).

When selected for divination or guidance, the message from this ogham is to focus on the present rather than the past, especially if you want to gain control of the things that influence your life. Where emotions are concerned, stabilizing them will provide clarity.

From January 21 to February 17, this ogham brings a period associated with the coming of new life and inspiration born from the darkness of winter. This is also a time to stoke creativity. Paint this ogham on a topaz, clear quartz, or tourmaline crystal to draw on the supportive energy of Luis during this time.

MUIN / MUINN

Muin is associated with the bramble or blackberry vines that populated the hedgerows of Britain in the past. Its bird is the titmouse. The color associated with Muin is usually called *variegated* and sometimes *speckled*, which makes me think of how light filters through a hedgerow. Rambling blackberry vines form thickets, and *muin* is a Gaelic word meaning "thicket."[94] Like a vine, our paths do not usually follow a straight course, however, with the help of Muin, we can learn from the twists and turns. When seeking guidance, mark pieces of amethyst or jasper with the symbol of Muin and lay them in a winding vine pattern on your altar. Also like a vine, Muin can be restrictive, making it ideal for binding spells. The circle of a vine can also draw people together. Use Muin as a symbol that holds and strengthens the bonds of a relationship or community. Also associated with prophecy, inscribe this ogham into a candle to burn during divination sessions.

Whether learning divination or a psychic skill or determining your spiritual path, the titmouse along with this ogham aids in acquiring the knowledge you need. This bird is familiar with altered states and supports practices such as shamanic journeying and astral travel. Keep a picture of a titmouse marked with Muin with you during these practices.

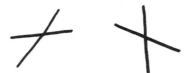

Figure 61: Muin is shown written horizontally (left) and vertically (right).

When selected for divination or guidance, this ogham indicates the need for introspection. It may be most apropos when seeking creative inspiration or self-discipline.

From September 2 to 29, Muin ushers in a period of inner growth and energy. With the help of this ogham, we can empower ourselves to adapt and make changes in our lives. Paint it on a piece of amethyst or jasper to keep with you during this time.

---

94. Niall Mac Coitir, *Irish Trees: Myths, Legends & Folklore* (Cork, Ireland: Collins Press, 2003), 167.

NGETAL / NGÉTAL / GÉTAL / NGÉADAL

This ogham is associated with reeds, the goose, and the color green. Like a reed, Ngetal represents adaptability and the ability to bend with circumstances rather than break. While this may seem like giving in or surrendering, Ngetal tells us to bide our time, because with determination we can reach our goals. Wear this ogham on a piece of jewelry as a reminder to remain aware of and proactive to changing situations. Inscribe Ngetal on the stalk of a reed or cattail or a green taper candle for spells to keep you on track and make your dreams come true. In addition, the energy of this ogham provides support for self-work, especially for healing and well-being. Paint Ngetal on a piece of green jasper, opal, or spinel to hold during meditation or to place on the altar of a healing circle.

This ogham with its bird, the goose, aids in working with spirits and can serve as a guide in otherworld journeys. This ogham/bird combination can be a guide for soul pathway working, deeply meaningful quests, and personal growth. Keep a goose figurine or picture marked with Ngetal in your workspace to spark inspiration and stoke your imagination.

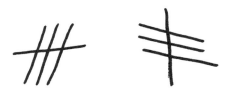

Figure 62: Ngetal is shown written horizontally (left) and vertically (right).

When selected for divination or guidance, the message of Ngetal is to learn when to go with the flow or grab the proverbial bull by the horns and take control. With the help of this ogham, you can avoid unpleasant surprises that can cause turmoil.

From October 28 to November 24, this ogham represents a period of unexpected changes and challenges that require adaptability. Ngetal helps us focus our minds and energy to ride out the storms that blow through life. It also aids in restoring our worlds to harmony.

NION / NUIN / NUINN

Nion is associated with the ash tree and the snipe, a type of long-billed wading bird. Its associated color is sometimes said to be "clear" and sometimes "grass green." Like the mighty ash Yggdrasil of Norse mythology, in Celtic lore this tree and ogham are associated with the otherworld and the ability to access other realms. Nion helps us realize that the world is a lot bigger than we may have believed because of unseen places. Whether dreaming or journeying, it provides a connection with other realms. Light a green candle inscribed with Nion and place it on your desk or workspace when seeking creative inspiration. Use pale green beryl or aquamarine crystals to aid you in working with the energy of Nion. White quartz with iolite can also be used.

The combination of Nion and the snipe aids in unlocking magical abilities. Write this ogham's name, *NION*, on a small piece of paper, and then write the word *SNIPE* vertically, using the first letter *N* in Nion for the *N* in snipe so the two words form a right angle. Draw the ogham symbol within the right angle formed by the words. Keep the paper with you for support when engaging in magical practices.

Figure 63: Nion is shown written horizontally (left) and vertically (right).

When selected for divination or guidance, the message from Nion is to pause and assess a situation before acting because you may need to adjust your perspective. This ogham also tells us to be open to things that we may consider unusual as these might provide the key that unlocks a whole new world of which we were previously unaware.

From February 18 to March 17, the energy of Nion helps us discover that boundaries are not limitations because they also provide connections. Gaining a fresh perspective on the interwoven aspect of boundaries and connections can help fuel creativity and spark a sense of renewed purpose.

ONN / OHN

Onn is associated with the gorse bush, the scrat (cormorant), and the color yellow. It is also associated with Ostara and Samhain. Because gorse can bloom almost all year in some areas, Onn symbolizes fertility and vitality. Draw this ogham on a picture of a gorse bush in bloom to use in fertility spells if you are planning a pregnancy. Inscribe it on a yellow candle to use on your Ostara altar to welcome the sun. Until the eighteenth century in England, fires of gorse were lit to help lead departed souls back to their former homes. At Samhain, Onn inscribed on a candle can act as a welcoming beacon for ancestors. This ogham also represents determination and is especially helpful when dealing with change. Write this ogham on a piece of paper to keep with you when you need to foster resourcefulness. Also use Onn to boost the energy of a protection spell.

The associated bird for this ogham often appears as *scrat* or *odoroscrach* in some texts, referring to the Gaelic *odhra-sqairneach* for cormorant.[95] The common name *cormorant* comes from the Latin *corvus marinus*, which means "raven of the sea."[96] In Ireland and Wales this bird was regarded as a magical sea raven that weaves together the forces of air and water. In conjunction with Onn, this bird aids in finding and developing skills, especially those related to prophecy and divination. For ritual and magic, draw this ogham on a picture of a cormorant to help call on the forces of nature, particularly the elements of air and water.

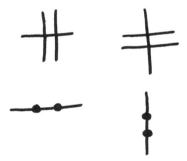

Figure 64: Onn is shown in its linear and dot forms
written horizontally (left) and vertically (right).

---

95. Alexander Robert Forbes, *Gaelic Names of Beasts (Mammalia), Birds, Fishes, Insects, Reptiles, Etc.* (Edinburgh, Scotland: Oliver and Boyd, 1905), 34.

96. Diana Wells, *100 Birds and How They Got Their Names* (Chapel Hill, NC: Algonquin Books of Chapel Hill, 2002), 34.

When selected for divination or guidance, the message from this ogham is to consider all angles in a situation before making a decision or taking action. Like the thorny gorse, something may appear to be an obstacle, however, it may also provide protection and lead you in an unexpected direction.

QUERT / CEIRT

Quert is associated with the apple and crabapple trees, the hen, and the colors green and brown. Draw this ogham on a picture of crabapple flowers to use in love spells or to boost fidelity. Place an apple leaf in a sachet marked with Quert to use as a charm when pursuing any kind of quest. Inscribe it on a green candle when sending healing energy to someone in need. Quert's association with the crabapple links this ogham with the legendary Avalon, the Isle of Apples, and the otherworld. Use this ogham to help you through the gateway between the worlds. Quert is also useful when contacting the fairies. Paint the ogham on a piece of white quartz to leave as an offering for them.

In combination with this ogham, the hen aids in spells for prosperity and fertility. Place an image or figurine of a chicken marked with Quert on the altar of a healing circle to boost the energy. For support during a divination session, draw the ogham on a piece of paper and attach it to a chicken feather. Keep this with you during the session and with your divination tools when they are not in use.

Figure 65: Quert is shown written horizontally (left) and vertically (right).

When selected for divination or guidance, this ogham represents an awakening that can expand your world even to the unseen realms. Choosing Quert can also serve as confirmation for a purpose you have chosen or an important decision you have made.

RUIS

Ruis is associated with the elder tree, the rook (a cousin to the crow), and the color red. This ogham brings recognition of the cycles that punctuate our lives and helps us accept the endings that occur, even though they may be painful. Of course, some endings bring a sense of completion and accomplishment. Burn a red candle on your altar for rituals to mark these events. Ruis also provides energy conducive for divination. Hold a stave or piece of paper inscribed with this ogham before a divination session to open the gates of awareness. For aid in accessing the otherworld, draw Ruis on a picture of an elder tree, and then safely burn it in your cauldron. Gently waft a little of the smoke over you before embarking on your journey. Malachite and moldavite crystals are especially effective for drawing on the power of this ogham.

When Ruis and the rook are used together, the darkness of this black bird becomes a cradle for creativity and intuition where talents can incubate. This ogham/bird combination is also instrumental in opening awareness for divination and all forms of communication. For support in past-life exploration or shamanic work, use a black pen to draw Ruis on a picture of a rook. Keep it with you during your sessions.

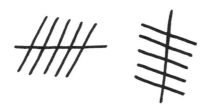

Figure 66: Ruis is shown written horizontally (left) and vertically (right).

When selected for divination or guidance, the message of Ruis is to be open to change, even if you are currently enjoying the status quo. Embracing the energy of this ogham is an aid for self-transformation.

From October 28 to November 24, this ogham represents the energy of the Crone. As we head into the darkest part of the year, Ruis bids us to look beyond the surface to explore what lies within. This exploration often helps us find what is truly meaningful.

SAILLE / SAILE

Saille is associated with the willow tree and the hawk. Its color is usually defined as fiery or bright. This ogham is particularly helpful in learning how to be adaptable, especially in personal relationships. Like the branches of a willow that sway in the wind, Saille helps us know when to stand fast or to go with the flow. Write this ogham on a willow leaf (or cut out a picture of one) and float it in a bowl of water. Gently stir the water with your finger, and then meditate on situations where you need to be adaptable. To foster inspiration, draw Saille on a piece of paper and place it in a small pouch with a ruby or pieces of calcite and lepidolite. Keep the pouch on your desk or wherever you engage in creative work.

In Celtic tradition, the hawk provides a link with the otherworld and the afterlife, bringing messages and representing omens. Combined with the power of Saille, this bird aids in learning to trust intuition, especially when interpreting visions. The hawk and willow can bestow illumination when seeking truth about a situation or oneself.

Figure 67: Saille is shown written horizontally (left) and vertically (right).

When selected for divination or guidance, the message of this ogham is to take your time. While we usually want to get where we are going fast, Saille tells us that slow and steady makes room for growth. It also suggests devoting more time for creativity.

From April 15 to May 12, Saille brings a time of balance and harmony. With the help of this ogham, you can learn how to listen to the subtle voice of intuition and gain a deeper meaning for the direction of your life.

STRAIF / STRAITH

Straif is associated with the blackthorn, the thrush, and the color purple. This ogham is instrumental for building the kind of strength and fortitude necessary to handle adversity. Like the thorny blackthorn tree, the energy of Straif is effective for protection and for dispelling negativity. Paint the ogham on a piece of black tourmaline to carry with you as a protective talisman. For protective energy around your home, paint it on four stones from your garden, and then place one at each corner of your house as you say:

> *"With these symbols that I now place;*
> *Negativity, be banned from this space."*

Draw this ogham on a piece of paper and burn it to give strength to any type of spell. Because the blackthorn is a legendary fairy tree, this ogham aids in contacting the wee folk.

Combining this ogham with its bird, the thrush, aids in bringing life into balance and focusing on what you want to achieve. As a symbol of commitment, the thrush combined with the protective powers of Straif is a boon to strengthen relationships. Incorporate this bird and ogham into spells for luck and to aid in making your wishes come true.

Figure 68: Straif is shown written horizontally (left) and vertically (right).

When selected for divination or guidance, the message of this ogham is to face the hard realities of life but not be daunted by obstacles that seem to block you from achieving your dreams. Instead, view challenges as a training ground for developing strength to control the direction of your life.

TINNE / TEINE

This ogham is associated with holly, the starling, and the color dark gray. With sharp spines, holly leaves are the epitome of protection, which is a major aspect of this ogham. Cut out a piece of paper in the shape of a holly leaf, and then draw the symbol of Tinne in the center. Tuck this leaf into your purse or wallet to carry with you as a protective amulet. It can also be burned in a spell for protection against hostile magic. For protection of your home, draw Tinne on the underside of your front door mat. Paint this ogham on a piece of smoky quartz, citrine, or zoisite to hold during meditation for guidance, especially when seeking resolution to a problem. Tinne is also an aid for making decisions and building courage. Carve this symbol into a gray candle to raise energy for any type of ritual or spell.

Also known as black star, the Gaelic name for the starling is *Druid*.[97] When combined with Tinne, this bird becomes a guiding star for accessing ancient wisdom. During times of change, carry a picture of a starling marked with this ogham for help in adapting to new situations.

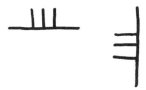

Figure 69: Tinne is shown written horizontally (left) and vertically (right).

When selected for divination or guidance, the message of Tinne is to respond wisely to problems rather than seek retributive justice. This ogham tells us that might does not make right; balance and courage are necessary to resolve conflict.

July 8 to August 4 is the time of Tinne and the time of year when holly comes into bloom with delicate, inconspicuous flowers. The energy during this period is associated with hearth and home. It is a time when problems that may occur are often best resolved through the power and unity of the family.

---

97. Forbes, *Gaelic Names of Beasts*, 335.

UR / UHR / URA

Ur is associated with heather, the lark, and the color purple. It is also associated with the summer solstice. Ur is an ogham of luck and passion. Draw this symbol on a little sachet stuffed with white heather flowers for good luck spells. Alternatively, draw it on a picture of white heather. Do the same with purple heather for spells to fan the flames of passion. Paint Ur on a piece of amethyst to use in meditation for clarity when seeking spiritual growth. This ogham and crystal combination is also instrumental in spiritual healing. To foster clarity and awareness while developing your psychic abilities, carve this ogham on a purple candle to burn during your sessions.

Since early times, the lark has been a symbol of joy. When combined in meditation with the ogham Ur, the lark can guide you to a deep level of introspection that can awaken the song that is in your heart. This combination of ogham and bird can lift your spirits and instill a deep sense of satisfaction and happiness.

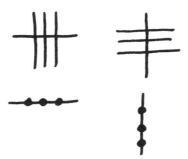

Figure 70: Ur is shown in its linear and dot forms written horizontally
(left) and vertically (right).

When selected for divination or guidance, the message of this ogham is that the mark of true success is expressed through generosity. Prosperity and abundance are best enjoyed when shared.

CHAPTER 12

WORKING WITH THE FORFEDA

WHILE THE CHARACTERS IN the fifth ogham group are not linked individually with birds, as a group they are sometimes referred to as the *crane bag*. According to legend, the forfeda was created by the sea god Manannán mac Lir who kept them in his magical bag made from the skin of a shape-shifting crane/woman along with other great treasures. Any of these oghams can be used with the energy of the crane for spells of abundance or reversal. They are also instrumental for stoking creativity. The combination of any of these ogham characters and the crane is especially powerful for divination and understanding the deep mysteries of this world and the otherworld.

Although the characters for Amhancholl, Ifin, and Uilleann have been used to represent Phagos, I have included it as a separate entry with its own symbol. Peith is also included.

AMHANCHOLL / EAMANCHOLL / EMANCOLL / MÓR

This ogham is associated with witch hazel and sometimes pine. Carve it on a small witch hazel twig or draw it on a picture of the tree to burn in a banishing spell. This ogham is also helpful for tapping into the subconscious mind for psychic work. Hanging a witch hazel or pine branch marked with Amhancholl over the front door provides protection for your home.

Although this ogham's first three names listed above are more traditional, it has become known as Mór and associated with the sea. In addition to resembling a fishing net, *mór* is the Welsh and Celtic Breton word for sea.[98] Associated with purification and release, like the cleansing ocean tides this ogham can carry away whatever is no longer needed in your life. Mór is especially potent for releasing emotions and providing a clean slate for renewal. Draw it on a seashell for aid in recovering from the breakup of a relationship.

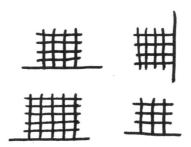

Figure 71: Amhancholl/Mór is shown on the top row as it is primarily written horizontally (left) and vertically (right). It is also commonly drawn with 5 x 5 lines and 3 x 3 lines.

When selected for divination or guidance, this ogham represents unexpected changes. While these changes may appear to come from outside sources, Amhancholl/Mór aids in accessing obscured information about them. It also aids in adapting to any kind of change.

EBAD / ÉABHADH / ALSO KOAD / GROVE

Ebad is associated with the aspen, honeysuckle, and elecampane. It symbolizes the ability to rise above the complexities and problems of everyday life. Inscribe this ogham on a white candle for spells or visualizations to attract what you desire. To foster happiness in your home, draw the symbol on a piece of paper, and then sprinkle it with a pinch of crumbled dried leaf from any of the plants associated with Ebad. Fold the paper to form a little bundle. Place it near your front door for three days, and then safely burn it as you visualize whatever represents happiness to you being drawn into your home. This ogham has also become known as Koad and Grove. In this respect, it is associated with a group of trees (a grove) rather than a specific type of tree.

---

98. J. P. Mallory and D. Q. Adams, *The Oxford Introduction to Proto-Indo-European and the Proto-Indo-European World* (New York: Oxford University Press, 2006), 127.

Figure 72: Ebad is shown written horizontally (left) and vertically (right).

When selected for divination or guidance, this ogham advises you to seek balance and to clear up any differences you may have with someone. Its message is to look for the small things that bring the most satisfaction in your life and to pursue them.

IFIN / IPHIN

Ifin is associated with the pine tree and gooseberry. Linked with prophecy and vision, this ogham is an aid for divination. To support your efforts, draw Ifin on a piece of paper, and then place a circle of pine cone scales around it on your altar during divination sessions or when you engage in any psychic or past-life work. This will also bring clarity to your readings and experiences. Inscribing the ogham on a candle for meditation aids in hearing your inner voice. Draw Ifin on a piece of paper, and then dab it with a tiny amount of pine essential oil. Place this on your bedside table to help remember dreams. Ifin also aids in the quest for knowledge and unlocking deeply held memories.

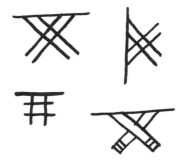

Figure 73: Ifin is shown on the top row written horizontally (left) and vertically (right). Two variations of Ifin are illustrated on the bottom row.

When selected for divination or guidance, Ifin tells us to follow the wisdom of the past, including ancient lore, to unravel the intricacies of the present. Once understood, it can be a guide for the future, as well.

OIR / OR

This ogham is associated with the spindle tree, ivy, and the color white. The small spindle tree is stronger and hardier than it looks. Its name comes from the popular use of its wood for spindles and lace-making bobbins, which links the tree and this ogham with domesticity and the magical arts of spinning, weaving, and lace making. These skills, and many others, rely on creativity and inspiration, which Oir can help you access. For a creative boost, draw this ogham on the tools you use for self-expression. Draw it on an ivy leaf (or picture of one) and place it on your altar for spiritual journeys that take you inward, as well as guide you back out.

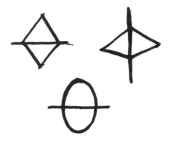

Figure 74: Oir is shown on the top row written horizontally (left) and vertically (right). It is also commonly drawn as a circle.

When selected for divination or guidance, the message of this ogham is to pay attention to family matters, especially if change is in the air. Use your talents to spin connections that draw loved ones closer.

UILLEANN / UILEN / UILLEAND

Uilleann is associated with the beech tree, honeysuckle, and ivy and the color yellowish white. This ogham's association with two plants that are vines makes it especially effective for binding spells. Write the objective of your spell on a piece of paper, and then roll it into a little scroll. Draw this ogham multiple times to make a spiral around the outside of the scroll. Hold it between your hands as you visualize your objective, and then burn it. While vines can hide things, Uilleann is also associated with revealing secrets. In addition, it is instrumental in spells to manifest what you seek.

Figure 75: Uilleann is shown written horizontally (left) and vertically (right).

When selected for divination or guidance, the message of this ogham is to seek what you desire. Although the means and methods to attain it may be currently hidden, continually working toward your goal will help you manifest it into reality.

PEITH / PETHBOC / PETHBOL

This symbol seems to have evolved from the early upturned arrow shape that was used in British inscriptions for the letter *P*. It is not difficult to see why the character Ifin became associated with this character because some inscriptions with the arrow-shaped symbol show a resemblance to it. Today, it is drawn as a short line parallel with the stem line. While guelder rose and dwarf elder are the plants often associated with Peith, older sources indicate pine as its tree.

Writings from the eighteenth and nineteenth centuries list the ogham Pethboc in place of Ngetal as a Brythonic substitute. According to eighteenth-century sources, *peth* comes from the Cornish *pethav* meaning "I am," signifying the essence of a person and *boc* had the meaning of "budding" or "springing forth."[99] The term *boc* was sometimes applied to a young buck because of its bounding energy. My interpretation for this ogham is that it aids us to look deep within to find who we are or can be when we allow ourselves to blossom. It also indicates the need for moving forward. When we know who we are, we know when to jump at an opportunity. Inscribe this ogham on a candle to use during meditation when seeking self-illumination.

Figure 76: Peith is shown written horizontally (left) and vertically (right).

99. Edward Davies, *Celtic Researches on the Origin, Traditions & Language of the Ancient Britons* (London: J. Booth, 1804), 461.

PHAGOS

As mentioned, this name has been associated with three different symbols and illustrates how the ogham has evolved and changed. While the characters Ifin, Amhancholl/Mór, and Uilliann have been used to represent Phagos, in more recent times it has been assigned its own symbol, a simple hook shape. It is associated with the beech tree and the color orange brown. Paint the hook symbol on a piece of orange calcite to wear as a protective talisman. Also meditate with it to stimulate creative inspiration. Associated with ancestors and ancient wisdom, include Phagos on your Samhain altar, especially if you plan to engage in divination. It is also instrumental for healing circles and binding spells.

Figure 77: Sometimes depicted as a simple hook, Phagos is shown
written horizontally (left) and vertically (right).

PART FIVE
THE RUNES

Like the Celtic ogham, there are several theories for the origin of these symbols, as well as the name *rune*. According to Webster's Dictionary, the word *rune* comes from the Old Norse and Old English *rūn*, which had several meanings: "secret," "mystery," "a character of the runic alphabet," and "writing."[100] This word is also akin to the Old English *rūnian*, meaning "to whisper"; the Old High German words *rūna*, "secret discussion," and *rūnēn*, "to whisper"; the Old Norse *reyna*, "to whisper"; and the Latin *rumor*.[101] Although often written in stone, they were not a static set of symbols. Over time, the runes evolved with the changing linguistics of Europe. Once they were incorporated into folklore, the mystic quality of the runes emerged.

---

100. Editorial Staff, *Webster's Third New International Dictionary*, 1989.
101. Ibid.

CHAPTER 13
RUNIC BEGINNINGS

ALTHOUGH OFTEN REFERRED TO as the Norse runes, the earliest evidence of a runic alphabet comes from the Germanic people who lived in an area that stretched from Denmark and northern Germany to southern Norway and Sweden. Most of the early inscriptions were carved into objects such as pieces of wood, stone, metal, or bone. One of the earliest objects marked with runes is a hair comb that dates to approximately 160 CE.[102] It was found in Denmark's Vimose bog, which is famous for a cache of ancient weapons and the abundant human and animal sacrifices found there.

There have been many ideas about where this alphabet originated. According to the three most prevalent theories, the runes were derived from the Latin, Greek, or Etruscan (Northern Italian) alphabets.

In 1874, Danish linguist and runeologist Ludvig Wimmer (1839–1920) launched the first scientific study to determine its origin.[103] According to his theory, runes were derived from the monumental script that the Romans used on their great buildings and structures. As his theory goes, this script could have been learned from the Romans who settled along the Rhine River. Wimmer based his idea on the similarities between several Roman letters and runes, such as the letter *F* and the rune Feoh. While it is also possible to see how the Latin letters *B*, *H*, *M*, *P*, *R*, and *X* could have had an influence on runic writing, most scholars today agree that letter shape, especially just a few, is not enough to link one alphabet with another. Linguistics must be compared to find commonalities.

Swedish scholar and university professor Otto von Friesen (1870–1942) was a leading proponent of the theory that runes were derived from Greek script. He claimed that the

---

102. Tineke Looijenga, *Texts and Contexts of the Oldest Runic Inscriptions* (Boston: Brill, 2003), 78.
103. Elmer H. Antonsen, "The Runes: The Earliest Germanic Writing System," *The Origins of Writing*, ed. Wayne M. Senner (Lincoln, NE: University of Nebraska Press, 1989), 145.

Goths—the early Germanic people who settled in an area around the Black Sea—knew the Greek alphabet. According to von Friesen, the Goths may have been familiar with the Greek language because of their service and travel with the Roman legions. The professor based his theory mainly on the fact that, like early Greek script, the runes could be written left to right, right to left, and boustrophedon (in an alternating direction). In addition, Greek and runes had been carved into a variety of surfaces including wood and metal. Like Wimmer, he based similarity of character structure on a handful of letters. The backup theory von Friesen had was that the runes came from the Latin alphabet.

Norwegian runeologist Carl Marstrander (1883–1965) believed that the runes had evolved from Etruscan because that civilization had the closest proximity with Germanic peoples. The problem is that no early runic writing has been found in southern Germany or any area bordering Etruscan territory. In addition, the Etruscan alphabet is still to be deciphered. Like the others, Marstrander's theory does not take linguistics into account.

To this day, no one knows for sure where the runes originated. One point of agreement by most scholars, however, is that the runes most likely resulted from the practical need for written communication related to trade.

RUNIC INSCRIPTIONS

Like the ogham, the runic alphabet is named for the beginning sequence of letters. It is called both *futhark* and *futhorc* from the first six letters of the Elder and Anglo-Saxon rune sets.

Unlike modern alphabets, runic writing is considerably quirky. A frequent feature of runic inscriptions is the lack of space between words. In fact, when a word began with the same letter that the previous word ended with, the rune was written only once, joining the two words. While we expect word breaks to be hyphenated, in runic inscriptions words were sometimes written in a run-on fashion from one line to the next. As mentioned, runes could be written left to right, right to left, and sometimes in alternating directions, complicating the deciphering process.

The first full runic alphabet was found in Gotland, Sweden, on part of a sarcophagus. Known as the Kylver stone, the inscription is usually dated to the fifth century CE.[104] This oldest of runic alphabets, called the *Elder Futhark*, is usually found on small, portable objects such as personal items, spears, and arrow shafts.

Also found in Sweden, the Vadstena bracteate also contains the full Elder Futhark but with variations in a few symbols and a slightly different order. A bracteate is a gold medal-

---

104. Jeremy J. Smith, *Old English: A Linguistic Introduction* (New York: Cambridge University Press, 2009), 124.

lion that has a decoration or inscription impressed on one side. Usually worn on a thin strip of leather around the neck, bracteates were common from 350 to 550 CE.[105]

Over a period of about five hundred years, Christianity was slowly accepted in the Germanic world. Early Christian converts did not seem to consider the runes as particularly Pagan and continued using them for inscriptions. Not only were runic inscriptions used on Christian gravestones, they have been found inside more than three hundred medieval Norwegian churches.[106] Carved graffiti-like on walls and columns, most inscriptions are prayer requests. Baptismal fonts, bells, chests, and other religious objects were also marked with runes.

In England, Celtic-style crosses dating between 650–750 CE hold runic inscriptions of Christian poems.[107] Along with Roman script, there is runic writing on the coffin of St. Cuthbert, circa 698.[108] Over time, runic writing in England evolved from short inscriptions to religious texts, some of which were inscribed on wooden sticks.

Of the over two thousand runic inscriptions found in Sweden, many include fragments of poetry.[109] In Scandinavia, runic writing continued into the late thirteenth century with isolated pockets, such as Gotland, carrying on until the seventeenth century.[110] Despite this longevity, the use of runes steadily declined. During this time, references to the runes began to appear in Norse literature and the alphabet acquired more of a supernatural connotation.

THE RUNIC ALPHABETS

The oldest runic alphabet, the Elder Futhark, consists of twenty-four characters and was used from approximately the first through the fifth centuries CE.[111] The first two full runic alphabets found on the Kylver stone and Vadstena bracteate have a slightly different order of characters, but there is no linguistic explanation for this. In addition, there is no

---

105. Antonsen, "The Runes," 148.

106. Ibid., 139.

107. Ibid., 137.

108. Victoria Symons, *Runes and Roman Letters in Anglo-Saxon Manuscripts* (Berlin, Germany: Walter de Gruyter GmbH, 2016), 9.

109. Ekkehard König and Johan van der Auwera, eds., *The Germanic Languages* (New York: Routledge, 2002), 5.

110. Terje Spurkland, *Norwegian Runes and Runic Inscriptions*, trans. Betsy van der Hock (Woodbridge, England: The Boydell Press, 2005), 4.

111. Richard L. Morris, *Runic and Mediterranean Epigraphy* (Philadelphia: John Benjamins North America, 2012), 107.

known reason for dividing the twenty-four symbols into three groups called *aettir*, which means "families."[112]

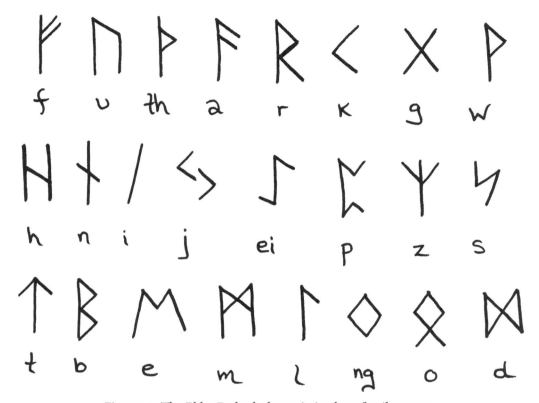

Figure 78: The Elder Futhark shown in its three family groups.

Each rune is composed of staves (upright strokes) and twigs (slanted lines extending from the stave). It is generally accepted that early rune shapes do not have curved or horizontal lines because the alphabet was developed for carving in wood. However, the shape of the characters does not necessarily relate to the age of inscription. Instead, it is thought that variations in form occurred between "schools" of writing. The differences seem to be a simple matter of style and preference.

The individual names of most runes are regular words. For example, *Fehu* and *Isa* are Old Germanic for "cattle" and "ice," respectively.[113] In some inscriptions, instead of the full

112. Antonsen, "The Runes," 142.
113. R. I. Page, *Runes* (Berkeley, CA: University of California Press, 1987), 15.

word, just the rune symbol was used. In most cases, the letter or sound represented by a rune corresponded to the first letter of the word used for its name, but there were exceptions. For example, Fehu represents the letter/sound *F*, but the rune Algiz represents *Z*. Runic alphabets do not have symbols for numbers; instead, they were written as words.

The Elder Futhark went through a transitional period from 500 to 700 as linguistic developments occurred in Germanic languages.[114] It was after this time that the languages in Scandinavia developed their Nordic traits with the shortening of words, reduction of unstressed syllables, and the development of new vowels.[115] As language changed, so, too, did the runic alphabet.

Odd as it may seem, as the number of spoken sounds increased, writing went the other way, decreasing from twenty-four to sixteen runes. Instead of one character equaling one sound, many of the runes represented multiple sounds. Although the Elder Futhark remained in use, by the eighth century the new alphabet, called the *Younger Futhark* was more widely used in Denmark and Sweden.[116]

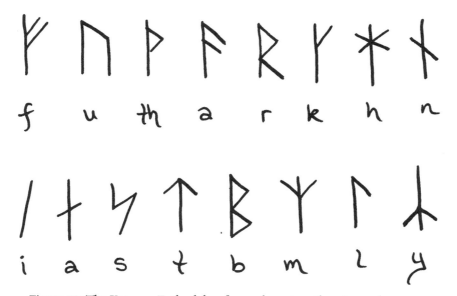

Figure 79: The Younger Futhark has fewer characters than its predecessor.

---

114. Morris, *Runic and Mediterranean Epigraphy*, 107.

115. Spurkland, *Norwegian Runes and Runic Inscriptions*, 78.

116. Oscar Bandle, et al., eds. *The Nordic Languages: An International Handbook of the History of the Northern Germanic Languages*, vol. 1 (New York: Walter de Gruyter, 2002), 700.

Denmark is generally considered the home of the Younger Futhark because it first appeared there in its complete form. Sometimes called the *Viking Runes*, this alphabet has two major variants: Danish and Swedish-Norwegian. The Danish variety is also called the *Long Branch Runes* and the Swedish-Norwegian variety, the *Short Twig Runes*, which is also known as the *Rök Runes* for the stone found in Rök, Sweden. There were variations within these two main divisions of the Younger Futhark, and by the medieval period, the Long Branch and Short Twig runes were mixed together.

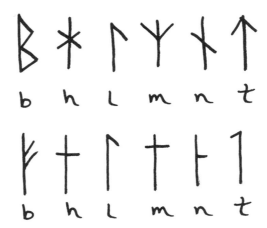

Figure 80: In the Middle Ages, a mix of Long Branch
and Short Twig runes were often used.

THE DOTTED RUNES

The Scandinavian sixteen-rune alphabet was in use for about four hundred years until roughly 1050 when they were replaced with the medieval *Dotted Runes*, which were also called *Pointed Runes* or *Stung Runes*.[117] With symbols representing more than one sound, the Younger Futhark became regarded as too ambiguous. The solution was to create new symbols by adding a dot to existing runes, thus indicating which sound was intended. For example, adding a dot to the letters *B* and *T* restored the letters/sounds *P* and *D*, respectively. That said, not all rune carvers used dotting, leaving ambiguities in some inscriptions.

117. Antonsen, "The Runes," 156.

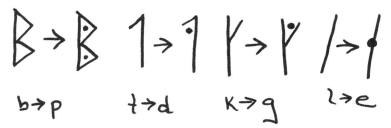

Figure 81: Dots were added to some runes to restore letters/sounds that had been dropped.

THE ANGLO-SAXON RUNES

Based on the first six letters, the English or Anglo-Saxon rune set is called the *futhorc* and sometimes *fuþorc*.[118] Although the third character in all three runic alphabets is *P*-shaped but represented the TH sound, the variation in the spelling of the rune set name is a peculiarity of later Anglo-Saxon manuscripts.[119]

The term *Anglo-Saxon* is a collective noun for the Angles, Saxons, Jutes, and Frisians who moved to Britain around the fifth century. Coming from northern Germany and the North Sea coast of Denmark and the Netherlands, they took the runes with them. However, changes to the alphabet had already begun on the Continent with the Frisian twenty-eight-character set.

---

118. Page, *Runes*, 38.
119. Antonsen, "The Runes," 140.

Figure 82: The Anglo-Saxon rune set was expanded by the regional Northumbrian additions (the last four characters on the bottom row).

Old English and Old Frisian shared the linguistic changes of the fifth century. With additions that adapted the complex vowel sounds of Old German, the Frisian runes worked well for the Anglo-Saxons. Regional tweaks and additions occurred, too, especially in the area north of the River Humber in England. Around the eighth or ninth century, the Northumbrian rune set reached thirty-three characters.[120]

THE RUNES REDISCOVERED

During the Middle Ages, runic stone inscriptions piqued the interest of antiquarians. One was Swedish librarian and tutor Johannes Bureus (1568–1652), who had a keen interest in languages. Because of his ability to decipher runes, he was given a post as the royal antiquarian and asked to make an inventory of rune stones. Despite having relatives jailed for dabbling in the occult, Bureus took an interest in the local sorcerers he had encountered during his travels. He was said to have acquired a Norwegian book of spells, some of which incorporated the use of runes. A self-styled Rosicrucian inspired by Agrippa and John Dee, Bureus developed his own system of magic that was based on the structure of the Kabbalah and incorporated the runes.

Not wanting to be left behind during a rise of nationalism in European countries during the nineteenth century, Scandinavians embraced their Old Norse sagas, which gave rise to a romanticized Viking revival. Despite being historical bad boys, all things Viking became fashionable, including furniture designed with sweeping lines and dragon's head finials that echoed their once-feared longboats. Both *Edda* poems were translated into multiple languages and German composer Richard Wagner (1813–1883) loosely based his epic four-opera Ring Cycle on Norse legends. Anything with a tinge of Norse history remained in vogue into the early twentieth century and quite naturally, the runes caught people's attention.

Austrian writer Guido von List (1848–1919) is credited with adapting the runes into the Western occult tradition. Seeming to echo Odin's ordeal, after an alleged period of blindness, von List claimed to have had a magical vision. He revised the Elder Futhark into a set of eighteen runes that he called the *Armanen Futharkh*. While List's theories on the occult and ancient Germanic religion may have brought runes into neopagan practice, according to history professor Michael Bailey (1971–) of Iowa State University, his intertwining them with nationalism and anti-Semitism may have also influenced some members of the Nazi party.[121]

---

120. Ralph W. V. Elliot, *Runes: An Introduction* (Manchester, England: Manchester University Press, 1980), 33.

121. Michael D. Bailey, *Magic and Superstition in Europe: A Concise History from Antiquity to the Present* (New York: Rowman & Littlefield Publishers, Inc., 2007), 235.

CHAPTER 14

RUNES FOR MAGIC AND GUIDANCE

ALTHOUGH THE RUNES WERE developed for practical reasons, they appear to have been used for magical purposes early on. Included in the fifth-century inscriptions on the Kylver stone is the enigmatic word *sueus*, which scholars have not been able to translate or discern any meaning.[122] Palindromes (words or phrases spelled the same forward and backward) with unknown meanings are often found in runic writing. According to Terje Spurkland, associate professor of medieval studies at the University of Oslo, Norway, these palindromes may have had a magical function.

During an excavation of the Viking-age village of Ribe on the west coast of Denmark, archaeologists discovered a piece of human skull that contained runic writing dating to approximately 720 CE.[123] While it was determined that the person was long-gone and the skull considerably old when runes were carved on it, the inscription has not been deciphered. Because a hole had been drilled through the piece of skull, archaeologists believe that it may have been worn as an amulet.

Also found in Ribe, but dating to much later is the Ribe stick, which is also referred to as a healing stick. The runic writing on this artifact contains a mix of Pagan and Christian incantations and a prayer calling for healing.

What appears to be a healing rhyme, known as the "thistle mistletoe formula," has been found in runic inscriptions in Scandinavia and Iceland. These words sometimes occur with names of people but most often they are accompanied by gibberish. What

---

122. Smith, *Old English*, 124.
123. Spurkland, *Norwegian Runes and Runic Inscriptions*, 72.

may appear as gibberish to us, of course, may have held a great deal of meaning. The words *thistle* and *mistletoe* have also been found on memorial stones in Denmark.

Pendants, rings, weapons, and other objects contain single, short inscriptions believed to have a talismanic meaning or function as charm words. The repetition of a single rune is also thought to be a charm. For example, the repetition of Fehu, "wealth, wealth, wealth," could serve as an incantation.[124]

Raymond Ian Page (1924–2012), who was a runeologist and professor of Anglo-Saxon studies at Cambridge University, England, regarded the letter combination *alu* as a magical word related to protection.[125] The word *alu* occurs alone and with other un-deciphered words that some have discounted as gibberish.

TWENTY-FIRST CENTURY RUNIC MAGIC

Because the runes and their related lore is a vast topic, this section is intended as a basic introduction to help you get started using the runes. First, choose which runic alphabet you want to use, the Elder, Younger, or Anglo-Saxon. Next, make or purchase a set of sticks, cards, wooden tiles, or stones. Before using them, consecrate them with water or smudge with incense or herbs. You may want to dedicate them to Odin or another Norse or Germanic deity. If you are working with the Anglo-Saxon runes, you may want to choose a deity from the British Isles.

Before using your runes for magic or divination, get to know each symbol so you understand its significance. Carry it with you, meditate with it, and attune to its message. While there are fundamental meanings for each rune, they can also convey something very personal.

Because it is an alphabet, runes are easy to incorporate into spells by writing your intention, keywords, or incantation. Keep in mind that runic writing lacks a fixed direction and the first line of an ancient inscription was often written right to left and the second left to right. Be creative.

---

124. Mindy MacLeod and Bernard Mees, *Runic Amulets and Magic Objects* (Woodbridge, England: The Boydell Press, 2006), 112.
125. R. I. Page, *Runes and Runic Inscriptions: Collected Essays on Anglo-Saxon and Viking Runes*, ed. David Parsons (Woodbridge, England: The Boydell Press, 1998), 154.

TABLE 5.1 THE THREE MAJOR FAMILIES OF RUNES

Elder Futhark			Younger Futhark			Anglo-Saxon Futhorc		
Symbol	Name	Sound	Symbol	Name	Sound	Symbol	Name	Sound
			ᛏ	Ar	a	ᚠ	Aesc	ae
ᚠ	Ansuz	a	ᚠ	As	ą	ᚠ	Ac	a
ᛒ	Berkanan	b	ᛒ	Bjarkan	b	ᛒ	Beorc	b
						ᚳ	Cen	c
ᛞ	Dagaz	d				ᛞ	Daeg	d
ᛖ	Ehwaz	e				ᛖ	Eh	e
ᛃ	Iwaz	ei				ᛃ	Eoh	ei
						ᛠ	Ear	ea
ᚠ	Fehu	f	ᚠ	Fe	f	ᚠ	Feoh	f
ᚷ	Gebo	g				ᚷ	Gyfu	g
						ᚸ	Gar	g/gh

TABLE 5.1 THE THREE MAJOR FAMILIES OF RUNES

Elder Futhark			Younger Futhark			Anglo-Saxon Futhorc		
Symbol	Name	Sound	Symbol	Name	Sound	Symbol	Name	Sound
	Hagalaz	h		Hagall	h		Haegl	h
	Isa	i		Iss	i		Is	i
							Ior	io
	Jera	j					Ger	j
	Kenaz	k		Kaun	k		Calc	k
	Laguz	l		Logr	l		Lagu	l
	Mannaz	m		Madhr	m		Mann	m
	Naudiz	n		Naudhr	n		Nyd	n
	Ingwaz	ng					Ing	ng
	Oþila	o					Ethel	oe

TABLE 5.1 THE THREE MAJOR FAMILIES OF RUNES

Elder Futhark			Younger Futhark			Anglo-Saxon Futhorc		
Symbol	Name	Sound	Symbol	Name	Sound	Symbol	Name	Sound
						ᚩ	Os	o
ᛈ	Perþ	p				ᛈ	Peorþ	p
						ᛢ	Cweorþ	q/kw
ᚱ	Raido	r	ᚱ	Reidh	r	ᚱ	Rad	r
ᛋ	Sowilo	s	ᛋ	Sol	s	ᛋ	Sigil	s
						ᛥ	Stan	st
↑	Tiwaz	t	↑	Tyr	t	↑	Tir	t
ᚦ	Thurisaz	th	ᚦ	Thurs	th	ᚦ	Thorn	th
ᚢ	Uruz	u	ᚢ	Ur	u	ᚢ	Ur	u
ᚹ	Wunjo	w				ᚹ	Wynn	w

TABLE 5.1 THE THREE MAJOR FAMILIES OF RUNES								
Elder Futhark			Younger Futhark			Anglo-Saxon Futhorc		
Symbol	Name	Sound	Symbol	Name	Sound	Symbol	Name	Sound
			ᛦ	Yr	y	ᛦ	Yr	y
ᛉ	Algiz	z				ᛉ	Eolh	z

Choose an appropriate rune to carry with you to bolster the energy of something you are working toward. Calling on the power of three, use a single rune three times as in the example previously mentioned with Fehu to attract wealth. Single or multiple runes can be carved into candles and used for spells or ritual. You can also punctuate a spell by drawing a rune character in the air as you visualize its power, giving your willpower a boost.

As in the past, it is common to use runes as talismans. A word or two can be spelled out or make bind runes that suit your intention. Found in old inscriptions, bind runes are regarded as having a magical purpose. A bind rune is a combination of two or more characters that are created with one stave (upright line). Often the characters were repeated on a long stave.

Combine a couple of them to create your own bind runes for special purposes. For example, combine Gebo and Kenaz if you are seeking the gift of clarity, knowledge, and inspiration. Algiz and Raido can be combined for a travel protection talisman.

Figure 83: A bind rune is a combination of two or more characters.

A famous example of a bind rune comes from the Kylver stone where the character Tiwaz was repeated one above the other, resembling a fir tree. Because the inscriptions on the Kylver stone (which was part of a sarcophagus) were facing the interior, they have been interpreted as protecting the grave or serving its occupant in some way.

RUNES FOR GUIDANCE

Runes are for guidance, not for fortune telling or predicting the future. Functioning with the subconscious, the energy of these symbols provides information. Our job is to interpret how this information applies to the questions or situations for which we seek guidance. Runes can offer guidance in helping us examine the past for a better understanding of the present. Whatever you are using the runes for, be clear in your question or in thinking about a situation or issue. Runes can also help you explore what you hold in your heart.

Keeping runes in a pouch makes it easy to select them randomly without seeing them. Prepare to use them by sitting quietly for a few minutes to clear your mind. Hold the pouch as you think of your question or a situation, and then draw one. Hold it as you contemplate your question and how the meaning or associations of the rune may point to a resolution.

Take a day or two to consider a rune's information, especially if you are unsure of how it fits the situation. If you cannot figure out what it's telling you, re-do the rune draw. If you draw the same one, spend more time and consider all aspects of the rune. Keep in mind that your first interpretation or impression of what it may mean is most often the correct one.

Another method for guidance is to cast the runes by gently tossing them onto a soft surface. The runes that land face up are the ones to examine. Alternatively, once you cast them, close your eyes and hold your hands over them. Let your intuition guide you to select one or more.

When selecting two runes, look for similarities between them, which means the information of each symbol supports or adds to the other. If they seem to be opposites, one will provide insight to your question/situation and the other will help guide you to a resolution. Two opposite runes can also reveal the root of a conflict.

A three-rune draw is also called *casting the Norns*. Like the Greek Fates, the Norns were Norse goddesses who represented the past, present, and future. Working with three runes provides clarity but do not predict the future; instead, they present possibilities. These possibilities may include challenges. It is your potential talent, endeavors, and actions that create your future.

Another way to work with the runes is to select one at a time and lay them out in a pattern. For example, in a five-rune layout, the first three are placed in a horizontal row, and then one is placed above and one below the center rune. When laying them out, place them face down so you cannot see the rune characters. Turn them over in the following order to do your reading: Begin with the center rune, which represents the current state of your issue or situation. The rune to the left of center shows past influences that caused or contributed to the issue. The rune above the center indicates either help or speed bumps that you may encounter during the process of resolving the issue. The rune below center reveals something that is unchangeable. It does not mean that you must accept something; it offers more clarity and potential workarounds. The final rune, to the right of center, represents a potential outcome or the key to procure a desired outcome.

Journaling your rune castings or single draws can be an aid for interpretation. Over time, a journal can reveal patterns in the runes that present themselves. There are many other layouts for reading the runes that you may want to try. Tarot layouts can also be used.

CHAPTER 15

WORKING WITH THE ELDER AND YOUNGER FUTHARK

THE RUNES ARE LISTED alphabetically according to their names in the Elder Futhark with a cross-reference to their Younger Futhark and Anglo-Saxon names. Because of the bewildering difference in some of the Elder Futhark names, it is important to remember that they were recorded centuries after the early runic inscriptions. The names I have used come from the work of Professor Raymond Ian Page and other runic scholars. The only exception is the rune Thurisaz, for which I have used its later name with the letters *TH* instead of *Þ* to avoid confusion.

Even though the Elder Futhark name is used throughout each entry, the information applies to the corresponding characters in the other futharks unless otherwise noted. The symbols that are found exclusively in the Younger Futhark and Anglo-Saxon rune sets are included in the next chapter.

In addition to the meaning and interpretation of each rune, details on the runic half months are also included. I first read about the half months in *The Pagan Book of Days* by Nigel Pennick (1946–), an authority on ancient belief systems. Like the Celtic ogham/tree calendar, the runic half months are a modern construct associated with the energy and wisdom of their respective symbols.

Although runes are sometimes described as having dual meanings based on being upright or reversed, this is impractical when casting runes as they may land at various angles. In addition, the rune poems and other runic sources do not indicate dual meanings for them. According to runic scholars, the occasional reversed (mirror image) or upside-down rune found in inscriptions seem to have been a whim with no relevance to its meaning.[126] Of course, if you are already using runes and working with dual meanings, follow your preference.

ALGIZ

Anglo-Saxon name: Eolh

Also known as: Elhaz

According to runic scholars, the original name for this rune is unknown and the current one was applied later. The names *Algiz* and *Eolh* are Old Germanic and Old English, respectively, for "elk."[127] Rather than the animal, the Old English rune poem relates it to the plant elk sedge, which has sharp leaves that can cut when trying to pull it up with bare hands.

Defense and protection are the core aspects of this rune. Algiz also signifies new opportunities or challenges and a need to keep emotions under control. Give yourself room to maneuver during challenges and keep tabs on feelings that get stirred up to avoid going to pieces in times of transition. On a personal note, I strongly associate this rune with the gesture of epiphany and the manifestation of deity, which dates to the ancient Great Mother Goddess.

When selected for divination or guidance, Algiz advises awareness of unwanted influences. Don't be in denial about or ignore negative things; set things right or turn them around and use them for positive opportunities. Amethyst, clear quartz, garnet, and onyx are especially effective crystals for working with the energy of Algiz.

Figure 84: The same symbol is used in the Elder Futhark and Anglo-Saxon runic alphabets.

The runic half month of Algiz runs from January 28 to February 11. It ushers in a time that is conducive to contacting spirit guides, especially for protection. It helps open the channels of communication and provides guidance for issues that may arise during this time.

---

126. Page, *Runes*, 9; Marie Stoklund et al., eds., *Runes and Their Secrets: Studies in Runology* (Copenhagen, Denmark: Museum Tusculanum Press, 2006), 175.

127. Looijenga, *Texts and Contexts of the Oldest Runic Inscriptions*, 7.

ANSUZ

Younger Futhark name: As

Anglo-Saxon name: Os

Also known as: Asa, Asc

The names for this rune are generally noted as meaning "god" or "mouth." While the word *ansuz* from Old Germanic and *oss* from Old Icelandic both mean "god," *óss* from Old Norwegian means "estuary" or "river mouth."[128]

This rune is often regarded as a messenger that brings sacred wisdom and aids in connecting with the Divine. Ansuz is especially helpful for exploring inner and outer worlds and initiating self-change. Be aware of unusual things that seem like chance because something may be calling you. The energy of this rune also stokes the fires of creativity.

When selected for divination or guidance, Ansuz's message is to expect the unexpected and watch for omens. The answers are apparent if you stop and pay attention. Clear quartz, red and blue tourmaline, and emerald are effective for working with the energy of Ansuz.

Figure 85: The same symbol is used in the Elder and Younger Futharks (left).
The Anglo-Saxon alphabet (right) has its own symbol.

The runic half month of Ansuz runs from August 13 to 28. This period is conducive to receiving blessings and inspiration. It is a time of communication—giving power to words and finding truth. Ansuz also helps to understand the meaning of messages you may receive.

---

128. Page, *Runes*, 43.

BERKANAN

Younger Futhark name: Bjarkan

Anglo-Saxon name: Beorc

Also known as: Berkana, Berkano

The names of this rune come from the Old Germanic *berkana* and Old Norwegian *bjarkan*, meaning "birch twig," and Old English *beorc*, "birch tree."[129] Like the birch tree, this rune relates to fertility, growth, and new beginnings. With nurturing energy, Berkanan aids both actual and symbolic growth. It is especially supportive when seeking rebirth of the spirit or any form of personal blossoming. Berkanan advises patience and clarity of purpose. Draw this rune on a piece of paper or paint it on an amulet to wear during shamanic work.

When selected for divination or guidance, Berkanan may be telling you that growth sometimes needs to be coaxed. With gentleness and patience, whether it is a situation or relationship, or even an aspect of life, it will bloom and grow at the appropriate time. The crystals citrine, green tourmaline, and moonstone aid in working with the energy of this rune.

Figure 86: The same symbol is used in all three runic alphabets.

The runic half month of Berkanan runs from March 14 to 29. It is a time of beginnings, which can relate to a pregnancy and the birth of a child, a new relationship, or the start of a business venture. It can be associated with the early stages of a creative project as well. This is also a time of self-renewal and personal growth.

---

129. Bandle, *The Nordic Languages*, 636.

DAGAZ

Anglo-Saxon name: Daeg

Also known as: Dag

This symbol is not used in the Younger Futhark.

Dagaz is an Old Germanic word, meaning "day."[130] This rune is about beginnings and endings and the cycles that drive our lives. It often indicates that a major shift in the form of something good may be heading your way. That said, it also cautions to be wise about gains, as recklessness often causes loss. Use this rune in ritual to initiate transformation or hasten completion of a cycle, situation, or project. Personifying day, it serves as a reminder that there is light at the end of the tunnel even when life is in turmoil. Dagaz also represents a breakthrough when struggling to understand something.

When selected for divination or guidance, Dagaz advises you to greet the dawning of something new with optimism. It beckons you to trust your intuition and grasp opportunities that seem right. Amethyst, azurite, chrysolite, and kyanite are effective for working with the energy of Dagaz.

Figure 87: The same symbol is used in the Elder Futhark and Anglo-Saxon runic alphabets.

The runic half month of Dagaz runs from June 14 to 28. Starting just before the summer solstice, this period is associated with light, growth, and transformation. Although Dagaz is a rune of change, it also brings stability and provides a foundation upon which something new can be built.

---

130. Looijenga, *Texts and Contexts of the Oldest Runic Inscriptions,* 7.

EHWAZ

Anglo-Saxon name: Eh

This symbol is not used in the Younger Futhark.

The words *ehwaz* and *eh* are Old Germanic and Old English, respectively, for "horse."[131] While in Norse legend this rune was linked with Odin's magical eight-legged horse, the Old English rune poem associates it with a warrior's horse.

Ehwaz is concerned with movement, making progress, and improvement in all aspects of life. It is particularly helpful in relationships, especially marriage. Reflecting the bond between a horse and rider, this rune is symbolic of trust, loyalty, and mutual support. Ehwaz helps move toward goals and speeds up transitions. Although it is linked with movement, this rune is also an aid when steadfastness is called for.

When selected for divination or guidance, Ehwaz indicates that gradual and steady effort maintains progress. By taking your time, you can manage changes in your business or personal life. Amazonite, clear calcite, lapis lazuli, malachite, and phenacite are especially effective for working with the energy of Ehwaz.

Figure 88: The same symbol is used in the Elder Futhark and Anglo-Saxon runic alphabets.

The runic half month of Ehwaz runs from March 30 to April 13. This period brings in a time for focusing attention on progress, especially when it relates to relationships or general improvements. It also relates to travel and provides protection.

---

131. Ibid.

FEHU

Younger Futhark name: Fe

Anglo-Saxon name: Feoh

The names for this rune come from Old Germanic, meaning "cattle" or "goods," Old Norwegian, "goods" or "wealth," and Old English, "cattle" or "wealth."[132] This is a rune of abundance, wealth, and creating a comfortable life. The Old Norwegian rune poem warns that wealth can be a source of friction, however, according to the Old English poem, prosperity that is freely shared brings honor. The energy of this rune is effective for boosting creativity and achieving success.

When selected for divination or guidance, Fehu advises mindful conservation, even if you are well off. In other words, don't squander resources. It emphasizes the importance of sharing with others and is effective for attracting luck. Moss agate, aventurine, and green tourmaline are effective for working with the energy of this rune.

Figure 89: The same symbol is used for all three runic alphabets.

The runic half month of Fehu runs from June 29 to July 1. Associated with wealth and prosperity, the underlying energy of this period is concerned with the power to attain and hold onto what you have. It is also about having enough control over your life to be independent and self-reliant. Spells for abundance, prosperity, and success at this time can get a boost from Fehu.

---

132. Bandle, *The Nordic Languages*, 626; R. I. Page, *An Introduction to English Runes*, 2nd ed. (Woodbridge, England: The Boydell Press, 2006), 14.

GEBO

Anglo-Saxon name: Gyfu

This symbol is not used in the Younger Futhark.

The names *Gebo* and *Gyfu* come from Old Germanic and Old English, respectively, and mean "gift."[133] As expected, this rune concerns gifts. The act of giving and receiving a gift brings a form of unity between people. It can signify a contract, either written or social. Marking a gift envelope or box with this rune symbolizes unity, and of course, represents the old-fashioned "sealed with a kiss" symbol. Gebo, and the act of giving and receiving, is concerned with balance, especially in relationships. It aids in giving thanks for the gifts—actual or symbolic—that you have received.

When selected for divination or guidance, this rune indicates that a relationship (love or business) is at hand. However, Gebo also instructs you to be yourself; don't be absorbed by the other person. Hold your power of self. Crystals to use when working with this rune include angelite, cat's eye, chrysoberyl, chrysocolla, garnet, and opal.

Figure 90: The same symbol is used for the Elder Futhark and Anglo-Saxon runic alphabets.

The runic half month of Gebo runs from September 28 to October 12. The emphasis during this time is generosity and the gift of hospitality. It is a period of balance, sharing, and building harmony.

---

133. Looijenga, *Texts and Contexts of the Oldest Runic Inscriptions*, 7.

HAGALAZ

Younger Futhark name: Hagall

Anglo-Saxon name: Haegl

The names of this rune come from Old Germanic, Old Norse, and Old English and mean "hail."[134] Although named for something disruptive and potentially dangerous, in essence, Hagalaz is a catalyst. Disruption can occur in any aspect of life; it may be from an outside source or of your own making. Whatever form it takes, it can bring an awakening and a sense of freedom. As the saying goes, "when life gives you lemons, make lemonade." Use disruption to make positive changes in your life or to adjust an outmoded way of thinking. One of this rune's important lessons is to rely on your inner strength.

When selected for divination or guidance, this rune advises that when the proverbial rug is pulled out from under you, take it as an opportunity to learn how to land on your feet and come into your own power. To help work with the energy of this rune, use onyx, tiger's eye, selenite, or sodalite.

Figure 91: Different symbols are used for the Elder Futhark (left), Younger Futhark (middle), and Anglo-Saxon (right) runic alphabets.

The runic half month of Hagalaz runs from October 28 to November 12. This rune brings a period that is potentially chaotic and unsettling. Like the Celtic ogham Ngetal, Hagalaz can bring a time of change that requires the ability to adapt to evolving situations. It can be a time of awakening or reawakening through which you can find freedom and inner harmony.

---

134. Page, *An Introduction to English Runes*, 69.

INGWAZ

Anglo-Saxon name: Ing

Also known as: Inguz

This symbol is not used in the Younger Futhark.

This rune's name comes from the Old Germanic *ingwar,* meaning "fertility god."[135] While the core meaning of this rune relates to fertility and growth, it also extends to the family and harmonizing relationships. Sharing and working together as a household are hallmarks of Ingwaz. Preparation is the key to success. Ingwaz supports the ability to bring plans to fruition. This completion also allows forward movement to a new beginning.

When selected for divination or guidance, this rune advises you to plan with an eye to the future, so you can reap the positive rewards of the seeds you now sow. Amber, calcite, garnet, and jasper are especially effective for working with the energy of Ingwaz.

Figure 92: Different symbols are used for the Elder Futhark (left) and
Anglo-Saxon (right) runic alphabets.

The runic half month of Ingwaz runs from May 14 to 28. The energy of this rune focuses on the family and home, especially protecting the home and property. Although Ingwaz supports individual growth, it also indicates that the love and warmth of family helps bring success. Also associated with male fertility, Ingwaz provides a time for men to evaluate their roles as fathers and caregivers.

---

135. Bandle, *The Nordic Languages,* 636.

ISA

Younger Futhark name: Iss

Anglo-Saxon name: Is

From the Old Germanic, Old Norse, and Old English, the names of this rune mean "ice."[136] Isa may bring challenges that require a period of introspection or withdrawal. Instead of putting plans on hold, use a brief withdrawal to review the past and make plans for the future. Isa aids in storing energy so when you are ready, you can move forward. Trust in yourself and your intuition. When selected for divination or guidance, this rune tells you that a chill wind from the past may be holding you back. Explore what it may be, and then let it go. Because they resemble icicles, long clear quartz or clear calcite crystals are effective for working with the energy of Isa.

Figure 93: The same symbol is used in all three runic alphabets.

The runic half month of Isa runs from November 28 to December 12. Associated with ice, this rune ushers in a time for stillness; however, it does not mean that we become frozen. While this period may present challenges, it also provides an opportunity for clarity. This rune also helps us appreciate the depth and beauty of approaching winter.

---

136. Page, *Runes*, 14.

IWAZ

Anglo-Saxon name: Eoh

Also known as: Eihwaz, Ihwiz

This symbol is not used in the Younger Futhark.

The names *Iwaz* and *Eoh* are Old Germanic and Old English, respectively, for "yew tree."[137] In the Old English rune poem, this rune is referred to as the keeper or guardian of fire. Iwaz's association with the yew also brings a relationship with the legendary longbow, hunting, and defense. It is symbolic of strength, skill, and responsibility. Although the association of the longbow may seem to represent combat or a combative attitude, the power of Iwaz lies in the skilled tactics of averting head-on conflict. Perseverance and foresight are instrumental in overcoming brute force. This is a rune of empowerment that can signal a person's worthiness and reliability.

When selected for divination or guidance, this rune of action counsels you to avoid rushing. Have patience because delay often results in a more easily achieved and beneficial outcome. Angelite, blue lace agate, and blue topaz are especially effective to draw on the power of Iwaz.

Figure 94: The same symbol is used for the Elder Futhark and Anglo-Saxon runic alphabets.

The runic half month of Iwaz runs from December 28 to January 12. It ushers in a period of strength and trust. During this time, we may be called upon to serve as a guardian or defender of others. The energy of Iwaz can be called upon for protection as we fulfill these roles. This is also a time to acknowledge and accept responsibility for how we conduct our lives.

---

137. Page, *Runes and Runic Inscriptions*, 135.

JERA

Anglo-Saxon name: Ger

Also known as: Jara

This symbol is not used in the Younger Futhark.

The Elder Futhark name of this rune comes from Old Germanic and means "year."[138] This rune relates to the year, cycles, and harvests. While it relates to accomplishments and reaping rewards, it also applies to any type of endeavor. Jera is a reminder of the seasons, the importance of living in harmony with the green world, and respecting the natural order. It is also a rune of prosperity that helps cultivate the knowledge required for success. Jera is an effective symbol to use in the garden to honor the seasons and encourage a good harvest.

When selected for divination or guidance, Jera advises you have patience and not expect quick results. Often, things need to run their full course before success can be achieved. Use carnelian, moonstone, or blue topaz to aid in working with the energy of this rune.

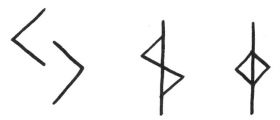

Figure 95: The symbol for Jera has variations in the Elder Futhark (left and middle). The Anglo-Saxon runic alphabet (right) has its own symbol.

The runic half month of Jera runs from December 13 to 27. It brings a period of recognizing cycles—not just seasonal ones but the recurring events in our lives. This is a time to look back at what you have accomplished and to enjoy the rewards your work has brought. Although the cycles of life constantly change, Jera serves as a reminder to pause and appreciate success, prosperity, and peace whenever they occur.

---

138. Bandle, *The Nordic Languages*, 636; Looijenga, *Texts and Contexts of the Oldest Runic Inscriptions*, 7.

KENAZ

Younger Futhark name: Kaun

Anglo-Saxon name: Cen

Also known as: Kano, Ken, Kaunaz

The names for this rune are from the Old German *kenaz* and Old English *cen*, both meaning "torch," and Old Norwegian *kaun*, meaning "boil" or "sore."[139] The earliest name for this rune in the Elder Futhark is unknown.

In the Elder and Anglo-Saxon Futharks, this rune represents illumination, knowledge, and clarity. Part of this is due to the rune name meaning "torch." Quite likely, it is also because of the Old English and Germanic words *cennan* and *kennen*, which mean "to tell" and "to know," respectively.[140] This rune stokes inspiration and supports creativity. It is sometimes related with spiritual enlightenment.

Because of the Norwegian connotation, this rune has been associated with sickness and death. However, taking the Germanic word into consideration, this has evolved to imply the destructive and purifying power of fire.

When selected for divination or guidance, Kenaz indicates the importance of seeking knowledge that will lift away darkness and allow clarity for informed action. Amber, blue tourmaline, bloodstone, jade, and opal are especially effective for working with the energy of this rune.

Figure 96: Different symbols are used for the Elder Futhark (left), Younger Futhark (middle), and Anglo-Saxon (right) runic alphabets.

The runic half month of Kenaz runs from September 13 to 27. This half month focuses on the type of knowledge that illuminates and enlightens. It is a time for finding clarity and for igniting creativity. Let the energy of this rune kindle deep knowledge and spark your imagination.

---

139. Morris, *Runic and Mediterranean Epigraphy*, 141.
140. Angus Stevenson, ed., *Oxford Dictionary of English*, 3rd ed. (New York: Oxford University Press, 2010), 960.

LAGUZ

Younger Futhark name: Logr

Anglo-Saxon name: Lagu

The names for this rune come from the Old Germanic, Old Norwegian, and Old English words for "water."[141] The association with water links Laguz with the emotions and intuition. Representing the ebb and flow of life's challenges, this rune shows that with emotional balance our lives flow more easily. Laguz helps to deal with sensitivities and attune to one's own rhythms. It symbolizes potentials and the development of psychic abilities. Laguz also represents the subconscious or any unseen force that ripples through life. Like a towering ocean wave or very deep water, certain situations may seem frightening, but with a belief in self and with inner strength any storm can be weathered.

When selected for divination or guidance, Laguz advises you to relax and swim with the flow rather than struggle against overwhelming currents. Listen for your intuition to tell you when it's safe to go in the direction you want. Jade, moss agate, pearl, and rose and smoky quartz work well with the energy of this rune.

Figure 97: The same symbol is used in all three runic alphabets.

The runic half month of Laguz runs from April 29 to May 13. The energy of this period centers on creativity, re-aligning energy, and maintaining emotional balance. This is a dynamic time when life seems to flow naturally and magic can be exceptionally powerful.

---

141. Page, *Runes*, 15.

MANNAZ

Younger Futhark names: Madhr, Man

Anglo-Saxon name: Mann

The name of this rune means "man." While it can symbolize all of humankind, it most often relates to the individual or self. It is concerned with social relationships, companionship, and one's place in community. Mannaz is about finding one's true self and being aware of how personal actions can influence others. It also represents an individual's intelligence and creativity. American author and cultural anthropologist Ralph Blum (1932–) suggested that Mannaz could represent a mirrored doubling of Wunjo, the rune of joy.[142] While this mirrored doubling can illustrate the importance of balance, it also indicates that true joy is found within. The Old Norwegian rune poem associated the Younger Futhark Madhr with the claw of the hawk.

When selected for divination or guidance, Mannaz advises you to look at yourself in the proverbial mirror. Do you see and know who you truly are? If not, spend time in meditation on this symbol. It also helps you to hold onto the important things in life. While turquoise is the most effective crystal for working with Mannaz, garnet, loadstone, obsidian, and smoky quartz also work well.

Figure 98: The same symbol is used in the Elder Futhark and Anglo-Saxon runic alphabets (left). The Younger Futhark (right) has its own symbol.

The runic half month of Mannaz runs from April 14 to 28. It offers a period for developing goals and achieving success. Through self-work you can increase knowledge, expand skills, and employ creativity to reach your full potential. In addition to advancing yourself, the message of this rune is to foster the same abilities in others.

---

142. Ralph H. Blum, *The Book of Runes. A Handbook for the Use of an Ancient Oracle: The Viking Runes* (London: Headline Book Publishing, 1993), 88.

NAUDIZ

Younger Futhark name: Naudhr

Anglo-Saxon name: Nyd

Also known as: Nauthiz

In Old Germanic, Old Norse, and Old English, the names of this rune mean "need."[143] Naudiz relates to needs, constraints, and the lessons they teach. It is also associated with obstacles and pain. While this rune symbolizes the proverbial school of hard knocks, its core message is to view setbacks and problems as teachers and guides. When hard work does not seem to pay off, Naudiz beckons for perseverance. It may be important to examine and explore any reason that constraints or obstacles occur or to look for something that is lacking within you or in your life. Spirituality should also be examined.

When selected for divination or guidance, this rune indicates that you may be your own worst enemy. Look for negative aspects, weaknesses, or areas of life that may have stagnated to figure out if you are attracting difficulties. Hematite, lapis lazuli, peridot, and sugilite work well with the energy of this rune.

Figure 99: The same symbol is used in all three runic alphabets.

The runic half month of Naudiz runs from November 13 to 27. This period presents the opportunity to see that assumed obligatory limitations may be self-imposed obstacles. Naudiz helps to review these situations with clarity. It also helps muster the power to make the necessary changes to overcome obstacles.

---

143. Morris, *Runic and Mediterranean Epigraphy*, 142.

OÞILA

Anglo-Saxon name: Ethel

Also known as: Othala, Othila

This symbol is not used in the Younger Futhark.

The names for this rune evolved from the Germanic ōþalan and ōþila and the Old English ēþel and æþel, meaning "property."[144] Oþila is the rune of acquisition and benefits. It is associated with heritage, the home, and ancestral lands. It also relates to the home as a place of retreat—your home is your castle, so to speak. Most importantly, this rune is a reminder that home is a source of prosperity, happiness, and safety. In other words, there's no place like home.

When selected for divination or guidance, Oþila indicates that the home is a place to withdraw from the world, but it also cautions for a judicious use of this to avoid isolation. Calcite, malachite, and spinel are effective for working with the energy of this rune.

Figure 100: The same symbol is used in the Elder Futhark and Anglo-Saxon runic alphabets.

The runic half month of Oþila runs from May 29 to June 13. The prosperity associated with this period is concerned with the rich spiritual and cultural heritage that provides the foundation of who we are. Contemplate how all your inheritances—material, physical, spiritual—have made you uniquely you.

---

144. Spurkland, *Norwegian Runes and Runic Inscriptions*, 47; Looijenga, *Texts and Contexts of the Oldest Runic Inscriptions*, 7.

PERÞ

Anglo-Saxon name: Peorþ

Also known as: Peorth, Perth, Perthro

This symbol is not used in the Younger Futhark.

Rarely occurring in early Continental inscriptions, the names for this rune recorded in later manuscripts include Perþ, Perþu, and Perþō; however, runic scholars have found no meaning in them.[145] In the Old English rune poem, its name varies from Peorþ to Peorth and is associated with a dice cup for gaming.

Without knowing the meaning of its name, this rune in the Elder Futhark has become associated with mystery and secrets. Perþ represents the power of inner transformation, which can seem mysterious. It also relates to making important decisions even if all the facts are not known. This rune's association with a dice cup suggests that it has something to do with luck and probability. While events may seem like random incidents, unforeseen forces may be at work. Perhaps, therein lies the message of this rune.

When selected for divination or guidance, Perþ advises you to have faith in your abilities and the courage to deal with the unknown. In other words, learn to work with the hand life has dealt you and you may be rewarded with an unanticipated gain. Agate, aquamarine, aventurine, and sodalite work well with the energy of this rune.

Figure 101: The same symbol is used in the Elder Futhark and Anglo-Saxon runic alphabets.

The runic half month of Perþ runs from January 13 to 27. This is a period of illumination when information that was previously obscured may come to light. In addition, the energy of this rune is an aid for making choices and solving problems.

---

145. Page, Runes, 7; Spurkland, *Norwegian Runes and Runic Inscriptions*, 11; Looijenga, *Texts and Contexts of the Oldest Runic Inscriptions*, 7.

RAIDO

Younger Futhark name: Reidh

Anglo-Saxon name: Rad

Also known as: Raed, Raidho

The Elder Futhark name, Raido, comes from Old Germanic and means "riding" or "a carriage."[146] The Younger Futhark and Anglo-Saxon names were most likely derived from the Old Norse *reidi*, meaning "equipment," and the Anglo-Saxon *râd* for "riding," respectively.[147] Rad is also the German word for "wheel."

As expected, this rune relates to travel and journeys, however, these can take different forms. In a broad sense, it can represent life's journey or the soul's journey through the afterlife. It can symbolize the journey toward self or union with the Divine. Raido can also represent mundane travel and serve as a charm for a smooth journey. On another level, this rune represents progress and the means for achieving it. Raido also relates to guidance that may be available for special travel or quests.

When selected for divination or guidance, this rune tells you that even if your journey may be a difficult or challenging one, you do not have to rely only on your own power to reach your destination or goal. Use chrysoprase, malachite, or turquoise to work with the energy of Raido. Sapphire with sodalite also works well.

Figure 102: The same symbol is used in all three runic alphabets.

The runic half month of Raido runs from August 29 to September 12. This period fosters and supports movement in all aspects of life. Related to travel, Raido marks a time for reaching personal objectives, which may require some form of travel. Pay attention to communication skills, as they are an integral part of achieving the things you are striving for.

---

146. Page, *Runes*, 15.

147. Page, *An Introduction to English Runes*, 69.

SOWILO

Younger Futhark name: Sol

Anglo-Saxon name: Sigil

Also known as: Sowelu

The Elder and Younger Futhark names come from Old Germanic and Old Norse, meaning "sun."[148] The word *sigil* in Old English refers to a small image that was usually used as a charm.[149] Symbolizing the sun, this rune represents its power and the energy of life. It relates to well-being and wholeness. Symbolizing success, Sowilo represents all the pieces (or aspects) of life coming together. This rune pertains to guidance and self-realization helping to bring your true self forward. Sowilo also relates to healing; both emotional and spiritual.

When selected for divination or guidance, this rune advises that no matter how dark the day or how difficult a situation, there is always hope to guide you. Amber, aventurine, labradorite, ruby, and zircon work well with the energy of this rune.

Figure 103: The same symbol is used in all three runic alphabets.

The runic half month of Sowilo runs from February 12 to 26. This is a period to foster untapped talents, achieve success, and move forward. It is no time for resting on your laurels, especially if you want to reach important goals. With the help of this rune, you can come into wholeness and fulfill your potentials.

---

148. Morris, *Runic and Mediterranean Epigraphy*, 142.

149. Joseph T. Shipley, *Dictionary of Early English* (Lanham, MD: Rowman & Littlefield Publishers, Inc., 2014), 597.

THURISAZ

Younger Futhark name: Thurs

Anglo-Saxon name: Thorn

Although earlier Elder and Younger Futhark names are often said to have been Þurisaz and Þurs, meaning "giant" or "demon" in their respective Germanic and Norse languages, the current forms may have originated in the Old Norse *thurse* meaning "goblin," which in turn may have come from an Old Germanic name that is now lost.[150] The Old English word *þorn*, meaning "thorn," actually began with a unique type of letter called a *diagraph*, and while it looked like the letter *P* it represented the TH sound.[151]

This rune symbolizes defense and changes that often come from disruptive influences. Although disruptions may seem gigantic and come from out of the blue, they are often inner demons. In regard to a thorn, this rune carries a protective quality and the strengthening of willpower.

When selected for divination or guidance, Thurisaz advises to be aware of an inner voice that may instill self-doubt. Such a goblin or ogre can be dispatched with truth and willpower. Citrine, lepidolite, rutilated quartz, and sapphire work well with the energy of this rune.

Figure 104: The same symbol is used in all three runic alphabets.

The runic half month of Thurisaz runs from July 29 to August 12. It is a time for initiating changes and quests. This is a period for developing and strengthening willpower, which is instrumental when making major changes. The energy of Thurisaz also supports spells for protection and defense.

---

150. Ibid.; Bandle, *The Nordic Languages,* 626.

151. Richard Hogg, *An Introduction to Old English,* 2nd ed. (Edinburgh, Scotland: Edinburgh University Press, 2012), 4.

TIWAZ

Younger Futhark name: Tyr

Anglo-Saxon name: Tir

Also known as: Teiwaz

The name *Tiwaz* was derived from the Old Germanic *Tiw*, a supreme sky god whose name survives in the weekday name Tuesday.[152] Odin superseded him. Sometimes associated with divine power, this rune most often represents personal battles. While it is related to victory, achieving it with honor is of paramount importance. Tiwaz bolsters courage, especially when seeking justice. Perhaps because of its arrow shape, the Old English rune poem regarded this rune as a faithful guide pointing the way. In this regard, it also points inward. Tiwaz is a symbol of reliability, dedication, and perseverance.

When selected for divination or guidance, it advises you to look inward for resources, especially if you are involved in any type of conflict. Chances are, you will find strength and abilities you may not realize you have. While bloodstone is the most potent crystal to work with the energy of Tiwaz, jet and tiger's eye are also effective.

Figure 105: The same symbol is used in all three runic alphabets.

The runic half month of Tiwaz runs from February 27 to March 13. It is a period associated with fairness and justice. The message of this rune is that regardless of the type of battle you are called to fight, it must be done with honor and integrity. These battles or challenges may be of a spiritual nature.

---

152. Page, *Runes*, 15.

URUZ

Younger Futhark name: Ur

Anglo-Saxon name: Ur

While the Old Germanic *uruz* and Old English *ur* mean "auroch" and "wild ox," respectively, in Old Norse *ur* meant "slag," and in Icelandic, "drizzle," illustrating how a common root word could acquire various meanings in different languages.[153] The dichotomy can be seen in the stanzas from the Norwegian and Icelandic rune poems—that are concerned with slag from poor iron and rain that destroys hay—and the Anglo-Saxon poem that expressed wonder at a magnificent beast. Early Germanic rune writers would have been familiar with the wild ox because it survived in Eastern Europe until the seventeenth century. Legends about this animal would have travelled with people to the British Isles.

While Uruz symbolizes vitality, strength, and power, it is also considered a rune of passage. It indicates that some sort of trial may be necessary to initiate change; the Norwegian and Icelandic rune poems would seem to indicate challenges.

When selected for divination or guidance, Uruz advises that facing fears can be like confronting a big scary auroch, but only if you let them grow out of proportion. The same goes when faced with unexpected challenges or setbacks; get all the facts and put them into perspective. Garnet, hematite, jasper, lepidolite, and sunstone work well with the energy of Uruz.

Figure 106: The same symbol is used in the Elder and Younger Futharks (left); the Anglo-Saxon runic alphabet (right) has its own symbol.

The runic half month of Uruz runs from July 14 to 28. Symbolizing strength and the vitality of life, this is a period of high energy and action. This rune is also an aid for maintaining well-being and healing. The power of Uruz can be employed to manifest what you seek and to help others.

---

153. Ibid.

WUNJO

Anglo-Saxon name: Wynn

Also known as: Wen, Wyn

This symbol is not used in the Younger Futhark.

From Old German and Old English, the names for this rune means "joy."[154] As the rune of joy, Wunjo is associated with happiness, friendship, inner peace, and well-being. Its shape is often compared to a banner or weathervane. As such, it is an aid for moving in harmony with the prevailing winds of life, which also helps to weather the storms and turmoil that invariably occur. However, as those winds calm, troubles come to an end, and the energy spent dealing with them can be applied to positive change. Wunjo shows that true joy comes from within and is not something that can be bought or given by others.

When selected for divination or guidance, this rune advises you to pay attention to issues and conflicts because they may point you in a new and rewarding direction. Crystals to use when working with the energy of this rune include aventurine, diamond, or iolite.

Figure 107: The same symbol is used in the Elder and Anglo-Saxon runic alphabets.

The runic half month of Wunjo runs from October 13 to 27. This is a period of joy and happiness, success, and prosperity. It is an opportune time to foster friendships and build community cooperation.

---

154. Morris, *Runic and Mediterranean Epigraphy*, 142.

CHAPTER 16

WORKING WITH RUNES UNIQUE TO THE YOUNGER AND ANGLO-SAXON FUTHARKS

INFORMATION ABOUT THESE runic alphabets comes from the rune poems. Written in the late tenth century, the Anglo-Saxon rune poem—also known as the Old English rune poem—contains twenty-nine stanzas. It does not include the regional Northumbrian additions. Concerned with the Younger Futhark, the Norwegian and Icelandic rune poems were written in the thirteenth and fourteenth centuries, respectively.[155] Although the Younger Futhark has fewer characters than the Elder, it has a couple that do not occur in the older rune set.

AC

This rune is unique to the Anglo-Saxon alphabet.

Although the symbol for Ac was derived from Ansuz in the Elder Futhark, its meaning is unrelated. The name of this rune was derived from the German *eiche*, meaning "oak."[156] Associated with the oak, it carries many of the attributes such as strength, power, stability, and endurance. Like the acorn, it serves as a metaphor for future potential.

The Anglo-Saxon rune poem also associated the oak with providing nourishment and timber for ships. Because of this, Ac indicates that basic needs will be met and that a time

---

155. Looijenga, *Texts and Contexts of the Oldest Runic Inscriptions*, 6.
156. Page, *An Introduction to English Runes*, 44.

of plenty may be on the horizon. Also associated with long-term growth, this rune advises about the wisdom of long-term plans rather than jumping for immediate gains.

Figure 108: The runic symbol of Ac is unique to the Anglo-Saxon alphabet.

When selected for divination or guidance, this rune tells you to look within because the seeds of what you need lie in your heart. This is especially true when you need strength to weather the storms of life like a seaworthy ship.

AESC

This rune is unique to the Anglo-Saxon alphabet.

Associated with the ash tree, Aesc uses the same symbol as Ansuz in the Elder Futhark. It has some of Ansuz's characteristics, such as acting as a conduit for sacred wisdom as well as stoking creativity. Like the ash tree, this rune serves as a shield against attack. It can also be an anchor, bringing order and stability.

Figure 109: The runic symbol of Aesc is unique to the Anglo-Saxon alphabet.

When selected for divination or guidance, the message of Aesc is to stand your ground in the name of fairness and against those who would injure others unable to defend themselves. It advises that compassion is an important tool for the warrior.

AR

This symbol is unique to the Younger Futhark.

The meanings and associations of this rune are akin to Jera, which does not appear in the Younger Futhark. Ar represents nature's cycles, good harvests, and times of plenty. By extension, it also represents generosity and sharing of one's bounty and is a symbol of achievement.

Figure 110: The runic symbol of Ar in the Younger Futhark has variations.

When selected for divination or guidance, this rune indicates the importance of planning ahead, especially if you want to live up to your potentials and enjoy abundance. Its association with the harvest serves as a metaphor for reaping what you sow.

CALC

This rune is one of the Northumbrian additions to the Anglo-Saxon alphabet.

Although it is usually said to represent an offering cup or chalice, runic scholars note that Calc also means "chalk." It is easy to see how the words for chalk and chalice could be confused. The Old English words *cealc* and *calc* were derived from the Latin *calx* (chalk) and *calic* and *cælc* from the Latin *calix* (chalice).[157]

Since an explanation of this rune does not survive in the Old English rune poem, I am offering a new interpretation. While ancient Britons used chalky mud as plaster for interior walls in some of their buildings, they also created spectacular chalk figures on hillsides. Two of the most famous, the White Horse of Uffington and the Cerne Abbas Giant, can be seen for miles. As a result, I believe the rune Calc could relate to important

---

157. Robert K. Barnhart, ed., *The Barnhart Concise Dictionary of Etymology* (New York: HarperCollins, 1995), 115.

or sacred messages. Because some versions of the Anglo-Saxon runes show Calc and gar to be similar, Calc could also relate to warning messages.

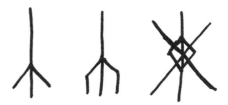

Figure 111: The Northumbrian runic symbol of Calc has variations.

When selected for divination or guidance, this rune advises careful study of messages—even if they may seem obscure at first—because they may hold important information.

CWEORÞ

Also known as: Cweorth, Cweord

This rune is one of the Northumbrian additions to the Anglo-Saxon alphabet.

Although this symbol was included in runic manuscripts, no meaning of its name was offered and epigraphical use of it has not been found. Several runic scholars have suggested that its intended use may have been to rhyme with the rune Peorþ. While Cweorþ has become associated with fire in popular literature, no explanation for this has been offered. A suggestion has also been made to eliminate Cweorþ from use, which would allow for a more uniform grouping of runes. I'm not comfortable with this, because the symbol exists; we just don't know what it was intended to represent. I am comfortable with accepting Cweorþ as an enigma; after all, there are things in this world that we don't understand or cannot explain.

Figure 112: The runic symbol of Cweorþ may have been intended as a rhyme word.

When selected for divination or guidance, this rune indicates the importance of working to develop a body of knowledge or master a skill. Cweorþ may also be telling you to accept something you cannot change, make alternate plans, and move on with your life.

EAR

Also known as: Eor

This rune is unique to the Anglo-Saxon alphabet.

Runic scholars have suggested that the use of the word *ear* in the rune poem comes from the Old Norse *aurr*, meaning "wet clay, loam, or mud."[158] The stanza in the poem is concerned with death; earth (clay, loam, mud) becomes a bed for final sleep and everything comes to an end. However, just as at Samhain we acknowledge death as a natural part of the cycle, we also acknowledge it being followed by rebirth.

Figure 113: The Anglo-Saxon runic symbol of Ear has variations.

When selected for divination or guidance, this rune indicates the need to let go of something or someone in your life to make room for something new. Although difficult, the change will be rewarding.

GAR

This rune is one of the Northumbrian additions to the Anglo-Saxon alphabet.

Gar was not included in any rune poem and so interpretation of it is based on the Old English word meaning "spear." As such, Gar is usually equated with the spear of Odin. It is tempting to stop there; however, the word had a couple other meanings. Gar also meant "sharp," and is one of the root words for garlic: *gar,* "sharp" and *lēc,* "leek," sharp leek.[159] Another meaning was "storm."[160]

Before his shamanic endeavor, Odin performed an initiatory cutting by piercing himself with his spear. The spear is also symbolic of sharpness of mind or the opening of oneself to receive wisdom. And, of course, when we have a brainstorm we are struck by inspiration.

---

158. Page, *Runes and Runic Inscriptions,* 72.

159. Laurel J. Brinton, ed., *English Historical Linguistics: Approaches and Perspectives* (New York: Cambridge University Press, 2017), 23.

160. George Watson, ed., *The New Cambridge Bibliography of English Literature: 600–1600,* vol. 1 (New York: Cambridge University Press, 1974), 1821.

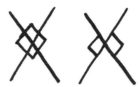

Figure 114: The Northumbrian runic symbol of Gar has variations.

When selected for divination or guidance, this rune indicates the need to take time for introspection and to be open for inspiration. It can also mean that you may gain from a new perspective.

IOR

Also known as: Iar

Although the symbol for Ior is the same as Hagall in the Younger Futhark, it has a different connotation. The name of this rune is not found in the Old English language. As a result, it is often regarded as a riddle. Although the verse in the Anglo-Saxon rune poem refers to an eel or river fish that takes its food on land, the creature has been interpreted as a range of aquatic/land animals, from a beaver to a newt and a sea serpent. Of course, the animal could be a metaphor for walking between the worlds or a symbol of how something can have a dual nature. Overall, the rune verse is about a creature that is happy and comfortable with its surroundings.

Figure 115: The symbol of Ior is the same as Hagall in the Younger Futhark,
but it has a different connotation.

When selected for divination or guidance, this rune indicates that the key to happiness often lies in the ability to be adaptable to circumstances and surroundings.

STAN

This rune is one of the Northumbrian additions to the Anglo-Saxon alphabet.

Like Cweorþ, this symbol was included in runic manuscripts but does not occur in the rune poem and no epigraphical use of it has been found. The name of this rune is believed to have come from the Old English *stān*, meaning "stone."[161] It has been interpreted to represent an altar stone or standing stone as well as stability.

Figure 116: The runic symbol of Stan is a Northumbrian addition.

When selected for divination or guidance, this rune indicates the importance of building a strong foundation for life and for keeping grounded. It may also indicate a need to be steadfast in a situation.

YR

The Younger and Anglo-Saxon alphabets use the same name for this rune.

In the Younger Futhark, Yr is associated with the yew tree and endings; in Anglo-Saxon it is associated with battle gear. Although it is sometimes considered to be a battle-axe, runic scholars note that the Anglo-Saxon rune poem refers to more elegant gear and identify it as a bow. This is befitting because the English bow was usually made of yew wood. In the Icelandic rune poem, this character was noted as the bent bow. In addition, Yr is sometimes referred to as the rune of the archer. Representing a bow, it is natural to associate this rune with protection and defense; however, there is more to it. To be an archer required a great deal of practice, which indicates that this rune may be more deeply associated with craft and skill.

Figure 117: The Younger Futhark (two on the left) and
Anglo-Saxon (three on the right) rune sets have variations.

When selected for divination or guidance, Yr indicates the importance of taking time to focus on and develop abilities.

---

161. Hogg, *An Introduction to Old English*, 28.

PART SIX
SIGILS

Sometimes shied away from because they may seem complicated or associated with ceremonial magic, sigils have become a popular form of magic. The word *sigil* comes from the Latin *sigillum*, meaning "a seal or signet" and "a symbol or device of power."[162] In Old English, the word *sigil* referred to a small image that was usually used as a charm.[163] Unlike most symbols, however, sigils are a BYO (bring your own) system in which you create your own unique symbols.

While sigil magic is often regarded as fairly new, this section traces its roots to magic squares and their evolution with astrology. During ancient times, a magic square was the device of power; however, from the Middle Ages through the Renaissance, a magic square became the means to create a device of power—a sigil. The following chapters explore methods for creating sigils: the old (medieval) method using magic squares and the new (early twentieth century) method using words. In addition to providing details on how to make and use sigils, this section also introduces several new methods for creating them that are a mix of old and new.

---

162. Editors, *Webster's Third New Dictionary*, vol. 3, 2,115.
163. Shipley, *Dictionary of Early English*, 597.

CHAPTER 17

SIGILS FROM MAGIC SQUARES

A MAGIC SQUARE CONSISTS of a grid of numbers that, when added horizontally, vertically, or diagonally, produces the same total. The grid can be 3 x 3 squares, 4 x 4, 5 x 5 or larger. Grids with numbers that only total the same when added horizontally and vertically (not diagonally) were regarded as semi-magic. The most famous magic square is a 3 x 3 grid known as the Lo Shu grid. According to Chinese legend, Emperor Yu (2200–2101 BCE) noticed a remarkable pattern on the shell of a tortoise that he spotted along the banks of the Luo River. After extensive analysis, Chinese scholars believed that the markings on the tortoise provided a perfect 3 x 3 magic square.

4	9	2
3	5	7
8	1	6

Figure 118: The legendary Lo Shu grid found on the shell of a tortoise.

The Lo Shu grid was first mentioned in the writings of Taoist philosopher Zhuang Zhou (369–286 BCE). Also called the *Nine Halls* and the *Nine Palaces Diagram*, the grid was used to represent various concepts and served as an emblem of harmony. Used in astrology and divination, it eventually became a fundamental part of feng shui. A turtle with this magic square also appeared in Tibetan cosmology. In medieval European astrology, the Lo Shu served as the magic square for the planet Saturn.

Revered in China, magic squares were believed to provide access to higher knowledge. They were employed in divination, Taoist magic, and used as talismans. Information about magic squares reached India sometime between the second and fifth centuries CE where they were incorporated into medical practices to help cure illness. They were also worn as amulets to ward off negative energy.

The ancient Romans used magic squares with letters instead of numbers as protective amulets. These usually consisted of five words that contained five letters. The Sator square is the most famous and is a super palindrome with words that can be read right to left, left to right, and vertically up and down.

S	A	T	O	R
A	R	E	P	O
T	E	N	E	T
O	P	E	R	A
R	O	T	A	S

Figure 119: The Sator square is a super palindrome.

Found on wall graffiti, amulets, and potsherds throughout the Roman empire, the Sator square has been most commonly translated as: "The sower Arepo holds fast the wheel." [164] However, Serbian-American professor of philosophy Miroslav Marcovich (1919–2001), regarded the name Arepo as a Greco-Roman aspect of Horus or a shortened form of Harpocrates, the Greek god of silence, secrets, and good luck. He translated the Sator square as "The sower Arepo keeps [protects from] toils and torments." [165] Marcovich believed the message to be a call to a god for luck in being spared from hard work and discomfort. Some of the uses for the Sator square discerned by archeologists include healing and recovering lost items.

Arab traders are credited with transporting the concept of magic squares from China and India to the Middle East, where they were incorporated into astrology and other prac-

---

164. Barbara I. Gusick and Edelgard E. DuBruck, eds., *Fifteenth-Century Studies*, vol. 32 (Rochester, NY: Camden House, 2007), 200.

165. Miroslav Marcovich, *Studies in Graeco-Roman Religions and Gnosticism*, vol. 4 (Leiden, The Netherlands: E. J. Brill, 1989), 34.

tices. As information and knowledge flowed back into Europe after the Dark Ages, mathematicians, scholars, astrologers, and occultists discovered magic squares. Although the magic square would remain a device of power, it was around this time that the magic square also became the means to create a device of power in the form of a sigil.

FROM SQUARE TO SIGIL

By the Middle Ages, magic squares were appearing in the writings of well-known people working in astrology, alchemy, and magic, including Pietro d'Abano, Cornelius Agrippa, Frances Barrett, Paracelsus, and Johannes Trithemius. Magic squares were also cropping up in the work of Italian mathematician and astrologer Girolamo Cardano (1501–1576), German artist Albrecht Durer (1471–1528), Byzantine teacher and grammarian Manuel Moschopulus (c. late thirteenth/early fourteenth century), and Dutch Jesuit missionary and astronomer Ferdinand Verbiest (1623–1688).

Because of the enthusiasm for astrology, magic squares for the seven planets were especially popular and reflected a mélange of cultures and wisdom. Although associating magic squares with the planets came from eleventh-century Arabic texts, the most frequently used grid sizes and numbers relating to the planets were based on the Hebrew Kabbalah. However, variations in the magic squares occurred because of different Kabbalistic interpretations.

Also called *planetary tables*, these magic squares were used widely for talismanic magic. Alchemists and ceremonial magicians used them to create three types of sigils: a planet's seal and two lesser sigils for entities referred to as a planet's spirit and intelligence. The names of the two entities were used to create their respective sigils, which were then used in rituals to summon them. Although various methods were used to create the planetary seals, most of the techniques remain unknown. For more details, refer to Appendix V in Agrippa's *Three Books of Occult Philosophy,* edited and annotated by occult scholar and author Donald Tyson (1954–).[166]

The lesser sigils were created in a straightforward manner by converting the entity's name to numbers. Every letter in the Hebrew alphabet has a number equivalent that runs from 1 to 10 and then jumps by 10s (20, 30, 40, etc.) to 100, and then it jumps again by 100s. Several letters that have more than one sound also have more than one number. For example, the letter named *Pe* has the sound P, which has the number equivalent of 80, and

---

166. Agrippa, *Three Books of Occult Philosophy,* 733.

the sound PH, 800. On the other hand, the letter *Shin* has S and SH sounds but only one number equivalent of 300.

After converting an entity's name to numbers, it was plotted on the magic square in a connect-the-dots fashion. For example, the name of the spirit for the planet Jupiter is Hismael, spelled *HSMAL* in Hebrew. The number equivalents work out to $H=5$, $S=60$, $M=40$, $A=1$, $L=30$. For numbers above 10, additional zeros are dropped. In figure 120, the table of Jupiter is shown with the sigil of the planet's spirit. Beginning and ending circles are placed in the squares for H and L, respectively. Occasionally, a short line that crossed the sigil replaced the end circle.

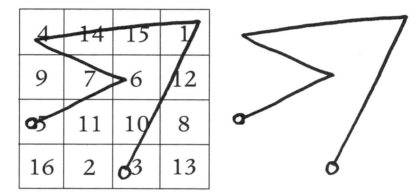

Figure 120: The magic square of Jupiter with the sigil of its spirit Hismael.

In addition to alchemists and magicians, others such as English physicians Richard Napier (1559–1634) and Simon Forman (1552–1611) used the planetary sigils in their practices. Not only were planets believed to influence people's affairs, they were also thought to have an effect on the physical body. While Napier employed them as talismans for treating different medical conditions, Forman used them for a range of purposes including warding off ghosts. Medieval astrologers crafted and sold pendants with symbols and planetary sigils to attract luck, ward off evil, or to provide other influences. Although this practice was widespread, it was controversial and regarded as black magic by the Church.

Not all medieval and Renaissance sigils were related to the planetary tables. Swiss physician and alchemist Paracelsus wrote explicit instructions on how and when to create magical pendants for physical ailments. Along with astrological symbols and letters of the alphabet, the inscriptions included sigils that he provided. Paracelsus did not mention the source of the sigils or explain the methods he may have used to construct them. (For more about Paracelsus see Part Seven.) Although the origin of sigils for the fifteen fixed stars is most likely Arabic, the method for crafting them is unknown.

Although the use of magic squares for creating sigils did not go far beyond planetary tables, it is a method that can be easily adapted for modern use. We will come back to them after learning about the word method, which is popularly used today.

CHAPTER 18
SIGILS FROM WORDS

FOUNDED IN THE LATE nineteenth century, the Hermetic Order of the Golden Dawn included the Enochian system of magic in its curriculum. While the system's use of large, complex squares appealed to some, it was too esoteric for many. In the early twentieth century, English artist Austin Osman Spare (1886–1956) began working on a method for creating sigils that became an easy-to-learn form of magic.

Spare trained as an artist and enjoyed early success. He worked as an editor for several art magazines and wrote books on art and magic. His developing ideas on magic were reflected in his artwork with unearthly beings, arcane suggestions of Egyptian mythology, and overt sexuality. Spare's art caught the attention of Aleister Crowley (1875–1947), an English writer and occultist who famously called himself *Beast666*. Although Crowley's devoted group of followers was small, after his death he became a cult figure. For a time, Spare was a member of Crowley's mystical order, but he did not like the structured approach to magic. He left the group and developed his own system of magic that he called *Zos Kia Cultus*, which was the forerunner of chaos magic.

Spare was intrigued by medieval grimoires, especially the magical symbols associated with spirits. Rather than summoning entities, however, Spare sought to develop a way to customize sigils for personal use. The cornerstone of his sigil method was included in his work entitled *The Book of Pleasure (Self-Love): The Psychology of Ecstasy*, which he self-published in 1913.[167] The book was a treatise on his various occult practices, which incorporated the emerging theories of psychology. Despite his early success as an artist,

---

167. Shirley Dent and Jason Whittaker, *Radical Blake: Influence and Afterlife from 1827* (New York: Palgrave Macmillan, 2002), 162.

Spare sank into obscurity painting portraits in pubs for beer money and eventually dying in poverty.

Even though Kenneth Grant (1924–2011), an assistant to Aleister Crowley, recorded Spare's sigil magic techniques and helped him publish more of his work, Spare's ideas on sigil magic did not catch on. It wasn't until the early 1990s that Spare's work gained wide attention through the book *Practical Sigil Magick* by Belgian magician and occult author Frater U∴D∴, born as Ralph Tegtmeier (1952–). Since then, Spare's word method for crafting sigils has taken off.

CREATING A SIGIL

In a nutshell, the word method is to write a sentence about your purpose (Spare called it a statement of desire), delete any duplicate letters, and then use the remaining ones to form a design—the sigil. After that, charge the sigil with energy, implant it in your mind, destroy the physical sigil, and then push it from your mind. Taking one step at a time, we will see how Spare's methods and today's sigil craft vary.

It is important to keep your attention focused and put your intention into words. Make sure to allow plenty of time when you won't be interrupted. You may want to start by grounding and centering your energy as you think about your reason for creating a sigil. Although not necessary, if you usually cast a circle for anything related to magic work, cast one when creating sigils.

With your purpose in mind, clearly state what you want in one sentence. If you're not sure how to start, use Spare's suggestion of "I wish" for a straightforward beginning. More recent schools of thought suggest using a sentence beginning with "I will," or simply making a statement such as "My life is filled with love." Alternatively, keywords or phrases can be used instead of a full sentence or statement. Whichever way you choose to work, remember the KISS principle: Keep It Simple, Silly. While it is important to be specific, too much detail can bog things down.

Use positive words and phrases and avoid words such as *not* or *don't*, as these are ineffective for directing energy. Say what you want, not what you don't want. For an example, we'll use the sentence, "I will pass my next math test." The next step is the reduction process where all duplicate letters are removed. The result for our example is *IWLPAS-MYNEXTH*. That leaves a lot to work with and can be a challenge, especially when first learning to craft sigils.

Deleting the vowels except for the leading letter I can reduce the sentence further, which produces: *IWLPSMNXTH*. In this case, the letter *Y* was used as a vowel and can be eliminated. I kept the leading letter *I* because it emphasizes the important personal connection and driving force of the purpose. However, this is an individual preference and you should follow what your intuition tells you

The *W* and *M* in the example are interchangeable when turned upside down so both letters do not need to be represented in the sigil. As you begin to think about how to put the sigil together, look for common lines that can be used to anchor multiple letters. For example, the straight lines in the letters *I*, *L*, *T*, and *P* can be used to combine letters. Also keep in mind that letters can be drawn backward or rotated in any direction. Work on fusing a few letters into small groups. For example, use the letters *N*, *M*, and *H* as one group, and *I*, *L*, *T*, *P*, and *S* as another. As you try various arrangements, the sigil may suddenly start to emerge. Don't be concerned about artistic talent. Magic is about intent and willpower, not artistic ability. On the other hand, if you have the skill, be as creative as you want.

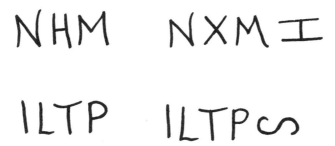

Figure 121: Group letters together, and then combine them into one design.

Once you have combined all the letters, consider placing a border around the sigil to contain the image. Sometimes, this can help focus the mind. As always, follow your intuition. A couple of little flourishes can be added as a decorative touch. However, remember to keep it simple and avoid a cluttered look, as that can become a distraction. When you are finished creating your sigil, spend a few minutes gazing at it; get to know it. This unique little design is full of meaning that only you understand.

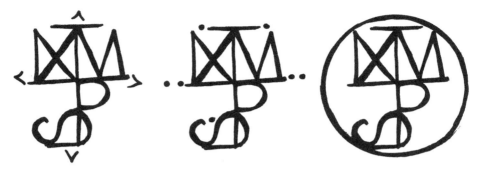

Figure 122: Little flourishes can be added to a sigil or it can be enclosed with a border.

ACTIVATING A SIGIL

Activating or charging a sigil is the process of focusing the intent for your purpose and sending your energy into the sigil. Just as with a spell or ritual, energy can be raised through various methods. According to Frater U.·.D.·., Spare's preference was through orgasm. Keep in mind, it is important to follow a method that is effective for you and one that you are comfortable with because sigils are very personal works of magic. Also, Spare was rather focused on his sexual life.

Like raising energy during ritual, any kind of movement, dancing, chanting, and drumming are effective processes. Place the sigil on your altar or wherever you will be able to see it while engaging in these activities. When you feel that your energy has reached a peak, pick up the sigil, gaze at it, and visualize your energy going into it.

If you prefer a subtler approach to magic, use meditation. Sit in front of your altar and breathe deeply and slowly as you study the sigil. Let your gaze soften, close your eyes, and bring the image into your mind's eye. Repeat this several times until your mental image of the sigil is clear. To aid the process, use your sentence, phrase, or keyword like a mantra. Slowly repeat it until the sigil is clear in your mind.

An especially powerful method for charging a sigil is to raise energy through your chakras. Come to a straight but comfortable stance in front of your altar and rub your hands together to activate the energy of your palm chakras. When your palms feel warm, place your left hand on your stomach and your right over your heart. The left hand is over the solar plexus chakra, which is the center of courage and power. This will activate the energy of this chakra and move it up to the heart chakra, which is being activated with the right hand. The heart chakra is the center of love and compassion. When channeled together, these chakras produce a flow of powerful energy. With your hands in these positions, visualize the energy of both chakras growing and merging. When the energy feels like it is expanding beyond your body, pick up the sigil and gaze at it, fixing the image in your mind. Think of your purpose for it, and then visualize your energy moving from your heart center, down your arms, and into the sigil to pattern it with your willpower.

Whichever method you use to charge the sigil, gazing at it and visualizing its purpose will implant the image in your subconscious mind, which responds more readily to pictures than words. By translating words into images, our conscious and subconscious, inner and outer worlds are united in a single purpose.

TO DESTROY OR NOT?

There is disagreement these days about the necessity to destroy a sigil to make it work. Spare noted that because it is intended for one-time use, a sigil is fleeting in nature. He stressed the importance of removing a sigil from the conscious mind. Destroying its physical form and not thinking about it was key in making this happen. According to Frater U∴ D∴, Spare believed that working with sigils was a way to direct the subconscious using a form of reverse psychology and Freud's theory of repression.[168]

On the one hand, we can think of a sigil like a sand mandala; even after it is swished away, the intent and energy behind it goes on to fulfill its purpose. However, like other magical objects a sigil can serve as a reminder to bring our minds back to a purpose and in doing so it repeatedly adds energy to it. Like many aspects of magic, whether a sigil should be destroyed is a personal choice. If you choose to destroy a sigil, burning it is the usual method because it is quick and uses the transformative power of fire.

Although the word method for creating sigils has become well-known, it is not the only one Spare developed. As an artist, it is fitting that his other method is based solely on imagery.

---

168. Frater U∴ D∴, *Money Magic: Mastering Prosperity in its True Element* (Woodbury, MN: Llewellyn Publications, 2011), 103.

CHAPTER 19

SPARE'S PICTORIAL METHOD

BECAUSE SYMBOLS WORK WITH the inner psyche, Spare developed a way to craft sigils without using words. This method does not require a statement of purpose; instead, images are used to express an intention. That said, it does not mean that a few letters, such as a person's initials, or short words can't be used in a sigil.

A pictorial sigil can include other symbols if they have meaning for you. If you often use astrological or elemental symbols, oghams, or runes, these can add dimension to the idea you want to express. For example, when seeking love and romance combine the symbol of Venus with a rose. For extra measure, draw it in pink or red. Alternatively, use the symbols of Venus and Mars, which also represent male and female, and a heart shape. Of course, this can be adapted to two Venus or two Mars symbols depending on your sexual orientation.

Figure 123: Astrological symbols and the initials SG
are used in a sigil to attract love.

For prosperity, craft a sigil using a dollar sign or other symbol that represents abundance, along with the outline of a house or your house number. To send healing energy to someone, incorporate that person's initials. If you are seeking peace of mind, consider creating a sigil with the elemental symbol of air, which is associated with the mind, and the outline of a lotus flower. Follow your intuition and let your creativity flow. If it feels appropriate, stylize it to make it personal, but like the word method, keep it simple. Follow the same procedure as with the word method to charge the sigil and decide whether you want to destroy it.

Figure 124: The rune Feoh is used with a dollar sign
and house number to attract prosperity.

COMBINING SPARE'S METHODS

Once you work with Spare's pictorial method, you may find that combining it with the word method can provide greater flexibility and specificity. As in the word method, a full sentence, simple statement, phrase, or keyword can be used to express your intention. As an example, we'll use the phrase "Isis, protect me" and combine it with the ankh, which is a symbol of Isis and protection. The phrase reduces to *SPRTCM*. A couple of variations would be to let the ankh represent Isis, drop her name, and use the letters *PRTCM*. Or, since the ankh represents Isis and protection, simply use the letter *M*. Another alternative would be to use the letters *I* and *S* for her name. In addition, enclosing the sigil with a border suggests an Egyptian cartouche.

Figure 125: Experiment with variations for
combining words and pictures in a sigil.

INCORPORATING MAGICAL SYMBOLS

The magical symbols that you already use for rituals, spells, or other purposes can
enhance the power of a sigil. Some of the symbols, such as the pentagram or triple moon,
can serve as borders to enclose a sigil. The following table lists eight frequently used magical symbols and their meanings.

TABLE 6.1 POPULAR SYMBOLS TO INCORPORATE INTO SIGILS	
	Pentagram The most important symbol for modern Pagans and Wiccans, the pentagram represents the four elements plus spirit. It is a symbol of power and blessings that is also used for protection and banishing.
	**Triple Moon** As our nearest celestial neighbor, the moon has caught people's attention since the beginning of time. Showing the waxing, full, and waning aspects of the moon, the symbol represents the magical stages of inspiration, manifestation, and receiving. It represents the Great Mother Goddess and women's power. It is the feminine principle of spirituality and life.

TABLE 6.1 POPULAR SYMBOLS TO INCORPORATE INTO SIGILS

	**Horned God** Just as the triple moon represents the goddess, this symbol represents the god, especially horned gods such as Cernunnos. It represents the hunter/provider and the wildness of nature. In addition to showing the full moon, the crescent holds the magical energy of the waxing and waning phases. This symbol represents men's power and the male principle of spirituality and life.
	Triskele A symbol of movement and energy, the triskele carries the magical power of three. It represents the three-fold cycle of life, death, and rebirth; the goddess as maiden, mother, crone; and the god as youth, father, sage. Its energy provides vision for the past, present, and future. This symbol represents the physical world and the three permanent elements: air (sky), earth (land), and water (sea).
	**Brigid's Cross** At Imbolc, Brigid's cross symbolically stimulates the energy of life to begin a new cycle. This symbol can be used to honor Brigid or to call on her for help. A venerated goddess of healing and fertility, she also presides over the power of crossroads and sacred waters. Use this symbol to call on her for guidance, inspiration, and knowledge.
	**Faery Star** This symbol is also known as the elven star, witch's star, and astrologer's star. Associated with the sacred number seven, it represents the cardinal directions, center, above, and below. The points of the star represent honor, truth, justice, service, faith, hope, and love. This symbol is instrumental in working with the faery realm.
	Spiral The spiral represents a continuum that stretches from our most ancient ancestors, to the present, and on into the future. It is one of the most common motifs in a wide range of cultures from around the world and throughout time. Representing the cosmos and cyclic time, it is a dynamic symbol of primary life-force energy, balance, and wisdom.

TABLE 6.1 POPULAR SYMBOLS TO INCORPORATE INTO SIGILS

	**Hammer of Thor** Associated with thunder, lightning, and storms, Thor is also a god of the household and fertility. Thor used his prized possession, the hammer, to protect the home of the gods in Asgard. Wearing it as an amulet is a call for his protection. Found on several rune stones, this symbol is thought to have had an early function for consecration too.

Magical symbols can be drawn small to fit within the letters used in a sigil, or they can serve as the structure for it. For example, when requesting help from Brigid you may start with the phrase "Brigid's Blessings." Instead of the usual method of reduction, the cross can be used in place of her name since it is her symbol. You can choose whether to remove vowels or duplicate letters. In the sample (Figure 126), the complete word *BLESS* was used.

Figure 126: Brigid's cross in a sigil calling on her blessings.

CHAPTER 20

NEW METHODS
AND FURTHER USES

EVEN THOUGH MAGIC SQUARES have been around for thousands of years, they continue to fascinate us mathematically and mystically. This has prompted me to develop a few new methods for creating sigils from magic squares. Once created, activate the sigil before using it and, as previously mentioned, whether to destroy a sigil or not is your decision.

BACK TO LO SHU

Regarded as a mathematical harmonic, the Lo Shu grid has eight permutations that all add up to the sum 15. When combined with gematria, the Lo Shu magic square can be used to create sigils. Gematria—the art of assigning numbers to letters—was used in ancient times in the belief that a lost word of great power could be revealed. The Babylonians in eighth century BCE and medieval Kabbalists used Gematria.[169] In numerology, each letter of the alphabet is assigned a number from 1 to 9, which works well with this magic square.

---

169. John McLeish, *Number: The History of Numbers and How They Shape Our Lives* (New York: Fawcett Columbine, 1992), 51.

1	2	3	4	5	6	7	8	9
A	B	C	D	E	F	G	H	I
J	K	L	M	N	O	P	Q	R
S	T	U	V	W	X	Y	Z	

Figure 127: To use the Lo Shu grid, letters are converted to numbers.

In this method, use a keyword or short phrase to express your purpose, and then convert it to its numerical equivalent. For example, if you are seeking a new home and use "new home" as your phrase, the numbers work out to 5558645. Delete consecutive duplicates and the result is 58645. Another example for a little magical help selling your home, use the phrase "sell home." The number equivalents for this phrase are 15338645 or 1538645 when consecutive duplicates are removed. Place a circle in the box for the beginning and ending numbers, and then draw a line to each number in consecutive order.

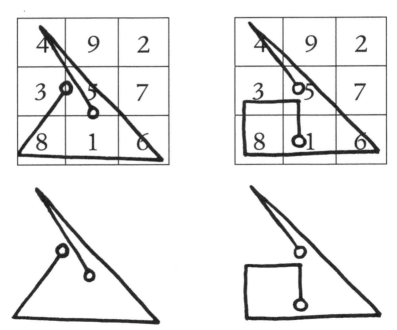

Figure 128: Sigils created with the Lo Shu grid using the phrases
"new home" (left) and "sell home" (right).

THE ALPHABET MAGIC SQUARE

This method skips numbers altogether and uses the alphabet in a 5 x 5 grid. Obviously the 26 letters of the English alphabet do not fit the grid, so the letters *U* and *W* share a square. Using the same example of finding a new home, the letters reduce to *N, W, H, M*. As in the previous example, use beginning and ending circles, and then draw a line to each letter in consecutive order.

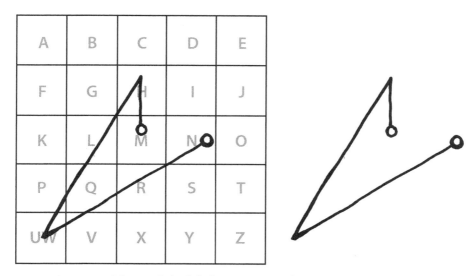

Figure 129: The English alphabet square can be used for creating sigils.

In regard to the letters *U* and *W* sharing a square, there are a couple of options. The letter *U* can have its own square and *V* and *W* can be doubled up. Or, the letter *W* can have its own square and *U* and *V* can share one.

Since the planetary table for Mars is a 5 x 5 grid, it can also be used for creating sigils. To make it easier to use, translate the Mars table into letters by assigning the numbers 1 to 25 to them according to their position in the alphabet. For example, *A* is 1, *B* is 2, and so forth. Again, *U* and *W* share a square and, in this case, they share the number 21. This planetary table is also appropriate because Mars is associated with action, which can add extra energy to a sigil.

11	24	7	20	3
4	12	25	8	16
17	5	13	21	9
10	18	1	14	22
23	6	19	2	15

K	Y	G	T	C
D	L	Z	H	P
Q	E	M	U/W	I
J	R	A	N	V
X	F	S	B	O

Figure 130: The Mars planetary table can be adapted for using the alphabet

Although the alphabet magic square and the Mars planetary table both use letters instead of numbers, the resulting sigils are different. Following is an example that uses the phrase "healthy child" for a healing spell. After reduction, it works out to *HLTCD*.

As previously mentioned, deleting the vowels is part of the reduction process to simplify and streamline a sigil. However, for short phrases or names or anytime you feel it would enhance your sigil, vowels can be kept.

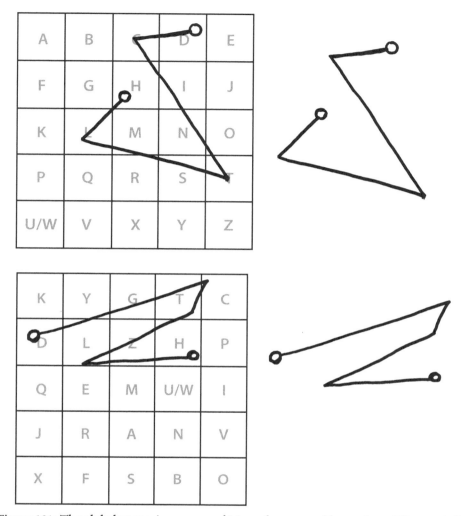

Figure 131: The alphabet magic square and Mars planetary table produce different sigils.

FROM SQUARE TO CIRCLE AND KEYBOARD

Just as the Golden Dawn used a stylized rose with Hebrew letters to create sigils, so too can a circle of the English alphabet be used. The circle is one of humankind's oldest and most elemental symbols. When we gather in a circle, we create a very special and powerful space:

a space where energies become focused and strengthened. When we use the circle for magic, we put the power of this symbol into our endeavors.

To use it for creating sigils, simply draw a circle, and then write the letters of the alphabet around the perimeter. For an example, we will use banishing negative energy as a purpose and the phrase "clear away negativity," which reduces to the letters *CLRWYNGTV*. Beginning and ending circles are placed by the *C* and *V*, and then connected with a line according to the order of letters.

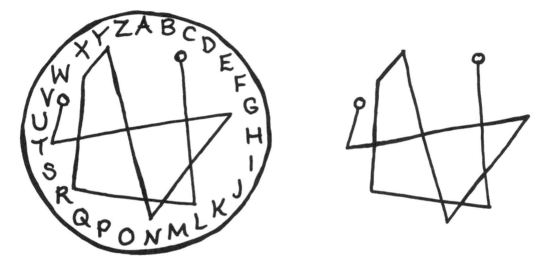

Figure 132: Sigils can be created with a circle instead of a magic square.

For a novel approach to sigil creation that is especially apropos for the twenty-first century, arrange the alphabet in the "qwerty" layout of a keyboard. It could be effective, especially if you are hoping for a piece of technology for your birthday or the holidays. For that purpose, be sure to include the words *please* or *I wish* to avoid making it sound like a demand. For an example, we'll use the phrase "I wish for a phone this birthday." This reduces to *IWSHFRPNTBDY*.

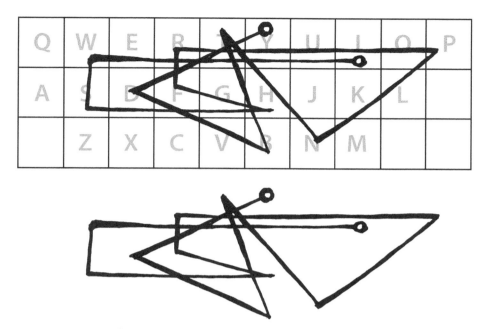

Figure 133: The qwerty keyboard layout can be used to create sigils.

Experiment with the various methods for creating sigils to find which ones work best for you. Sometimes, you may find that trying different approaches will produce one that resonates more deeply with you. Figure 133 is a sigil sampler illustrating the various sigils that can be produced using the five new methods. The sentence used for the example is "I wish to protect this house and all within," which reduces to the letters *IWSHTPRCNDL*. As previously noted, keeping the initial letter *I* is a personal choice.

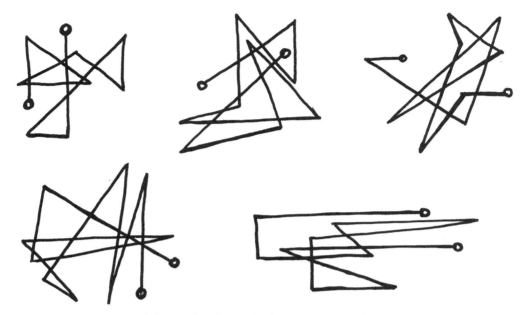

Figure 134: From left to right, the methods used to create the sigils: Lo Shu grid, alphabet square, Mars planetary square (top row), circle, and keyboard (bottom row).

I used several methods to create new sigils for the fifteen fixed stars in Part Four. Most of them were crafted using the alphabet magic square. Because their medieval counterparts are very linear, I used the qwerty keyboard layout to create sigils for Ala Corvi, Spica, and Vega. For the Regulus sigil, I used the circle. Because these sigils are for names and are much shorter than a phrase or sentence, I used the vowels and, in some cases, I kept duplicate letters.

OTHER WAYS TO USE SIGILS

As previously mentioned, the decision to destroy a sigil is a personal one, which may vary according to your purpose. However, rather than one-time use, you may want to create sigils for repeated use in rituals or for other occasions.

A sigil can be used like any other symbol to create a talisman and draw energy into an object. Create a sigil for business or employment purposes to stimulate opportunities and achieve success. Draw it on a piece of paper and keep it where you work on finances to aid in building wealth. A sigil can be used for spells or rituals or placed around the home to enhance the energy and hold your intention. Paint a sigil on something in your garden to attract abundance. Create a binding sigil for use in a handfasting ritual or make one to mark other special rites of passage.

A sigil can be used to foster traits or strengthen certain characteristics. Create a personal power sigil to use as an insignia. Make a pendant with it to wear or have a jeweler engrave it on a crystal. Use your personal sigil like a signet to sign a piece of artwork or anything else you create. You may even consider turning it into a tattoo. In addition, a sigil insignia can be created for a coven or any close-knit group. Like other objects used in magic, a multi-use sigil becomes more powerful over time. Let your intuition guide you in developing personal ways to incorporate the use of sigils into your life.

Sigils for Deities

Create a sigil using the name of a god or goddess and carve it into a candle when you call on him or her for help. In addition to the symbols of Brigid and Thor in Table 6.1, other deities have simple emblems that can be incorporated into sigils. For example, use a trident for Poseidon or Neptune, a thunderbolt for Zeus, or the moon for Artemis or Diana.

Design sigils for the deities you call on during ritual to keep on your altar. If a sigil becomes a piece of ritual gear, draw it on a piece of good parchment paper or inscribe it in clay or wood. Consecrate it with the smoke of sage, lavender, or mugwort. Because constructing a sigil for a god or goddess creates a special bond with that deity, always treat it with respect and special care.

If you work with deities associated with the sea, paint the sigil on a seashell or an object with an ocean theme. For forest deities, carve your sigil into a piece of wood or draw it on the picture of a tree associated with that deity such as an oak for the Dagda or Jupiter, an ash for Odin, or a sycamore for Hathor. When seeking protective energy, create a sigil with the name of a god or goddess and include an ogham, rune, or the word *protect*. Hang the sigil in your home somewhere out of sight or draw it on the underside of a doormat.

Sigils and Crystals

Since ancient times in China, India, and the Middle East, crystals have been associated with celestial bodies. Roman naturalist and author Gaius Plinius Secundus, known more widely as Pliny the Elder (23–79 CE), wrote about gems and all things associated with them. Although he referred to symbols associated with gems as *sigilla*, the descriptions he provided are standard intaglio images rather than abstract sigils.

During the Middle Ages in Europe, astrologers also associated gemstones with the planets and constellations. Becoming all the rage, lapidaries—books about minerals— included information on their magical properties and astrological associations. One of the most famous, *Speculum lapidum* (*Mirror of Stones*) by Italian physician and astrologer Camilli Leonardi (c. 1455–1532), was published in 1502.[170] Along with their magical properties, he described the astrological and magical symbols to carve on them. Despite the Church railing against astrology and magic, gemstone rings with astrological symbols and planetary sigils were popular and openly worn.

Even though we are not limited to planetary sigils and can craft them for whatever purpose we want, we can still give them a powerful energy boost by combining them with crystals. If the crystal is large enough, the sigil can be inscribed on it with a felt tip pen. If you are working with an expensive gemstone or the shape of a crystal is not conducive for drawing on it, use a fabric marker to draw your sigil on a small pouch to hold the crystal. As an alternative, use a small piece of paper to wrap around the crystal. Create a sigil to represent a wish or goal, and then coordinate it with the properties of a crystal. Use the crystal as you normally would in a spell, to keep with you, or place somewhere in your home.

As an example for a healing sigil, we'll start with the sentence "Please heal my broken toe," which reduces to PLSHMBRKNT. Any method for creating the sigil can be used; however, crafting it with a magic square, circle, or qwerty layout will most likely result in a simple design that is easier to paint on a crystal than one created with the word method. When it is finished, charge the sigil crystal, and then meditate with it either by gazing at it or placing it against the area of the body that needs healing; in this example, a broken toe. Afterward, wear or carry the sigil crystal until the healing is complete.

As an alternative, lay crystals associated with healing on your altar in the pattern of the sigil. After charging it, hold your hands above the crystals as you visualize healing energy surrounding you, and then center it on the part of your body that needs healing.

---

170. Lynn Thorndike, *A History of Magic and Experimental Science* (New York: Columbia University Press, 1958), 229.

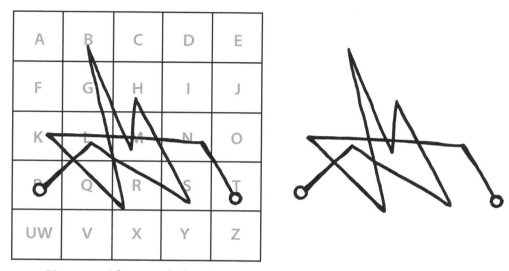

Figure 135: The example for a healing sigil was crafted with the alphabet square.

Like any type of crystal grid, laying out stones in the shape of a sigil creates a power-house of energy. Whether your purpose is a specific goal or a call for guidance, follow the same procedures for creating and charging your sigil. After working with a sigil crystal layout, leave it in place for as long as it seems appropriate. Afterward, be sure to cleanse the crystals.

As with other aspects of magic, experiment to see what works best for you.

PART SEVEN

THE WITCHES' ALPHABET AND OTHER MAGICAL SCRIPTS

As we have seen in previous chapters, magic and astrology were practiced regardless of the Church's stance, which was often to look the other way when it suited. Nevertheless, popular views waxed and waned and could be manipulated, as with the witch hysteria. This prompted a need for secrecy. To keep work safe, practitioners used symbols and magical alphabets in their grimoires. Alphabets that were ascribed to earlier traditions were given a great deal of credence and used for talismans and magical circles. Agrippa regarded them as an aid to revealing the great mysteries.

Magical alphabets not only help to maintain secrecy should a grimoire be stolen but add power to spells and other information contained in a grimoire. Another equally important reason for using a magical alphabet is that it helps to focus attention. Because it is not for everyday use, writing in a different alphabet requires more time and effort, which in turn helps raise energy that can be directed into a magical intent.

CHAPTER 21

THE WITCHES' ALPHABET

SINCE MAGIC, ASTROLOGY, AND alchemy went hand in hand during the Middle Ages and Renaissance, we find some of the same people using and writing about magical alphabets. Although use of the witches' alphabet has waxed and waned over the centuries, it is one that Pagans and Wiccans recognize and use today.

The witches' alphabet has also been known as the Theban alphabet, the Honorian script, and the runes of Honorius. The last name is misleading because there is no link between the Theban alphabet and the runes. While the alphabet's origin remains a mystery, trying to trace its roots takes us on a round-robin trail that seems to intentionally obscure its creator.

The alphabet first came to light in the work of Johannes Trithemius, the astrologer and magic-practicing abbot mentioned in Part One of this book. Born as Johann Heidenberg, he took the name *Trithemius* from his birthplace of Trittenheim, Germany. He became known as a scholar throughout Europe and initially denounced the practices of witches and magicians. His attitude seems to have changed when he began to study ancient texts and developed an interest in magical practices.

According to legend, Trithemius gained notoriety in a Faustian manner in the presence of Holy Roman Emperor Maximilian I (1459–1519) by raising the spirit of the emperor's dead wife. In addition to dabbling in necromancy, Trithemius formulated magical theories and searched for a way to unite magic and Christian theology. Two of his favorite pursuits were steganography— hiding a secret message within a regular form of communication—and deciphering codes.

Although Trithemius wrote numerous manuscripts, he often held them back from publication. Written in 1508, his work entitled *Polygraphia*, which is a set of six books, was published posthumously in 1518.[171] Regarded as the first book on cryptology, the Latin title relates to encipherment and comes from the Greek *polygraphos*, meaning "much writing."[172] Contained in the final book of *Polygraphia* is the earliest known publication of the witches' alphabet. Trithemius noted it as an alphabet from the Theban Honorius that was discovered by Petries de Apono (Pietro d'Abano).

Calling it the Theban alphabet, Trithemius's student Agrippa included it in his work. Referring to d'Abano as Apponus, Agrippa noted that the script originally came from Honorius of Thebes. Agrippa seemed to believe that the Theban script dated to a very early time because d'Abano was known to have translated ancient manuscripts, including the work of Greek physician Galen. During the Middle Ages and Renaissance, works of ancient origin had an appealing mystical quality. Agrippa also noted that magical alphabets were "delivered by Cabalists."[173]

As mentioned in Part One, the Paduan physician Pietro d'Abano had gained magical notoriety and was tried twice by the Inquisition. Prior to his fall from grace in the eyes of the Church, he was in high demand for teaching and medical consultations. One of his most well-known patients was Pope Honorius IV, Giacomo Savelli (1210–1287).

The association between d'Abano and the pope has led to claims that Honorius IV was his source for the Theban alphabet. However, Honorius's granduncle, Pope Honorius III, Cencio Savelli (1150–1227), has also been a contender. Honorius III's connection to the alphabet comes from a manuscript that circulated in Paris called *Grimoire du Pape Honorius*. A copy of it dating to 1670 from the Bavarian State Library is available online through Google Books.[174] However, that edition of the grimoire does not contain the Theban alphabet. In addition, earlier copies of the grimoire dating to the thirteenth century are not associated with Honorius III or any other pope.

Because "the older the better" was a theme for sources of magical information, attention shifted to someone who seemed more mystical than a pope. A fourteenth-century

---

171. J. M. van der Laan, Andrew Weeks, *The Faustian Century: German Literature and Culture in the Age of Luther and Faustus* (Rochester, NY: Camden House, 2013), 101.

172. Editorial Staff, *Webster's Third New International Dictionary*, vol. 2, 1758.

173. Agrippa, *Three Books of Occult Philosophy*, 560.

174. *Grimoire du Pape Honorius*, (Rome, 1670), https://books.google.com/books?id=4cY5AAAAcAAJ.

manuscript called *The Sworn Book of Honorius* was reputedly a copy of a much earlier text written by Honorius of Thebes. The earliest-known copy of this manuscript is believed to date to the early thirteenth century. References to it were made in numerous books throughout the Middle Ages and Renaissance. One reference to it was by Trithemius and another by John Dee (1527–1608/09), English astrologer and advisor to Queen Elizabeth I (1533–1603).

Although Honorius of Thebes was reputed to be the son of Greek mathematician Euclid (c. 300 BCE), who lived in Alexandria, Egypt, this is generally dismissed as fiction to give the book more credence. Scholars who have studied *The Sworn Book of Honorius* have noted that the assemblage of magicians mentioned in the prologue were all from the Continent—Spain, Italy, and Greece—and have theorized that instead of Egypt, the eponymous Honorius was from Thebes, Greece. Known as Thiva today, the ancient city was central to many Greek myths, and during medieval times it was an important cultural crossroads. At one time, Thebes, Greece, was equally as exotic as Thebes, Egypt.

The Harry Potteresque account of a gathering of grand wizards is also regarded as an attempt to give the book more glamour. As the story goes, the purpose of the meeting was to pool magical knowledge and record it in three copies for safekeeping. According to the legend, the Theban Honorius was the scribe who took down the information.

The only surviving remnant of *The Sworn Book of Honorius* that includes the Theban alphabet is part of the Sloane 3854 manuscript. The Sloane collection of manuscripts in the British Library is a miscellany of texts—many about magic—that date from the fourteenth to sixteenth centuries. The collection is named for its second owner Sir Hans Sloane (1660–1753), a British physician and naturalist. The curious thing about the document in the Sloane collection is that it notes the Theban alphabet as having come from Agrippa.

REVIVAL AND NEW LIFE FOR THE ALPHABET

Although magical practices did not completely disappear, they remained low-key. The Theban alphabet seemed to have been unused until Francis Barrett (1774–1818) published *The Magus or the Celestial Intelligencer*, which dealt with elemental and ceremonial magic, herbs, crystals, and celestial scripts. Barrett billed himself as a student of chemistry, metaphysics, and natural and occult philosophy. With a keen interest in mysticism and magic, he translated the Kabbalah and other texts into English and gave private instruction in occult subjects. *The Magus* served as an advertisement for his magic school.

Published in 1801, Barrett's book didn't catch on until decades later when there was a surge of interest in the mystical arts.[175] In particular, archaeological finds in Egypt helped fuel an interest in magic. A cache of magical books found near the city of Thebes was eagerly bought and translated into English. Along with the Jewish Kabbalah, Egyptian hieroglyphs piqued interest in symbols and alphabets. By the mid-Victorian period, even ordinary, "respectable" people were dabbling and studying magic. Societies were formed to learn about it and practice. When Barrett's book was reprinted, it became a major influence for magical societies, including the Hermetic Order of the Golden Dawn.

English author and amateur archaeologist Gerald Gardner (1884–1964) is regarded as the father of modern Witchcraft and Wicca. With a keen interest in the Old Religion, he wanted people to know its history and keep it from dying out. Delving into Agrippa's work, he found the Theban alphabet and re-introduced it to the world. This time, it caught on.

THE WITCHES' ALPHABET IN THE TWENTY-FIRST CENTURY

Since Gardner brought the alphabet into the light of day, its popularity has ebbed and flowed, but it hasn't sunk into obscurity again. In fact, it seems to be gaining popularity. It can be the perfect tool for enhancing spells, writing magical names, and inscribing candles. Because it is not an alphabet for everyday use, working with it helps focus attention. This is effective for directing energy when making talismans and magical tools or when creating magic circles. Magical alphabets are available as downloadable fonts that can be fun to use for some things; however, computer-generated text defeats the purpose of enhancing focus and energy for magic.

When the alphabet was published in *Polygraphia*, Trithemius provided the equivalent Latin letters; however, there were no symbols for the letters *J*, *V*, and *W*. One theory for this is that the Theban alphabet was based on Hebrew, which uses one symbol for the letters *I* and *J* and one for *U*, *V*, and *W*. While the Kabbalah was used by avid magic practitioners of the time, it may have been a little too esoteric for wider use.

It seems more likely that a learned person devised the Theban alphabet in early medieval times. Because Latin was the language of the clergy, scholars, and magicians, it would

---

175. Alison Butler, *Victorian Occultism and the Making of Modern Magic: Invoking Tradition* (New York: Palgrave Macmillan, 2011), 101.

have been the alphabet on which to base another one. Not only were the letters *J*, *V*, or *W* not in Latin but early Latin didn't have *Y* and *Z* either, until around the first millennium.[176] They were finally added to accommodate the sounds in Greek words that were being adopted into Latin.

As for the letter *J*, classical Latin used a hard G and had no need for a soft G sound. It wasn't until the influence of medieval French that the soft G, or letter *J*, came into use.[177] The letter *J* began to appear in English writing in the 1600s.[178]

In modern versions of the Theban alphabet, the same character is used for the letters *I* and *J* and another for *U* and *V*. Doubling the *U* accommodates the letter *W*. In other versions of the alphabet, a dot was added to the *J* and *V* to distinguish them from the *I* and *U*, respectively.

The Theban alphabet has a curious letter at the end that has been used in two ways. It is often called a *full stop/period* symbol and was used as such. This dates to Agrippa's version where he showed the equivalent character as the Greek letter *Omega*. Omega came to be understood as marking the end of something, even by non-Greek speakers, because of the passage in the Book of Revelations in the Bible: "I am the alpha and omega, I am the beginning and the ending."[179]

In the *Polygraphia*, Trithemius shows an ampersand (&) as the equivalent to the final Theban character. While this may seem odd, the ampersand—a ligature of the letters *E* and *T* for the Latin word *et* meaning "and"—appeared after the letter *Z*, along with several other ligatures in a textbook written in 1011 by English Benedictine monk and scholar Byrhtferth (c. 970–1020).[180] Over the centuries, the other ligatures were dropped but the ampersand remained the final letter in the English alphabet until the mid-1800s.[181]

176. Norma Goldman and Jacob E. Nyenhuis, *Latin Via Ovid: A First Course*, 2nd ed. (Detroit: Wayne State University Press, 1982), xix.

177. David Sacks, *Letter Perfect: The A-to-Z History of Our Alphabet* (Toronto, Canada: Vintage-Canada, 2004), 137.

178. Ibid.

179. Ibid., 77.

180. Stanley B. Greenfield and Daniel G. Calder, *A New Critical History of Old English Literature* (New York: New York University Press, 1986), 119.

181. Stephen Webb, *Clash of Symbols: A Ride Through the Riches of Glyphs* (New York: Springer Publishing, 2018), 9.

Figure 136: The Theban alphabet is also called the Witches' alphabet.

Since Theban is a magical alphabet, set aside time to practice writing with it. You can choose whether to use the final character as an ampersand, stop/end, or not at all. Gaze at the characters for a few minutes, and then focus on the letter *A*. Study its shape until you can see it in your mind's eye, and then practice writing it. Don't worry about getting it perfect; in fact, as you work with the alphabet you may develop your own way of writing the letters.

THREE OTHER
MAGICAL ALPHABETS

IN ADDITION TO THEBAN, other magical alphabets were recorded in medieval texts with claims of mystical or divine origins. Some of these alphabets show a mix of influences, especially Hebrew. The deep mysteries of the Hebrew alphabet are integral to the Kabbalah (also spelled Kabalah, Cabala, Qabala), an esoteric philosophy and mystical interpretation of the Hebrew Bible and Rabbinic literature that includes the use of magic. Those who dabbled in magic and alchemy would have had some exposure to Kabbalistic literature, which reached a high point in Europe between the thirteenth and sixteenth centuries.

Characters in the three alphabets covered in this chapter have the squarish appearance of Hebrew letters and similar letter names. A feature of these alphabets not found in Hebrew is the placement of circles at the ends of some lines. Because of this peculiarity, these alphabets have been referred to as eye-writing and eyeglass symbols because the circles are thought to resemble eyes or monocles. All three alphabets have been referred to as angelic alphabets.

While the angelic alphabet from the *Sefer Raziel*, "Book of the Angel Razial," contains eyeglass characters and resembles the alphabets discussed here, there is no information about the letter names or what their sound assignments were. According to legend, the alphabet was used in a book given by the angel Razial to Adam when he left the Garden of Eden. The *Sefer Raziel* is believed to have been written during the thirteenth century.

Despite an ongoing debate about angels and Paganism, I thought it was important to include these alphabets. While some people believe that angels are Christian entities and have no place in Wiccan or Pagan practice, others claim that angels pre-date Christianity and Judaism. Because of my personal experiences, I believe angels are a type of spiritual being that bring messages, provide guidance, and protect us when in need. They act regardless of a person's religious orientation.

THE MALACHIM ALPHABET

Two sources have been given for the name of this alphabet: an order of angels—the Malachim—and the Book of Malachi in the Bible. The Book of Malachi, also known as the Prophecy of Malachias, is grouped with books of the Minor Prophets at the end of the Old Testament. The word *malachi* is Hebrew for "my messenger" or "my angel."[182] According to the Kabbalah, the Malachim rank sixth among the ten orders of angels.

Believed to be a secret alphabet of the Malachim, it was also said to have been a gift from these angels. Another story about the origin of this alphabet is that the laws given to Moses on Mount Sinai were written in it. From less lofty heights, some sources indicate that Agrippa created the alphabet.

Nineteenth-century occultist Samuel Liddell MacGregor Mathers (1854–1918) gave the alphabet an ancient but different origin. Mathers, who added *MacGregor* to his name to portray himself as Scottish, was one of the founders of the Hermetic Order of the Golden Dawn and a brilliant, eccentric scholar. He translated a number of occult texts including *The Key of Solomon*, which was the most famous grimoire in Europe for ritual magic. In his translation, Mathers mentioned that the alphabet was used to write the names of god and angels for conjuring and that Solomon had called it "the tongue of angels."[183]

John Johnson (1777–1848), an English printer and author on the history and art of printing also researched and wrote about ancient alphabets. In his 1824 book *Typographia*, Johnson illustrated several alphabets attributed to King Solomon that resemble the eye-writing alphabets, but do not match any of them.[184]

At any rate, because people were enchanted with antiquity, especially wisdom found in old texts, placing the alphabet's provenance with King Solomon (c. 1010–931 BCE) was as good as it gets. Renowned as a great sage, Solomon united the tribes of Israel and built the first temple of Jerusalem. He was of great interest to those pursuing the secrets of magic in the Middle Ages.

---

182. James D. Newsome, *The Hebrew Prophets* (Louisville, KY: Westminster John Knox Press, 1984), 189.

183. S. L. MacGregor Mathers, *The Key of Solomon the King* (Mineola, NY: Dover Publications, Inc., 2009), 38.

184. John Johnson, *Typographia, Or, The Printers' Instructor: Including a Series of Ancient and Modern Alphabets*, vol. 2 (London: Longman, Hurst, Rees, Orme, Brown & Green, 1824), 297.

The Wisdom of Solomon, a collection of sayings attributed to him, is part of the Apocrypha, a section of the Bible between the Old and New Testaments that does not fit the criteria for official canon. Other writing attributed to him includes a third-century text, *The Testament of Solomon*, which involves astrology, magic, angels, and demons. It tells the story about Solomon's ring and how it gave him power over the demons that plagued the building of the temple. Associating the alphabet with ancient magic and the famous biblical king gave the alphabet more mystique and glamour.

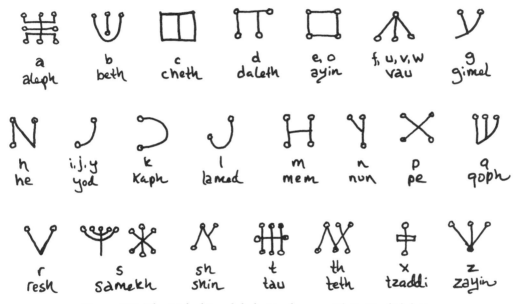

Figure 137: The Malachim alphabet is shown with its English letter
and sound equivalents and character names.

Whether or not the Malachim alphabet was delivered or used by angels, King Solomon, or simply created by Agrippa, it seems to have always had an association with prophecy and messages. If you choose to work with the Malachim, use it in conjunction with divination. Inscribe candles or mark tools with it. For dreamwork, write a few keywords on a piece of paper to slip under your pillow or keep on your bedside table. Let your imagination guide you for other ways to use this alphabet.

THE CELESTIAL ALPHABET

Similar in design to the Malachim, the Celestial alphabet is also referred to as the angelic alphabet. The Celestial alphabet gets its name from the belief that the stars formed the letters as they moved across the sky, forming messages and delivering prophecies. Other sources note that like the imagery associated with the constellations, the shape of the celestial letters could be seen by drawing imaginary lines between certain stars. English physician, astrologer, and Kabbalist Robert Fludd (1574–1637) likened the celestial letters to geomantic symbols, holding hidden knowledge discernible by those initiated into the ancient mysteries.

According to Francis Barrett in his work *The Magus*, the Celestial alphabet was devised by God or the angels to send messages to people who had been given the knowledge to understand them. Although Barrett presented the letters in a different order from Agrippa's, the character symbols were the same. Other sources indicate that this alphabet was used for secret teachings handed down from Adam to Seth, which became the basis for the Kabbalah.

American physician Albert Mackey (1807–1881), who wrote extensively about Freemasonry, also studied languages, symbolism, and the Kabbalah. He noted that while the alphabet does not have the exact appearance of Hebrew writing, it carries the power invested in the Hebrew alphabet. Mackey mentioned that medieval astrologers and alchemists used the Celestial alphabet. He also noted that through the centuries, Agrippa, Johnson, and others were instrumental in making the alphabet widely available.

In writing about the Celestial alphabet, Johnson noted that the earliest alphabets were symbols taken from objects in nature. He went on to say that the Chaldeans used the stars to form their alphabet and that it became known as the Celestial alphabet. Other references to a Chaldean Celestial alphabet indicate that it was intertwined with Hebrew. In fact, a book published in 1799 gives the Celestial alphabet the title of *Chaldean 1*. See the section on the Alphabet of the Magi for more on this.

As mentioned in Part One, the term *Chaldean* became synonymous with *Babylonian*, however, it was also a general term used by some ancient writers in reference to scholars and priests renowned for their knowledge of astronomy and astrology. After the Babylonian conquest of Judah in the sixth century BCE, the Hebrews were held in captivity until the Persians conquered Babylon. With no stretch of the imagination, it is possible to conclude that some of the Chaldean mages were Hebrew. An intermingling of ideas could have taken place, resulting in a mélange of Chaldean/Babylonian astrology and Hebrew Kabbalah. The planets and Hebrew alphabet are an integral part of the Kabbalah.

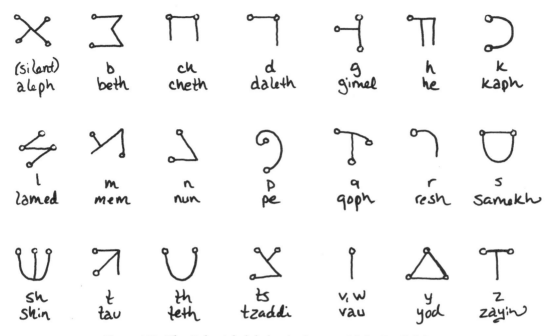

Figure 138: The Celestial alphabet is shown with its English letter
and sound equivalents and character names.

Regardless of its origin, if the Celestial alphabet captures your attention, incorporate it into your magical practices. Because of its association with the stars, you may find that it enhances astrology work. If you are doing readings for other people, write a person's name with the alphabet to place on the table with your other tools. When doing your own readings, use the alphabet to write a keyword or question that relates to the purpose of your reading.

CROSSING THE RIVER ALPHABET

This alphabet is known by other names including Passing the River, Passing Through the River, Passing of the River, Beyond the River, and *Transfluvial* and *Trans Fluvii* from the Latin *Fluvii Transitus*. While it has been noted as a talismanic script of King Solomon, alphabets attributed to him only have a slight resemblance with circles terminating the lines of some letters.

Like its name, the river referred to has several candidates. The four rivers of the Garden of Eden are sometimes mentioned; however, one is never singled out as *the* river, so that doesn't seem to make sense. There is a consensus that the river relates to the Babylonian exile of the Hebrews, making the Euphrates and Jordan Rivers prime contenders. However, noting that Kabbalistic Rabbis used the alphabet, Elena Petrovna Blavatsky (1831–1891) believed the river referred to the Chebar Canal.[185] Blavatsky was a Russian émigré author, philosopher, and co-founder of the Theosophical Society. She brought the alphabet into vogue in the late nineteenth century.

Blavatsky doesn't give her reason for selecting the Chebar, but it is an interesting choice. Sometimes referred to as the Chebar River, the waterway is a tributary of the Euphrates with a network of irrigation canals near the city Nippur, which is now located in present-day Iraq. The River Chebar is mentioned in the Book of Ezekiel in the Bible as an area where the Judean exiles stayed and the place where God appeared to Ezekiel, making it a sacred site. However, Nippur was the Sumerian city sacred to their supreme god Enlil. Even though names and religions may change, certain sites remain sacred.

While Crossing the River is often attributed to Agrippa, there are other contenders for creating or discovering and publishing this alphabet. Giovanni Agostino Panteo (d. 1535), an Italian priest interested in combining alchemy with the Kabbalah, couched his work in Christian terms to stay under the radar of the Inquisition. Crossing the River appeared in the second printing of his book *Ars et Theoria Transmutationis Metalicae* (*Art and Theory of the Transmutation of Metals*), published in 1530.[186] Panteo referred to it as the Beyond the River alphabet and associated it with Abraham, patriarch of the Jewish people.

Italian calligrapher Giovambattista (Giovanni Battista) Palatino (c. 1515–1575) was fascinated with alphabets, ciphers, and typefaces. The Palatino font was named in his honor. In 1550, he published a handbook of calligraphy and sample alphabets of Greek, Hebrew, Arabic, and others.[187] Crossing the River appears as *Alphabetum Hebraicum ante Esdram* (*Hebrew Alphabet before Ezra*). Ezra was a Hebrew priest and scribe who had been in exile in Babylon.

German Jesuit scholar Athanasius Kircher (1602–1680) studied linguistics and claimed to possess the secret for decoding Egyptian hieroglyphics. He included Crossing the River

---

185. H. P. Blavatsky, *The Theosophical Glossary* (New York: The Theosophical Publishing Society, 1892), 250.

186. Nadia Vidro, Irene E. Zwiep, and Judith Olszowy-Schlanger, *A Universal Art: Hebrew Grammar across Disciplines and Faiths* (Boston: Brill, 2014), 217.

187. Ibid., 216.

in his book *Turris Babel* (*Tower of Babel*), which was published in 1679.[188] In it, he noted that Abraham de Balmes was the first scholar who made the alphabet known. Abraham ben Meir de Balmes (c. 1440–1523) was a Jewish physician, grammarian, philosopher, and translator who was dedicated to Judaic scholarship. The alphabet was included in his treatise on the Hebrew language published in Venice in 1523.[189]

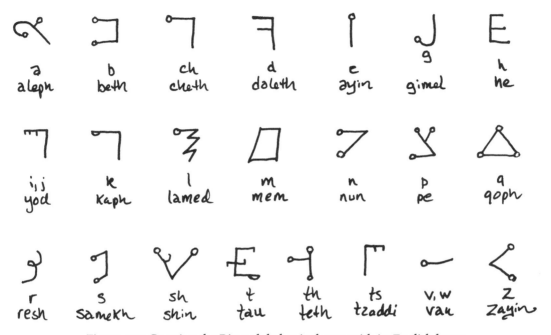

Figure 139: Crossing the River alphabet is shown with its English letter
and sound equivalents and character names.

Crossing the River can be used like any other magical alphabet; however, because of its association with rivers it is especially effective for spells involving water. Also use this alphabet on ritual objects that represent the element water.

188. Ibid., 231.

189. Israel Zinberg, *A History of Jewish Literature: Italian Jewry in the Renaissance Era*, trans. and ed. Bernard Martin (New York: KTAV Publishing House, Inc., 1974), 46.

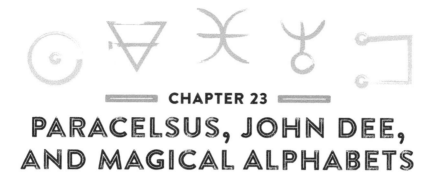

CHAPTER 23

PARACELSUS, JOHN DEE, AND MAGICAL ALPHABETS

IN THIS CHAPTER, WE WILL look at two other magical alphabets. Unlike Malachim, Celestial, and Crossing the River, these bear no relation to the Hebrew alphabet. The alphabet of the Magi and the Enochian alphabet are uniquely associated with well-known people. Although Paracelsus and John Dee are known for their interest in magic, astrology, and alchemy, their wider knowledge and contributions are often overlooked.

THE ALPHABET OF THE MAGI

Sometimes referred to as the alphabet of wizards, the alphabet of the Magi has been attributed to Paracelsus. Like other magical alphabets, its history is circuitous. Mentioned in Part Two of this book for his treatise on elementals, Swiss physician and alchemist Theophrastus Bombastus von Hohenheim called himself Paracelsus. He created his identity from the name of a highly acclaimed first-century Roman physician, Celsus, and then added the prefix so his name would mean "beyond Celsus."[190]

Paracelsus was influential in the development of chemistry as a science and is regarded as the founder of modern toxicology and the homoeopathic system of medicine. He was also influential in promoting the use of minerals for healing purposes. With astrology as an integral part of his medical practice, he is said to have used the alphabet of the Magi to inscribe the names of angels on talismans to aid in curing his patients.

---

190. Thomas F. X. Noble, et. al, *Western Civilization. Beyond Boundaries Volume I: to 1715*, 7th ed. (Boston: Wadsworth Cengage Learning, 2018), 488.

Paracelsus lived up to the connotation of his middle name and was exceedingly bombastic. Believing that he was more learned than classical physicians such as Galen, he astonished his colleagues at the University of Basel by throwing the most important medical books into a midsummer's eve bonfire. Although it is tempting to believe that the word *bombastic* related to Paracelsus, it was derived from the old term *bombast*, a stuffing for upholstery, which was extended to mean pompous and overblown.[191]

The curious thing about Paracelsus and the alphabet of the Magi is that according to some sources it does not appear in any of his writings. Not having access to all of his work, I am not able to confirm this. However, the 1656 edition of Paracelsus's book *Of the Supreme Mysteries of Nature,* translated by English writer Robert Turner (fl. 1654–1665), includes illustrations of his talismans with writing that could be mistaken for the alphabet of the Magi. Or they could be badly drawn examples of it.

The alphabet appears in the work of others. French linguist and philologist Claude Duret (c. 1570–1611) was an avid collector of old texts and alphabets. His book on the history and origin of languages entitled *Thresor de l'histoire des langues de cest univers* (*Treasure: the History of the Languages of this Universe*), was published posthumously in 1613.[192] In it, Duret refers to the alphabet of the Magi as the characters of the angel Raphael and cites Theseus Ambrosius (1469–1540) as his source.

Theseus Ambrosius is the Latinized name of Teseo Ambrogio Albonesi, who was also a linguist and taught Semitic languages at the University of Bologna. In his 1539 book *Introductio in chaldaicam linguam* (*Introduction to Chaldaean Languages*), Ambrosius presented a number of ancient alphabets including the alphabet of the Magi. Like Duret, he noted that it came from the angel Raphael. Ambrosius was reputed to have been working on a Christian version of the Kabbalah.

The Alphabet of the Magi turned up in numerous other manuscripts throughout the centuries, including the work of Englishman Edmund Fry (1754–1835). Although Fry had a medical degree, he chose to take over the family-type foundry and printing business with his brothers. Being a printer, he was interested in typefaces and alphabets and published a book entitled *Pantographia; Containing Accurate Copies of All the Know Alphabets in the World.* Included are two alphabets that he called *Chaldean 1* and *Chaldean 2*. Chaldean 2 is the Alphabet of the Magi, which Fry attributed to Duret. Chaldean 1 is the Celestial alphabet.

---

191. Barnhart, *The Barnhart Concise Dictionary of Etymology*, 77.

192. Florence Bretelle-Establet and Stéphane Schmitt, eds., *Pieces and Parts in Scientific Texts* (New York: Springer Publishing, 2018), 307.

Fry's source and reason for naming the two alphabets Chaldean is uncertain. It could not have been Ambrosius because the two Chaldean alphabets that he presented are completely different.

The Alphabet of the Magi should not be confused with the Mystic Alphabet of the Magi of Count Alessandro Cagliostro, the adopted name of Giuseppe Balsamo (1743–1795). Cagliostro was an Italian alchemist and charlatan who traveled around Europe healing people and practicing magic as he attempted to build his own Egyptian Masonic movement. He was arrested for swindling people and later attracted the attention of the Inquisition. Rather than being an alphabet *per se*, Cagliostro's mystic alphabet was a method of divination he devised by using a unique arrangement of letters.

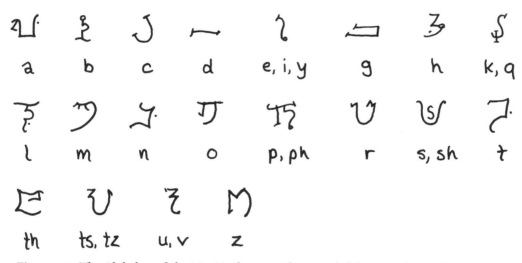

Figure 140: The Alphabet of the Magi is shown with its English letter and sound equivalents.

Like the other magical alphabets, the alphabet of the Magi can be used for any purpose that seems appropriate to you. Whether or not Paracelsus devised it for his medical practice, this alphabet has a long association with talismans and healing. Use it to inscribe candles or any other objects used for healing, protection rituals, or spells.

THE ENOCHIAN ALPHABET

The Enochian alphabet is unique from the others because of its legendary beginning with John Dee and Edward Kelley (1555–1597). Although this alphabet has not been linked with Hebrew, Dee and Kelley worked during a time when the Kabbalah was at its height of medieval popularity. Their work on the Enochian system lasted seven years.[193] According to Dee's notes, the alphabet was received over a thirteen-month period during numerous trance sessions by scrying in a crystal.

From the Middle Ages through the Renaissance, crystallomancy (crystal gazing) was a common form of divination because crystals were regarded as a bridge between matter and spirit. Sometimes credited with making it all the rage, Dee and Kelley used a rock crystal ball that they referred to as a *shewstone* ("show stone"), angelic stone, and *crystallo*.[194] Flat slabs of highly polished obsidian were also used as scrying mirrors. Dee's crystal ball and obsidian mirror are in the British Museum.

John Dee is best known for being a mathematician, astrologer, occult philosopher, and adviser to Queen Elizabeth I. It is often overlooked that he was also an antiquarian and inventor whose interests ranged from geography and navigation to the fine arts; a true Renaissance man. In the centuries since, his interest in occult philosophy, mathematical magic, and theurgy—the influence of supernatural powers—have obscured an accurate evaluation of his work. During his time, he was regarded as a respected and learned man, especially on the Continent where he was recognized for his contributions to mathematics and invited to lecture on Euclid at the University in Paris.

However, back home in England, mathematics was often thought to be associated with the black arts, and Dee's interest in astrology, magic, and alchemy did not help his reputation. For several months in 1555, he was imprisoned by Queen Mary (1516–1558) for conjuring spirits.[195] When her sister Elizabeth became queen, this liability became an asset when her privy council called on Dee's help for protection after an image of Elizabeth was found with a pin through the heart.

As an avid collector with an interest in learning, Dee amassed the greatest library in sixteenth-century England. He bought old manuscripts and books in England and the Continent to help preserve knowledge and acquired some of the manuscripts from the monasteries that Queen Elizabeth's father had dissolved. According to a catalogue in Dee's handwriting, his library contained nearly 4,000 works, many marked with his mar-

---

193. Egil Asprem, *Arguing with Angels: Enochian Magic and Modern Occulture* (Albany, NY: State University of New York Press, 2012), 11.

194. Eric G. Wilson, *The Spiritual History of Ice: Romanticism, Science, and the Imagination* (New York: Palgrave MacMillan, 2003), 13.

195. Peter French, *John Dee: The World of the Elizabethan Magus* (New York: Routledge, 2002), 6.

gin notes.[196] With so much knowledge at his fingertips, he became a go-to guy and drew many visitors, including the queen.

One text in Dee's library that is believed to have been influential to his work was *Voarchadumia* by Italian priest Johannes Pantheus (d. 1535), whose name was Latinized from Giovanni Agostino Panteo.[197] A handbook of mystical alchemy, it contains an alphabet that Pantheus noted as Enochian. A copy of the book in the British Museum is believed to have belonged to Dee because of the margin notes. While Dee's Enochian alphabet is different, there is a theory that *Voarchadumia* may have been an inspiration for him.

Seeking hidden wisdom about the universe, his detailed journals and books were an attempt to find links among alchemy, astrology, sacred geometry, and the Kabbalah. Using prayer and invocations, he called upon angels to appear in crystals. Unable to scry, he worked with several scryers/crystal gazers before meeting Edward Kelley. Trained as an apothecary, English alchemist and spirit medium Kelley (also spelled Kelly) occasionally went by the name Edward Talbot.

Dee's journals indicate that their sessions consisted of Kelley scrying and relaying information to Dee, who would record the details. Messages received by Kelley often consisted of letters arranged in squares. According to legend, when Kelley could not describe or accurately draw the alphabet and had trouble drawing the letters, the angels made them appear on paper as faint yellow characters so he could trace them.

Dee's transcripts of the sessions, called the *Five Books of Mystery*, are part of the Sloane manuscript numbers 3188 to 3191. Kelley also made a transcript of the alphabet and other notes, the *Sixth Book of Spirit*, which is also included in the Sloane collection. Both Dee's and Kelley's handwriting appear throughout the manuscript. The transcripts also contain a part that Dee called the *Book of Enoch* that he said had been delivered by the angel Raphael.

According to the Bible, Enoch was a prophesying patriarch who was conveyed to heaven without death. Along with the Kabbalah, the lost or forgotten mystical Book of Enoch was of high interest during the sixteenth century. A copy of the manuscript emerged in the seventeenth century and later in the Dead Sea scrolls. The Book of Enoch contains stories about a class of angels called *Watchers* who came to earth to teach humans

---

196. Ibid., 43.

197. There is a great deal of debate about the meaning of the word *Voarchadumia*, which is beyond the scope of this book.

alchemy, sorcery, and astrology. Along with visions and prophecies, the book also provides a description of hell.

Three versions of the Enochian alphabet appear in Dee's transcripts. According to Australian linguist and anthropologist Donald Laycock (1936–1988), the first two are said to slightly resemble Hebrew characters drawn by Dee.[198] However, no one has been able to trace the characters back to a Semitic source. The alphabet consists of twenty-one characters, each with its own name that has no relation to the letter's phonetic value. In addition to an alphabet, the messages received by Dee and Kelley included an Enochian language that Dee regarded as the lost language of Adam.

However, even with its own grammar, the Enochian language follows English patterns. For example, it contains both hard and soft sounds for the letters *C* and *G* and uses the combination of *S* and *H* to make the SH sound. According to Laycock, these are not characteristics of any ancient language.

In addition to an alphabet and language, the transcripts from their sessions also contained a complex system of magic. While it is unknown how widespread the use of Enochian magic was during the Renaissance, it seems to have disappeared for several centuries. In the nineteenth century the alphabet and system of magic gained attention through the writings of MacGregor Mathers. It became the heart of a magical system used by the Hermetic Order of the Golden Dawn, who added elemental and planetary attributes. Aleister Crowley is credited with bringing attention to the alphabet beyond the Golden Dawn. One small piece of the magical system that often spills over into popular ritual is calling on the four Enochian directional Watchtowers.

---

198. Donald C. Laycock, *The Complete Enochian Dictionary: A Dictionary of the Angelic Language as Revealed to Dr. John Dee and Edward Kelley* (York Beach, ME: Weiser Books, 2001), 27.

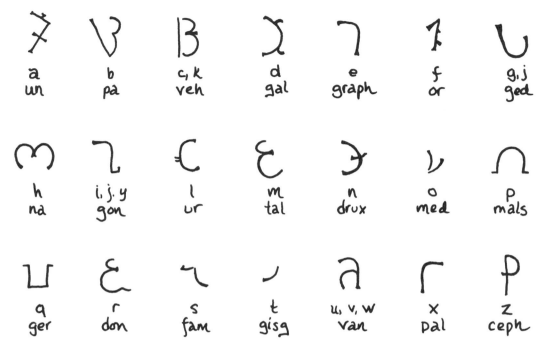

Figure 141: The Enochian alphabet is shown with its English letter
and sound equivalents and character names.

While the script was obviously integral to the Enochian language, Dee also used it to mark talismans, ritual gear, and scrying implements. We can use the alphabet for these purposes too. Because it was instrumental in Kelley's scrying, the script can also be used to mark tools, candles, and other objects used for divination. As with all magical alphabets, follow your intuition for other meaningful ways to use them.

SUMMARY

WHILE AN INDIVIDUAL SYMBOL can be meaningful, learning about it in context of a system and exploring its history adds depth and dimension to its use. Sometimes historical details can spark our imaginations and help us find personal relevance in the symbols we use.

As we have seen, some symbols and their meanings change through the centuries as successive generations of people find new significance in them. While we continue to adapt them to give them relevance in today's world, it is important to avoid distorting the past to make them fit our vision.

Whether or not you have previously worked with a group of symbols, explore them if you find them interesting. You don't have to be a rune master for the runes to speak to you. Start with a symbol that attracts you; get to know it, use it, and meditate with it. From there, explore other symbols in the system. You may find that a mix of Elder Futhark and Anglo-Saxon runes work well for you, or some of the alternative astrological symbols may resonate with you. Follow your intuition and let your heart guide you on your unique path as you explore the power of symbols.

BIBLIOGRAPHY

Agrippa of Nettesheim, Heinrich Cornelius. *Three Books of Occult Philosophy: The Foundation Book of Western Occultism*. Translated by James Freake. Edited and annotated by Donald Tyson. St. Paul, MN: Llewellyn Publications, 2004.

———. *Three Books of Occult Philosophy Or Magic: Book One—Natural Magic*. Translated by James Freake. Edited by Willis F. Whitehead. Chicago: Hahn & Whitehead, 1898.

Åkerman, Susanna. *Rose Cross Over the Baltic: The Spread of Rosicrucianism in Northern Europe*. Boston: Brill, 1998.

Allen, Richard Hinckley. *Star-Names and Their Meanings*. New York: G. E. Stechert, 1899.

Anonymous. "The Ogam Scales of the Book of Ballymote." *Epigraphic Society Occasional Papers*, vol. 22, part 2. Danvers, MA: The Epigraphic Society, 1993.

Antonsen, Elmer H. "The Runes: The Earliest Germanic Writing System." *The Origins of Writing*. Edited by Wayne M. Senner. Lincoln, NE: University of Nebraska Press, 1989. 137–158.

Asprem, Egil. *Arguing with Angels: Enochian Magic and Modern Occulture*. Albany, NY: State University of New York Press, 2012.

Austin, Daniel F. *Florida Ethnobotany*. Boca Raton, FL: CRC Press, 2004.

Bailey, Michael D. *Magic and Superstition in Europe: A Concise History from Antiquity to the Present*. New York: Rowman & Littlefield Publishers, Inc., 2007.

Bandle, Oscar, Kurt Braunmüller, Ernst Håkon Jahr, Allan Karker, Hans-Peter Naumann, Ulf Teleman, Lennart Elmevik, and Gun Widmark, eds. *The Nordic Languages: An International Handbook of the History of the Northern Germanic Languages*, vol. 1. New York: Walter de Gruyter, 2002.

Barnes, Michael P. *Runes: A Handbook*. Woodbridge, England: The Boydell Press, 2012.

Barnhart, Robert K., ed. *The Barnhart Concise Dictionary of Etymology*. New York: Harper-Collins, 1995.

Barrett, Francis. *The Magus: A Complete System of Occult Philosophy*. Book One and Two. Escondido, CA: The Book Tree, 1999.

Becker, Udo. *The Continuum Encyclopedia of Symbols*. Translated by Lance W. Garmer. New York: Continuum International Publishing Group Inc., 2000.

Berg, Walter. *The 13 Signs of the Zodiac*. London: Thorsons Publishing Group, 1995.

Berloquin, Pierre. *Hidden Codes & Grand Designs: Secret Languages from Ancient Times to Modern Day*. New York: Sterling Publishing Company, Inc., 2008.

Blavatsky, H. P. *The Theosophical Glossary*. New York: The Theosophical Publishing Society, 1892.

Block, Daniel I. *Beyond the River Chebar: Studies in Kingship and Eschatology in the Book of Ezekiel*. Cambridge, England: James Clarke & Co., 2014.

Blum, Ralph H. *The Book of Runes. A Handbook for the Use of an Ancient Oracle: The Viking Runes*. London: Headline Book Publishing, 1993.

Brady, Bernadette. *Brady's Book of Fixed Stars*. York Beach, ME: Red Wheel/Weiser LLC, 1998.

Brann, Noel L. *Trithemius and Magical Theology: A Chapter in the Controversy over Occult Studies in Early Modern Europe*. Albany, NY: State University of New York Press, 1999.

Bretelle-Establet, Florence, and Stéphane Schmitt, eds., *Pieces and Parts in Scientific Texts*. New York: Springer Publishing, 2018.

Brinton, Laurel J., ed. *English Historical Linguistics: Approaches and Perspectives*. New York: Cambridge University Press, 2017.

Brown, Michelle P. *The British Library Guide to Writing and Scripts: History and Techniques*. Toronto, Canada: University of Toronto Press, 1998.

Butler, Alison. *Victorian Occultism and the Making of Modern Magic: Invoking Tradition*. New York: Palgrave Macmillan, 2011.

Campbell, Joseph, with Bill Moyers. *The Power of Myth*. New York: Doubleday, 1988.

Campion, Nicholas. *A History of Western Astrology Volume II: The Medieval and Modern Worlds*. New York: Continuum US, 2009.

Capecchi, Danilo. *History of Virtual Work Laws: A History of Mechanics Prospective*. New York: Springer, 2012.

Carraher, Jr., Charles E. *Giant Molecules: Essential Materials for Everyday Living and Problem Solving*, 2nd ed. Hoboken, NJ: John Wiley & Sons Inc., 2003.

Chartrand, Mark R. *Night Sky: A Guide to Field Identification*. New York: St. Martin's Press, 1990.

Cirlot, Juan Eduardo. *A Dictionary of Symbols*. 2nd ed. Translated by Jack Sage. Mineola, NY: Dover Publications, Inc., 1971.

Classen, Albrecht, ed. *Magic and Magicians in the Middle Ages and the Early Modern Time: The Occult in Pre-Modern Sciences, Medicine, Literature, Religion, and Astrology*. Boston: Walter de Gruyter, 2017.

Cortés, Carlos E., ed. *Multicultural America: A Multimedia Encyclopedia*, vol. 4. Los Angeles: Sage Publications, Inc., 2013.

Crone, Hugh. *Paracelsus, The Man who Defied Medicine: His Real Contribution to Medicine and Science*. Melbourne, Australia: The Albarello Press, 2004.

Crowley, Vivianne. *Jung: A Journey of Transformation, Exploring His Life and Experiencing His Ideas*. Wheaton, IL: Quest Books, 1999.

Daniels, Peter T., and William Bright, eds. *The World's Writing Systems*. New York: Oxford University Press, 1996.

Danver, Steven L., ed. *Popular Controversies in World History: Investigating History's Intriguing Questions. Prehistory and Early Civilizations*, vol. 1. Santa Barbara, CA: ABC-CLIO, LLC, 2011.

Darling, David J. *The Universal Book of Astronomy: From the Andromeda Galaxy to the Zone of Avoidance*. Hoboken, NJ: John Wiley & Sons, Inc., 2004.

Davies, Edward. *Celtic Researches on the Origin, Traditions & Language of the Ancient Britons*. London: J. Booth, 1804.

Davies, Norman. *Europe: A History*. New York: Oxford University Press, 1996.

Davies, Owen. *Grimoires: A History of Magic Books*. New York: Oxford University Press, 2010.

Deming, David. *Science and Technology in World History: The Origin of Chemistry, the Principle of Progress, the Enlightenment, and the Industrial Revolution*, vol 4. Jefferson, NC: McFarland & Company, Inc., 2016.

Dennis, Geoffrey W. *The Encyclopedia of Jewish Myth, Magic and Mysticism*. 2nd ed. Woodbury, MN: Llewellyn Worldwide, 2016.

Dent, Shirley, and Jason Whittaker. *Radical Blake: Influence and Afterlife from 1827*. New York: Palgrave Macmillan, 2002.

DeSalvo, John. *The Lost Art of Enochian Magic: Angels, Invocations, and the Secrets Revealed to Dr. John Dee*. Rochester, VT: Destiny Books, 2010.

deVore, Nicholas. *Encyclopedia of Astrology*. New York: Philosophical Library, 1947.

Dobelis, Inge N., ed. *Magic and Medicine of Plants: A Practical Guide to the Science, History, Folklore, and Everyday Uses of Medicinal Plants*. Pleasantville, NY: The Reader's Digest Association, Inc., 1986.

Ede, Andrew, and Lesley B. Cormack, *A History of Science in Society: From Philosophy to Utility*, 3rd ed. Toronto, Canada: University of Toronto Press, 2017.

Editorial Staff, *Webster's Third New International Dictionary*, Unabridged, vol. 3. Chicago: Encyclopedia Britannica, Inc., 1981.

Editors of Encyclopaedia Britannica. "Babylonia." Encyclopaedia Britannica, Inc. July 12, 2016. https://www.britannica.com/place/Babylonia.

Elliot, Ralph W. V. *Runes: An Introduction*. Manchester, England: Manchester University Press, 1959.

Evans, James. *The History and Practice of Ancient Astronomy*. New York: Oxford University Press, 1998.

Evans-Wentz, W. Y. *The Fairy Faith in Celtic Countries*. New York: Citadel Press, 1999.

Findell, Martin. *Phonological Evidence from the Continental Runic Inscriptions*. Boston: Walter de Gruyter, 2012.

Finocchiaro, Maurice A. *The Routledge Guidebook to Galileo's Dialogue*. New York: Routledge, 2014.

Fontana, David. *The Secret Language of Symbols: A Visual Key to Symbols and Their Meanings*. San Francisco: Chronicle Books, 2003.

Forbes, Alexander Robert. *Gaelic Names of Beasts (Mammalia), Birds, Fishes, Insects, Reptiles, Etc*. Edinburgh, Scotland: Oliver and Boyd, 1905.

Forbes, John. *The Principles of Gaelic Grammar*, 2nd ed. Edinburgh, Scotland: Oliver and Boyd, 1848.

Fortson, Benjamin W. *Indo-European Language and Culture: An Introduction*, 2nd ed. Chichester, England: Wiley & Sons, Ltd., 2010.

French, Peter. *John Dee: The World of an Elizabethan Magus*. New York: Routledge, 2002.

Fry, Edmund. *Pantographia; Containing Accurate Copies of All the Known Alphabets in the World*. London: Cooper and Wilson, 1799.

Gallant, Roy A. *Constellations: How They Came to Be*. Cincinnati, OH: Four Winds Press, 1979.

Gettings, Fred. *The Book of the Hand: An Illustrated History of Palmistry*. New York: Hamlyn Publishing, 1971.

_____ . *Dictionary of Occult, Hermetic and Alchemical Sigils*. Boston: Routledge and Kegan Paul, Ltd., 1981.

Gimbutas, Marija. *The Language of the Goddess*. San Francisco: HarperSanFrancisco, 1991.

Glick, Thomas, Steven Livesey, and Faith Wallis, eds. *Medieval Science, Technology, and Medicine: An Encyclopedia*. New York: Routledge, 2005.

Goldman, Norma, and Jacob E. Nyenhuis. *Latin Via Ovid: A First Course*, 2nd ed. Detroit: Wayne State University Press, 1982.

Grande, Lance, and Allison Augustyn. *Gems and Gemstones: Timeless Natural Beauty of the Mineral World*. Chicago: The University of Chicago Press, 2009.

Graves, Charles. "On the Ogham Character." *Archaeologia Cambrensis, The Journal of the Cambrian Archaeological Association,* vol. 2, 3rd series. London: J. Russell Smith, 1856.

Graves, Charles. "On Ogam Inscriptions." *Hermathena: A Series of Papers on Literature, Science, and Philosophy*, vol. 6, 241–268. Dublin, Ireland: Hodges, Figgis, & Co., 1888.

Greer, John Michael. *The New Encyclopedia of the Occult*. St. Paul, MN: Llewellyn Publications, 2004.

Gregersen, Erik, ed. *The Milky Way and Beyond: Stars, Nebulae, and Other Galaxies*. New York: Britannica Educational Publishing, 2010.

Greenfield, Stanley B., and Daniel G. Calder. *A New Critical History of Old English Literature*. New York: New York University Press, 1986.

Gusick, Barbara I., and Edelgard E. DuBruck, eds. *Fifteenth-Century Studies*, vol. 32. Rochester, NY: Camden House, 2007.

Hock, Hans Henrich, and Brian D. Joseph. *Language History, Language Change, and Language Relationship: An Introduction to Historical and Comparative Linguistics*, 2nd rev. ed. Berlin, Germany: Mouton de Gruyter, 2009.

Hoeller, Stephan A. "On the Trail of the Winged God: Hermes and Hermeticism Throughout the Ages." *Gnosis: A Journal of Western Inner Traditions*, vol. 40, 20–28. Commack, NY: Gnosis, 1996.

Hogg, Richard. *An Introduction to Old English*, 2nd ed. Edinburgh, Scotland: Edinburgh University Press, 2012.

Holberg, Jay B. *Sirius: Brightest Diamond in the Night Sky*. New York: Springer, 2007.

Holden, James Herschel. *A History of Horoscopic Astrology*, 2nd ed. Tempe, AZ: American Federation of Astrologers, Inc., 2006.

Honorius, III, Pope. *Grimoire du Pape Honorius with a Collection of the Rarest Secrets*. Rome, 1670.

Honorius of Thebes. *The Sworn Book of Honorius: Liber Iuratus Honorii*. Translated by Joseph Peterson. Lake Worth, FL: Ibis Press, 2016.

Hulse, David Allen. *The Western Mysteries: An Encyclopedic Guide to the Sacred Languages and Magical Systems of the World*, vol. 2. St. Paul, MN: Llewellyn Publications, 2000.

Hume, Lynne, and Nevill Drury. *The Varieties of Magical Experience: Indigenous, Medieval, and Modern Magic*. Santa Barbara, CA: Praeger, 2013.

Johnson, John. *Typographia, or the Printers' Instructor*, vol. 2. London: Longman, Hurst, Rees, Orme, Brown & Green, 1824.

Jung, Carl G., M.-L. von Franz, Joseph L. Henderson, Jolande Jacobi, and Aniela Jaffé. *Man and His Symbols*. New York: Dell Publishing, 1968.

Jung, C. G. *Mysterium Coniunctions: An Inquiry into the Separation and Synthesis of Psychic Opposites in Alchemy*. Princeton, NJ: Princeton University Press, 1976.

Kassell, Lauren. *Medicine and Magic in Elizabethan London. Simon Forman: Astrologer, Alchemist & Physician*. New York: Oxford University Press, 2005.

Kenner, T. A. *Symbols and Their Hidden Meaning*. London: Carlton Publishing Group, 2007.

Koch, John T., ed. *Celtic Culture: A Historical Encyclopedia: M-S*, vol. 4. Santa Barbara, CA: ABC-CLIO, Inc., 2005.

Koch-Westenholz, Ulla. *Mesopotamian Astrology: An Introduction to Babylonian and Assyrian Celestial Divination*. Copenhagen, Denmark: Museum Tusculanum Press, 1995.

König, Ekkehard, and Johan van der Auwera, eds. *The Germanic Languages*. New York: Routledge, 2002.

Lachièze-Rey, Marc, and Jean-Pierre Luminet. *Celestial Treasury: From the Music of the Spheres to the Conquest of Space*. Translated by Joe Larado. New York: Cambridge University Press, 2001.

Laycock, Donald C. *The Complete Enochian Dictionary: A Dictionary of the Angelic Language as Revealed to Dr. John Dee and Edward Kelley*. York Beach, ME: Weiser Books, 2001.

Lehmann, Ruth P. M. "Ogham: The Ancient Script of the Celts." *The Origins of Writing*. Edited by Wayne M. Senner, 159–170. Lincoln, NE: University of Nebraska Press, 1989.

Leitch, Aaron. *The Angelical Language, Volume 1: The Complete History and Mythos of the Tongue of Angels*. Woodbury, MN: Llewellyn Publications, 2010.

Lipp, Deborah. *The Way of Four: Create Elemental Balance in Your Life*. St. Paul, MN: Llewellyn Publications, 2004.

Liungman, Carl G. *Symbols: Encyclopedia of Western Signs and Ideograms*. Stockholm, Sweden: HME Publishing, 1995.

Looijenga, Tineke. *Texts and Contexts of the Oldest Runic Inscriptions*. Boston: Brill, 2003.

Macalister, R. A. Stewart. *The Secret Languages of Ireland*. New York: Cambridge University Press, 2014.

MacCall, Seamus. *And So Began the Irish Nation*. Dublin, Ireland: The Talbot Press Limited, 1931.

Mac Coitir, Niall. *Irish Trees: Myths, Legends & Folklore*. Cork, Ireland: Collins Press, 2003.

MacDonald, Fiona. *The Plague and Medicine in the Middle Ages*. Milwaukee, WI: World Almanac Library, 2006.

Mackey, Albert G. *An Encyclopaedia of Freemasonry and Its Kindred Sciences: Comprising the Whole Range of Arts, Sciences and Literature as Connected with the Institution*. Philadelphia: Moss & Company, 1874.

Magill, Frank N., ed. *Dictionary of World Biography: Volume II The Middle Ages*. New York: Routledge, 1998.

MacKillop, James. *A Dictionary of Celtic Mythology*. New York: Oxford University Press, 1998.

MacLachlan, Bonnie, and Judith Fletcher, eds. *Virginity Revisited: Configurations of the Unpossessed Body*. Toronto, Canada: The University of Toronto Press Inc., 2007.

MacLeod, Mindy, and Bernard Mees. *Runic Amulets and Magic Objects*. Woodbridge, England: The Boydell Press, 2006.

Mallory, J. P., and D. Q. Adams. *The Oxford Introduction to Proto-Indo-European and the Proto-Indo-European World*. New York: Oxford University Press, 2006.

Marcovich, Miroslav. *Studies in Graeco-Roman Religions and Gnosticism*, vol. 4. Edited by H. S. Versnel. Leiden, The Netherlands: E. J. Brill, 1989.

Marshack, Alexander. *The Roots of Civilization: The Cognitive Beginnings of Man's First Art, Symbol and Notation*. Wakefield, RI: Moyer Bell Ltd., 1991.

Mathers, S. L. MacGregor, ed. *The Key of Solomon the King*. Translated by S. L. MacGregor Mathers. Mineola, NY: Dover Publications, Inc., 2009.

McCalman, Iain. *The Last Alchemist: Count Cagliostro, Master of Magic in the Age of Reason*. New York: HarperCollins, 2003.

McLeish, John. *Number: The History of Numbers and How They Shape Our Lives*. New York: Fawcett Columbine, 1992.

Mickey, Sam. *Whole Earth Thinking and Planetary Coexistence: Ecological Wisdom at the Intersection of Religion, Ecology, and Philosophy*. New York: Routledge, 2016.

Monk, Michael A., and John Sheehan, eds. *Early Medieval Munster: Archaeology, History and Society*. Cork, Ireland: Cork University Press, 1998.

Monod, Paul Kléber. *Solomon's Secret Arts: The Occult in the Age of Enlightenment*. New Haven, CT: Yale University Press, 2013.

Morris, Richard L. *Runic and Mediterranean Epigraphy*. Philadelphia: John Benjamins North America, 2012.

Nauert, Charles G. *The A to Z of the Renaissance*. Lanham, MD: Scarecrow Press, Inc., 2004.

Newsome, James D. *The Hebrew Prophets*. Louisville, KY: Westminster John Knox Press, 1984.

Noble, Thomas F. X., Barry Strauss, Duane J. Osheim, Kristen B. Neuschel, Elinor A. Accampo, David D. Roberts, and William B. Cohen. *Western Civilization. Beyond Boundaries Volume I: to 1715*. 7th ed. Boston: Wadsworth Cengage Learning, 2018.

Nozedar, Adele. *The Secret Language of Birds: A Treasury of Myths, Folklore and Inspirational True Stories*. London: Harper Element, 2006.

Ó Cróinín, Dáibhí, ed. *A New History of Ireland: Prehistoric and Early Ireland*, vol. 1. New York: Oxford University Press, 2005.

O'Kelly, Michael J. *Early Ireland: An Introduction to Irish Prehistory*. New York: Cambridge University Press, 2001.

Olcott, William Tyler. *Star Lore: Myths, Legends, and Facts*. Mineola, NY: Dover Publications, Inc., 2004.

Osborne, Kenan B. *Sacramental Theology: A General Introduction*. New York: Paulist Press, 1988.

Page, R. I. *Runes*. Berkeley, CA: University of California Press, 1987.

_____. *Runes and Runic Inscriptions: Collected Essays on Anglo-Saxon and Viking Runes*. Edited by David Parsons. Woodbridge, England: The Boydell Press, 1998.

_____. *An Introduction to English Runes*, 2nd ed. Woodbridge, England: The Boydell Press, 2006.

Page, Sophie. *Astrology in Medieval Manuscripts*. Toronto, Canada: University of Toronto Press, 2002.

Pankenier, David W. "On Chinese Astrology's Imperviousness to External Influences." *Astrology in Time and Place: Cross-Cultural Questions in the History of Astrology*. Edited by Nicholas Campion and Dorian Geiseler-Greenbaum. Newcastle upon Tyne, England: Cambridge Scholars Publishing, 2015. 3–26.

Paracelsus. *Of the supreme mysteries of nature*. Translated by Robert Turner. London: N. Brook and J. Harison, 1656.

Payne-Gaposchkin, Cecilia, and Katherine Haramundanis. *Introduction to Astronomy*. New York: Prentice Hall, 1970.

Pennick, Nigel. *Magical Alphabets*. York Beach, ME: Samuel Weiser, Inc., 1992.

Pogačnik, Marko. *Nature Spirits & Elemental Beings: Working with the Intelligence in Nature*. Forres, Scotland: Findhorn Press, 2009.

Pyle, Andrew. *The Dictionary of Seventeenth-Century British Philosophers*, vol. 1. Bristol, England: Thoemmes Continuum, 2000.

Remler, Pat. *Egyptian Mythology A to Z*. 3rd ed. New York: Chelsea House, 2010.

Rhys, John. *Celtic Britain*. New York: E. & J. R. Young & Co., 1882.

Ridpath, Ian. *Star Tales*. Cambridge, England: Lutterworth Press, 1988.

Robson, Vivian. *The Fixed Stars & Constellations in Astrology*. Abingdon, MD: The Astrology Center of America, 2005.

Roeckelein, J. E., comp. *Elsevier's Dictionary of Psychological Theories*. San Diego, CA: Elsevier Inc., 2006.

Ross, Anne. *Pagan Celtic Britain: Studies in Iconography and Tradition*. London: Constable and Company, Ltd., 1993.

Rudhyar, Dane. *The Astrology Of Personality: A Reformulation of Astrological Concepts and Ideals in Terms of Contemporary Psychology and Philosophy*. New York: Lucis Publishing Co., 1936.

Ruickbie, Leo. *The Impossible Zoo: An Encyclopedia of Fabulous Beasts and Mythical Monsters*. London: Little, Brown Book Group, 2016.

Sacks, David. *Letter Perfect: The A-to-Z History of Our Alphabet*. Toronto, Canada: Vintage-Canada, 2004.

Savedow, Steve, ed. *Sepher Rezial Hemelach: The Book of the Angel Rezial*. Translated by Steve Savedow. York Beach, ME: Weiser Books, 2000.

Schaaf, Fred. *A Year of the Stars: A Month by Month Journey of Skywatching*. Amherst, NY: Prometheus Books, 2003.

_____ . *The Brightest Stars: Discovering the Universe through the Sky's Most Brilliant Stars*. Hoboken, NJ: John Wiley & Sons, Inc., 2008.

Schmandt-Besserat, Denise. *Before Writing Volume I: From Counting to Cuneiform*. Austin, TX: University of Texas Press, 1992.

Shipley, Joseph T. *Dictionary of Early English*. Lanham, MD: Rowman & Littlefield Publishers, Inc., 2014.

Skeat, Walter W. *The Concise Dictionary of English Etymology*. Ware, England: Wordsworth Editions, Ltd., 1993.

Slavin, Michael. *The Ancient Books of Ireland*. Montreal, Canada: McGill-Queen's University Press, 2005.

Smith, Jeremy J. *Old English: A Linguistic Introduction*. New York: Cambridge University Press, 2009.

Sommers, Susan Mitchell. *The Siblys of London: A Family on the Esoteric Fringes of Georgian England*. New York: Oxford University Press, 2018.

Spurkland, Terje. *Norwegian Runes and Runic Inscriptions*. Translated by Betsy van der Hock. Woodbridge, England: The Boydell Press, 2005.

Stevenson, Angus, ed. *Oxford Dictionary of English*, 3rd ed. New York: Oxford University Press, 2010.

St. Fleur, Nicholas. "Oldest Known Drawing by a Human is Found in South Africa." *The New York Times*. September 13, 2018. 10.

Steingass, F. *Persian-English Dictionary: Including Arabic Words and Phrases to be Met with in Persian Literature*. New York: Routledge, 1998.

Stoklund, Marie, Michael Lerche Nielsen, Bente Holmberg, and Gillian Fellows-Jensen, eds. *Runes and Their Secrets: Studies in Runology*. Copenhagen, Denmark: Museum Tusculanum Press, 2006.

Swetz, Frank J. *Legacy of the Luoshu: The 4,000 Year Search for the Meaning of the Magic Square of Order Three*. Boca Raton, FL: CRC Press, 2008.

Swift, Catherine. "The Story of Ogham." *History Today* 65, no. 10, 4–5. London: History Today Ltd, 2015.

Symons, Victoria. *Runes and Roman Letters in Anglo-Saxon Manuscripts*. Berlin, Germany: Walter de Gruyter GmbH, 2016.

Tester, Jim. *A History of Western Astrology*. Woodbridge, England: The Boydell Press, 1996.

Thierens, A. E. *Elements of Esoteric Astrology*. London: Rider & Co., 1931.

Thorndike, Lynn. *A History of Magic and Experimental Science*. New York: Columbia University Press, 1958.

Torkelson, Anthony R. *The Cross Name Index to Medicinal Plants: Plants in Indian Medicine A-Z*, vol. 4. Boca Raton, FL: CRC Press, 1999.

Tyson, Donald. *Llewellyn's Truth About Runes*. Woodbury, MN: Llewellyn Publications, 2013.

U∴ D∴, Frater. *Money Magic: Mastering Prosperity in its True Element*. Woodbury, MN: Llewellyn Publications, 2011.

———. *Practical Sigil Magic: Creating Personal Symbols for Success*. Translated by Ingrid Fischer. Woodbury, MN: Llewellyn Publications, 2015.

van der Laan, J. M. and Andrew Weeks, eds. *The Faustian Century: German Literature and Culture in the Age of Luther and Faustus*. Rochester, NY: Camden House, 2013.

van der Poel, Marc. *Cornelius Agrippa: The Humanist Theologian and His Declamations*. New York: Brill, 1997.

Vidro, Nadia, Irene E. Zwiep, and Judith Olszowy-Schlanger. *A Universal Art. Hebrew Grammar across Disciplines and Faiths*. Boston: Brill, 2014.

Watson, George, ed. *The New Cambridge Bibliography of English Literature: 600–1600*, vol. 1. New York: Cambridge University Press, 1974.

Webb, Stephen. *Clash of Symbols: A Ride Through the Riches of Glyphs*. New York: Springer Publishing, 2018.

Wells, Diana. *100 Birds and How They Got Their Names*. Chapel Hill, NC: Algonquin Books of Chapel Hill, 2002.

Wilson, Eric G. *The Spiritual History of Ice: Romanticism, Science, and the Imagination*. New York: Palgrave MacMillan, 2003.

Wilson, Nigel, ed. *Encyclopedia of Ancient Greece*. New York: Routledge, 2010.

Zinberg, Israel. *A History of Jewish Literature: Italian Jewry in the Renaissance Era*. Translated and edited by Bernard Martin. New York: KTAV Publishing House, Inc., 1974.

ONLINE RESOURCES

Astronomical Applications Department of the U.S. Naval Observatory at http://aa.usno.navy.mil/data/docs/RS_OneYear.php.

The Internet Archive at https://archive.org/.

INDEX

S

T

TO WRITE TO THE AUTHOR

If you wish to contact the author or would like more information about this book, please write to the author in care of Llewellyn Worldwide Ltd. and we will forward your request. Both the author and publisher appreciate hearing from you and learning of your enjoyment of this book and how it has helped you. Llewellyn Worldwide Ltd. cannot guarantee that every letter written to the author can be answered, but all will be forwarded. Please write to:

Sandra Kynes
℅ Llewellyn Worldwide
2143 Wooddale Drive
Woodbury, MN 55125-2989
Please enclose a self-addressed stamped envelope for reply,
or $1.00 to cover costs. If outside the U.S.A., enclose
an international postal reply coupon.

Many of Llewellyn's authors have websites with additional information and resources. For more information, please visit our website at http://www.llewellyn.com.